The Experts and
the Evidence

T0337970

The Experts and the Evidence

A Practical Guide to Stock Investing

Charlie X. Cai

Kevin Keasey

WILEY

This edition first published 2022
Copyright © 2022 by John Wiley & Sons, Ltd.

Registered office
John Wiley & Sons Ltd, The Atrium, Southern Gate, Chichester, West Sussex, PO19 8SQ,
United Kingdom

For details of our global editorial offices, for customer services and for information about how
to apply for permission to reuse the copyright material in this book please see our website at
www.wiley.com.

All rights reserved. No part of this publication may be reproduced, stored in a retrieval system,
or transmitted, in any form or by any means, electronic, mechanical, photocopying, recording or
otherwise, except as permitted by the UK Copyright, Designs and Patents Act 1988, without the
prior permission of the publisher.

Wiley publishes in a variety of print and electronic formats and by print-on-demand. Some
material included with standard print versions of this book may not be included in e-books or
in print-on-demand. If this book refers to media such as a CD or DVD that is not included in the
version you purchased, you may download this material at http://booksupport.wiley.com.
For more information about Wiley products, visit www.wiley.com.

Designations used by companies to distinguish their products are often claimed as trademarks. All
brand names and product names used in this book are trade names, service marks, trademarks or
registered trademarks of their respective owners. The publisher is not associated with any product
or vendor mentioned in this book.

Limit of Liability/Disclaimer of Warranty: While the publisher and author have used their best
efforts in preparing this book, they make no representations or warranties with respect to the
accuracy or completeness of the contents of this book and specifically disclaim any implied
warranties of merchantability or fitness for a particular purpose. It is sold on the understanding
that the publisher is not engaged in rendering professional services and neither the publisher
nor the author shall be liable for damages arising herefrom. If professional advice or other expert
assistance is required, the services of a competent professional should be sought.

Library of Congress Cataloging-in-Publication Data

Names: Cai, Charlie X., author. | Keasey, Kevin, author.
Title: The experts and the evidence : a practical guide to stock investing /
   Charlie X. Cai and Kevin Keasey.
Description: Chichester, West Sussex, UK : Wiley, 2022. | Includes index.
Identifiers: LCCN 2021059920 (print) | LCCN 2021059921 (ebook) | ISBN
   9781119842552 (paperback) | ISBN 9781119842538 (adobe pdf) | ISBN
   9781119842569 (epub)
Subjects: LCSH: Stocks. | Investments.
Classification: LCC HG4661 .C317 2022 (print) | LCC HG4661 (ebook) | DDC
   332.63/22—dc23/eng/20220112
LC record available at https://lccn.loc.gov/2021059920
LC ebook record available at https://lccn.loc.gov/2021059921

Cover Design: Wiley
Cover Images: Expert: © CSA-Archive/Getty Images
            Evidence: Wiley

Set in 11.5/15pt STIX Two Text by Straive, Chennai, India

SKYFAC3B609-4DAD-4B44-857E-A242A4B7991A_032322

Contents

List of Practical Applications

- Practical Application I: Equity Screening and Backtesting
- Practical Application II: Understanding a Company's Realized and Potential Growth
- Practical Application III: A Closer Look at Portfolio Performance
- Practical Application IV: Beta Estimation and Factor Backtesting (FTST)
- Practical Application V: Factors to Watch
- Practical Application VI: A Walkthrough of Technical Analysis
- Practical Application VII: Quant Tools

Preface

This book explains how the investment philosophies of well-known investor experts can be tested and implemented with the data and analytical tools available on the BLOOMBERG PROFESSIONAL® platform.

We have brought the ideas (successes) of experts and the potential of data together in this book to give readers the opportunities to learn from the best and to put their insights into practice. Specifically, it covers two important aspects of financial investment: (1) the formulation of investment philosophies via learning from some of the best investors in history with many different styles; and (2) showing how to test and implement data-driven investment strategies on one of the most popular professional, financial, digital platforms. Readers will have the opportunity to learn from both the investment ideas of the experts and the tools used by investment professionals to start the construction of their own portfolios.

The purpose of writing this book is to create a learning resource that can connect abstract investment ideas and philosophies with measurable data and evidence. Existing investment textbooks provide excellent coverage of investment theory and offer an excellent foundation for undergraduate courses and MBA courses. However, even after learning the contents of a whole textbook, there is not an obvious route for the development of investment philosophies and strategies. While there are data-driven online exercises, there is little room for an in-depth development of technical and practical data skills that can translate investment ideas into implementable strategies. Similarly, the many books on investment experts (gurus), relating tales about these legendary investors, do not connect the various ideas with real practice and are usually shallow in depth and often unsystematic.

This book has been written against the backdrop of the growing digital economy. As educators, we try to keep our programmes relevant to the likely future demand for skills. Many schools have introduced the Bloomberg or Eikon platforms into their classrooms and we have personally initiated and managed such financial market labs in three different UK universities. It is during the process of integrating such resources into our teaching that we identified a huge gap in the market. This book draws on over 60 years of combined teaching and research experience – over the last seven years, we have been heavily investing in integrating the Bloomberg platform into our teaching, research, and investment practice.

Given the many experts we could have chosen, the coverage of this book is balanced by a consideration of the variety of investment styles and their effectiveness in demonstrating the use of data and in developing a broad set of skills in using the Bloomberg platform.

The discussion is kept at a practical level and only linked to appropriate theories when students might need a more structured view on what they can learn from the experts. The Practical Application sections throughout the book provide both explanations on the rationale of the chosen functionality and detailed step-by-step demonstrations.

One key feature of this book is the links between ideas and data. While the book is concerned with looking at the lessons to be learnt from investment experts, it is also interested in presenting relevant evidence on the various investment approaches (i.e. what could have been achieved by a specific approach over recent years). The presentation of evidence asks two questions: (1) do the claims of an expert now stack up?; and (2) how might an approach be quantified so it can be tested against the data? This allows the reader to look at an approach and shows how it can be applied to modern data and techniques of testing. The evidence in each of the chapters is a prelude to the Practical Application sections that accompany each chapter. These are a step-by-step guide to actioning a strategy that replicates that of an expert – not always perfectly but as close as we are able to. The intention being that by the end of the book, students and investors will be comfortable with accessing data and developing customized investment strategies.

After giving a brief introduction, the book starts with the two most popular styles of investing: value in Chapter 2 (Warren Buffett) and growth in Chapter 3 (Philip Fisher). It then introduces the contrarian approach in Chapter 4 (David Dreman). The theoretical foundations of portfolio investing are introduced in Chapter 5 (Harry Markowitz). The effect of investors' behavioural traits on investing are examined in Chapter 6 with applications linked to factor investment. The final two chapters cover technical analysis (Chapter 7) and more advanced quantitative investment with alternative data and techniques (Chapter 8). Here we will meet the one of the greatest Quant investors – Jim Simons.

This book is not intended to be a primer for those new to the financial markets, many of those already exist. Nor is it intended to be an in-depth guide to a particular investment approach. Instead, it is intended to introduce a range of investment approaches that have seen great success in the hands of individual experts. Some of the approaches are complementary, others are not. More importantly, lessons can be learned from each of the approaches and some can be combined to form a unique approach to fit the interests and attitudes of an individual student/investor.

We have given a reasonable amount of background on each of the experts as this helps to understand the context of the successes and what might be required to make them work. Each chapter also gives small insights to make the reader sit back and think, i.e. does the reader have the patience to make this work?, do they have the funds?, is the market the same?, have such gains now been competed away, etc.? Given all this, the book is aimed at students and interested amateurs.

This text is addressed to both graduate and advanced undergraduate students providing an in-depth discussion of investment ideas and practical training in applying the ideas via a real-life informational and analytical system. It introduces a systematic approach to investment strategy development which is not only relevant to individual DIY investment for growth or retirement but also the training of future professional fund managers. The quantitative aspect of this book is important but not overly demanding. It is important to understanding the underlying use of quantitative data for stock selection but less is demanded in the actual calculations. The Practical Applications are built on the tools we teach, with the complicated calculations and programming being done by the tool – thus, freeing up time to focus more on the ideas themselves.

Acknowledgements

This book was written over a period of about two years, possibly some of the most tumultuous and unsettling periods either of us has encountered. There was the ongoing saga of Brexit and it finally being pushed through Parliament by Boris Johnson, followed by the ongoing Covid-19 pandemic. While much has been written about Covid-19, we will look back on this period and wonder what happened to well-balanced scientific enquiry.

Covid-19 took away some of our time (as academics trying to navigate the chaos of shutting down universities) but also gave us time through those long months of being isolated. During this period, we locked ourselves away and finished this book. In doing this, we need to thank our families for showing understanding and patience . . .

About the Authors

Charlie X Cai is a Professor of Finance at the Liverpool University Management School. He is currently the Director of Research for the Accounting and Finance Group. Charlie's research career started from his PhD on the market microstructure of the London Stock Exchange. This research journey taught him the foundations of financial markets and provided him with solid empirical modelling skills. Since then, he has continued his research interest in examining the impact of technology on financial markets (issues such as algorithmic, high-frequency trading, crowdfunding) and developed expertise in Big Data analytics. His core research area is in investment, including machine learning and automatized investment and corporate financial and Environmental, Social and Governance (ESG) reporting. He has been published in leading finance and accounting journals including the *Journal of Accounting and Economics*, *Journal of Money, Credit and Banking*, and *Journal of Financial Econometrics*.

Charlie's informed and rigorous approach has benefited from his active collaboration with scholars from a wide range of academic, industrial and regulatory organizations. He has also worked outside academia as a research consultant, and he is committed to building research links with other disciplines and academic institutions worldwide.

Kevin Keasey has been a Professor at the University of Leeds for over 30 years. Previous to that, he held positions at the universities of Warwick, Nottingham, and Newcastle. He is Director of the International Banking Institute (IBI) and the Centre for Advanced Studies in Finance (CASIF) at Leeds. He was the long-term Head of the Accounting and Finance Division, stepping down in 2017.

Kevin is the author of 13 books, monographs, and edited volumes on corporate governance, banking, small firms and decision-making, and is the author of over 140 refereed articles in leading international journals. He has also published over 80 book chapters, reports, etc. His most recent books include *Size, Risk and Governance in European Banking* and *A Handbook of Corporate Governance* (both Oxford University Press, 2013). He is joint editor of the most comprehensive (14 volumes by leading international authors) series on corporate governance to date. Kevin's research has received international recognition and he is one of only four UK academics to be ranked both in the top 100 (top 1%) for the past 50 years of global accounting research output in the 25 leading accounting journals and in the top 4% for the past 50 years of global finance research output in the 25 leading finance journals.[1]

Kevin has taught across the whole range of accounting, finance, and banking subjects. He has supervised over 45 PhD students, with many progressing to senior academic and corporate positions across the globe.

Finally, Kevin has had substantial experience as a founder, executive, and non-executive – he has held positions in hi-tech holding, fast growth care, and venture capital companies, and IT and telecom plcs.

---

[1] J. Heck and P. Coole, Most prolific authors in the finance literature: 1959–2008. *SSRN Electronic Journal* (2009). 10.2139/ssrn.1355675.

CHAPTER 1

Introduction

Experts and Evidence

Investing in shares is challenging, even for experts, and it will always be so. This is because the movement of a share price and the eventual returns a share is able to provide are the result of a myriad of different influences (international, macro-economic, government actions, analysts' forecasts, general news, the actions of the company – to name but a few). At any one point in time, it is unclear how these various forces will come together and affect a share price and, even in the longer term, where there is a hope that the performance of the underlying company will shine through, there are lots of uncertainties and irrationalities that can bounce a share price in a downward (or upward) direction. At the time of writing this first chapter (May 2020 – as you will see throughout the book, different chapters have been written during different periods and we have decided to keep these time differences to illustrate how the world of investing is extremely dynamic, to say the least), the world is coming to terms with the economic consequences of Covid-19. In the UK, we are facing the biggest drop in GDP (possibly 25% – on 11 June 2020 it was announced that GDP in April had fallen by 20.4%, the biggest one-month drop ever recorded, and the FTSE 100 barely moved on the back of the announcement!!!) since the Great Frost of 1709.

However, we are getting ahead of ourselves (and we do this occasionally throughout the book when the logic/excitement of the argument takes hold) and we need to explain why investing can be rewarding and fun, albeit challenging. But before we do this, we should give you a bit of background on ourselves. Well, we are a couple of finance professors who also run investment portfolios and we have been doing both of these for six decades across the pair of us. You would have thought by now we would have all the answers but this is far from the case. Investing is always a challenge and there is always something to learn, shocks to deal with, and surprises to enjoy. This is why we have continued to teach and practise finance for such a length of time. In terms of the practice, we have learnt approaches and lessons that can be passed on to good effect – While not one of them is 100% foolproof, they should act as good guides and prevent too many costly mistakes. Our academic lives have given us the time and resources to analyse and reflect on a whole range of different approaches – their shortcomings and strengths. Furthermore, we do not have any axes to grind or services to sell – our advice is impartial.

This is not the first book we have written on share dealing. We wrote one back in 1998 to launch the Halifax share dealing service. This book was intended as a simple primer for people new to the world of financial markets and shares. It was also written in a different (pre-internet) era where access to the markets was not as easy and there was a lot less financial information and fewer computer programs to undertake any analysis. Essentially, we are now in a different world for the 'part-time' investor. Having said that, the information and analysis available do differ across different types of investors – professional investors having everything at their fingertips on a second-by-second basis, students having excellent access to online datasets and analytical programs, through to the amateur investor on a laptop in a bedroom. Even the last of these still has access to data and programs that were only a glint in the eye before the internet. And, possibly, most importantly, minute-by-minute business and financial news is available to everyone; this can be a blessing but it can also be a curse because a lot of the news is just noise, speculation, opinion, etc. and it can blind the investor to what is really going on. The stock markets are currently riding high in the midst of the biggest crisis the globe has seen for many a year. They are being driven by the cash being washed into the system via government and central bank actions, and the premise seems to be that the economies will benefit from a sharp recovery. We have our doubts, given the damage done to a lot of sectors, the record increases in unemployment and the changed (reduced) behaviours consequent on the Covid-19 virus (will a service economy bounce back, given all the fears and uncertainties?).

This moves us on to who this book is aimed at. It is not intended to be a primer for those new to the financial markets, many of those already exist. Nor is it intended to be an in-depth guide to a particular investment approach.

Instead, it is intended to introduce a range of investment approaches that have seen great success in the hands of individual experts. Some of the approaches are complementary, others are not. More importantly, lessons can be learned from each of the approaches and some can be combined to form a unique approach to fit the interests and attitudes of an individual investor. We have given a reasonable amount of background on each of the experts as this helps to understand the context of the successes and what might be required to make them work. Each chapter also gives small insights to make you sit back and think – i.e. do I have the patience to make this work?, do I have the funds?, is the market the same?, have such gains now been competed away, etc.? Given all this, the book is aimed at students and, to a lesser degree, interested amateurs (see the next paragraph) – these are the ones who have the potential to benefit from the approach taken here and this moves us on to the next, key feature of this book.

While the book is concerned with looking at the lessons to be learnt from investment experts, it is also interested in presenting relevant evidence on the approach (i.e. what could have been achieved by an approach over recent years). The presentation of evidence has two questions:

1. Do the claims of an expert now stack up?
2. How might an approach be quantified so it can be tested against data?

This allows the reader to look at an approach and shows how it can be applied to modern data and techniques of testing. The evidence in each of the chapters is a prelude to the Practical Applications that accompany each chapter. The Practical Applications are a step-by-step guide to actioning a strategy that replicates that of an expert – not always perfectly but as close as we are able to. The intention being that by the end of the book, students and investors will be comfortable with accessing data and developing customised investment strategies.

Through teaching quantitative methods and its many constituent parts, we have found it is best to give a bit of a feel for the theory and then to quickly follow this with practical examples students can work through. There is no replacement for learning by doing. The 'doing' allows the students to understand the intricacies of an approach, the key assumptions, what needs to be done to apply an approach and how it might be 'sensibly' tested – this is not as obvious as it might seem at first glance. Only by trying to apply an approach can an investor begin to appreciate its strengths and weaknesses. So, while the approaches of the various investment experts can be read on their own, the real 'wins' will be gained through trying to apply them to data.

THE PHILOSOPHY AND STRUCTURE OF THE BOOK AND ITS CHAPTERS

Novels are often best read through a series of sittings not too distant from each other; too distant and characters become muddled, as does the plot, and this is especially the case in some crime novels when there are a number of inter-woven subplots. This book is almost the reverse. Each chapter is largely self-contained and should be approached in a singular, focused manner (this sounds a bit heavy and it is not intended to be) and be seen as a starting point for exploring a particular approach to investing. The structure and style of each chapter are intended to whet the appetite of the reader and encourage further exploration. In other words, each chapter is not the end to learning an investment style but purely the beginning. The chapters should be seen as guides, simple highlights, focusing on the key elements and giving impetus to further reading and research. As we noted above, we have been doing this a long time and we keep on learning and exploring on a daily basis. To take an art metaphor, it is easy to understand the broad approach of an artist but it normally takes a lifetime to appreciate the intricacies of an artist and become something approaching an expert – just consider how many so-called art experts are fooled by forgeries/forgers.

To achieve the above objectives, each chapter has a common structure, with a few exceptions, given the specifics of a particular investment expert. After a brief introduction, each chapter has a **background** section on an expert. The intention here is to give a bit of colour and interest and, more importantly, the context of an expert. The particular style of an expert is often determined by their history and specific experiences, noting a number of the experts lived through many of the economic/financial trials and tribulations of the twentieth century. Experiencing a great depression must leave a lasting impression, as will living through the nightmare of Covid-19. Seeing the con-sequences of rampant speculation and betting on a market driven by the sheer volume of cash and speculation, rather than fundamental value, is bound to leave a taste for value, growth, and a contrarian perspective to investing. A number of the background sections clearly show how an expert's experience has had an influence on the nature of their investment philosophy. However, it is important to remember these sections just give brief highlights and there are a lot more insights to be gained by wider reading, and for most of the experts there is no shortage of reading material – with some having many books and articles about their lives and investment philosophies/successes/failures. What does shine through a number of the background sections is that the investment styles of experts often mirror their personalities and this needs to be borne in mind when considering your own approach – there is little point in trying to adopt a cautious, long-term value approach if you are a natural risk taker who enjoys the short-term ups and downs of gambles. The other characteristic that also shines through is the determination of the experts and the willingness to pick themselves up, again and again.

Once some interest has hopefully be gained in an expert through the background section, we then move on to describe their **key lessons**. The key lessons of an expert are our distillation of their fundamental insights. For example, let's take Warren Buffett (see Chapter 2), who has had many books and hundreds of thousands of words written about him and his investment philosophy. His approach is essentially very simple in outline but downright difficult to apply in practice. There are only three **key** lessons to Buffett's approach:

1. Understand the value of a stock (i.e. understand its fundamental investment value of the company and not its stock price/return based on speculation). At the moment of writing (June 2020), we are seeing a massive dislocation between underlying company values and their stock prices. The latter being driven by money being pumped into the system by central banks to counteract the effects of the Covid-19 virus. But a large number of companies are facing very difficult futures through massively restructured markets, dysfunctional supply chains, a reluctance to invest, and a reluctance to consume. Buffett, and a number of other Wall Street experts, have stated this is biggest dislocation between underlying corporate value and stock prices they have ever seen.

2. When purchasing any asset, attention needs to be given to its liquidity, i.e. the ease of disposing of the asset at not too great a loss. We have experienced this issue a number of times in our lives. Let's take the case of yachts. They are incredibly easy to buy but you try selling one. The market (excuse the weak pun) is extremely illiquid. It can take months and years to sell a yacht and many languish unsold for an inordinate length of time. It often takes a significant price reduction from the

'market price' to sell a yacht and this is the definition of an illiquid asset. Another asset that currently springs to mind is French chateaus. To the British investor, they look to offer remarkable value (not surprising given the prices in the British housing market) but there are normally good reasons why assets are priced at a specific level (ignoring speculation and bubbles). French chateaus suffer from the three obvious problems of very expensive repair and maintenance, a difficult-to-navigate state bureaucracy, and a complex tax system in terms of assets. Not surprisingly, these assets are difficult to sell and at the moment of writing, their prices are dropping significantly – even allowing for the TV programmes portraying their many advantages. These are definitely assets of the heart rather than the head.

3. Buffett is cautious and he demands a margin of safety between the fundamental value of a company and the price that is being asked for it. What level of safety is required will depend on the nature of the asset and its liquidity.

So, the key lessons of Buffett are fairly simple but their application is not so straightforward. However, with a bit of common sense it is possible to move some way towards the Buffett approach and that of the other experts. For example, and keeping with Buffett, we will describe how he is a cautious investor, as mirrored by the above key lessons. Therefore, he will want to consider companies that have a good information set on which to base his analysis. This means avoiding small companies and recent flotations (initial public offerings, IPOs) because the information is likely to be patchy and not always reliable. Buffett also wants to invest in solid performers, so here you could put in place some form of profit filter across a given time period and some measures of balance sheet strength.

Having explained the key lessons and application of an expert, we then look at the existing empirical **evidence**. We can again illustrate this with the example of Buffett in Chapter 2. The empirical evidence of Buffett's direct performance is relatively limited apart from the fact that he has made a lot of money for himself and the investors in his Berkshire Hathaway investment vehicle. But even here there is the argument that any investment approach will have a distribution of success, and Buffett's is just an extreme observation. He rightly counters this argument with the longevity of his success – no one beats the market every year, so there must something underpinning an approach that generates extremely positive returns decade after decade.

Due to existing empirical evidence often being limited, we provide our own quantitative assessment of an expert's approach on common datasets covering the US, the UK, and China. The common datasets allow us to compare the performance of the different experts discussed, but we need to accept that not all approaches are equally quantifiable and testable. Allowing for this caveat, we show that Buffett's approach, as quantified by us, achieved a cumulative return across the period 2004–2018 almost double that of a market benchmark – noting that with the exception of the Global Financial Crisis of 2007–2008, the markets have experienced one of the longest bull runs in financial history.

Of course, no expert is free from error and all of the ones discussed in this book have made major errors of judgement. We discuss the major (published) **mistakes** of each of the experts to see what can be learned. What is interesting is that the errors normally occur because the expert strayed from their own strict guidelines – showing it is difficult to maintain an approach when confronted with a range of opportunities and lots of conflicting data/information. In addition, each of the mistakes offers an insight on their own. For example, Buffett's mistimed investment in Tesco. His normal approach is to invest only in what he understands but he broke this rule with this investment because he did not appreciate the changing landscape of the UK grocery sector with the surge of the low-cost entrants, such as Aldi and Lidl.

After a brief conclusion, each chapter proceeds to a section describing how the approach of a specific expert can be applied and backtested. In Chapter 2 on Buffett, the Practical Application section describes some general matters, given this is the first expert chapter, of equity screening; for example, what should be the sample of companies and whether absolute or relative metrics should be used when considering the various filters applied to a given expert. Once these general issues have been discussed, Chapter 2 follows the pattern of all chapters and describes a worked example step-by-step. While the chapters are intended to be largely stand-alone, understanding how to apply various steps and filters will build up as the chapters are worked through. Once a given expert's approach has been built up, the final part of the chapter is the Practical Application section to show how to backtest and see how the approach has performed across various samples and time periods.

The Practical Application sections are critical to understanding an approach. Only by trying to apply an approach, can its intricacies, strengths, weaknesses, etc. be understood. It also gives readers the fun of tweaking an approach and seeing how its performance changes across different samples and time periods. With reflection, this is a quick and analytical means of gaining insights – just as much as watching the market and reading the financial news on a daily basis. Remember, no approach is ever the 'finished article' as the markets and its participants change through time – this is what makes the subject exciting and, hopefully, rewarding. An open mind and lots of reflection through testing are the only methodical ways to achieve ongoing success.

THE ROLE OF DATA AND TESTING

We connect experts' investment lessons with data in two ways. First, data enable us to produce evidence to evaluate and understand an expert's investment approach. This gives us a tangible idea of how great some of these investment achievements are but also allows us to appreciate the diversity of paths that one can take to get there. Second, data are the new fuel in the digital economy. We are connecting traditional philosophies with future developments in mind. To understand the relevance of those investment ideas to current and future investment environments, we need to reconsider the increasingly important role that data play in the economy and how we can harness the power of easy access to data for our investments.

To turn data into useful information, we need analytical tools that fit the purpose. As we will learn in Chapter 8 on Quants, complex computer algorithms are used to connect with millions of data points to produce an automated trading system. It was only possible to develop such systems in the past by bespoke software design and proprietary access to some hand-collected data. The internet has lowered the costs and technology development has enabled the collection of unstructured data (images, video) from many different sources (satellite images). Vast quantities of these data are released in real time. The traditional approach of watching the news and reacting is gradually being replaced by an algorithm to monitor the abnormal flow and tone of the news.

The ideas and techniques introduced in this book can be implemented via many data environments and we will use a few to illustrate the power of a structured, data-driven approach to developing and testing investment strategies.

CHAPTER 2

Warren Buffett

The World's Greatest Investor?

INTRODUCTION

If the man on the street was asked to name an investor, it is likely that he would say Warren Buffett. His fame (and fortune) arise because he is one of the richest people on the planet (he has been the richest and is normally included in the top 5) with an estimated wealth of approximately $90bn at the time of writing (July 2019). While his wealth has led to a lot of media attention, his style of investing and his willingness to speak simple 'business truths' have also helped – these might have contributed to him being referred to as the Sage, Oracle or Wizard of Omaha.

Given such fame, it will come as no surprise that there is no shortage of texts or books written about Buffett. This leaves us with a bit of problem, i.e. what can we hope to add to the reams of paper and lines of text written about Warren Buffett?

Well, following the structure of all chapters in this book, we intend to give the key lessons of Buffett as simply as possible and then consider how easy it is for a starter investor to apply them. Once we have covered these aspects, we then review two critical topics: (1) the available empirical evidence concerning the success of such an approach; and (2) the mistakes the expert investors have made across their career. We undertake this last topic because while we all know about their wealth and the successes, we tend to hear less about their failures. And there is as much to be learned from failure as there is from success, possibly more so. If such great investors are prone to failures, it raises questions over how easy it is to apply the lessons of a particular investment approach. Finally, the Practical Application section shows you how to apply the lessons of Buffett. As is the case for all of the other chapters, the best way of understanding an approach to investing is to try it out.

Before we get to these aspects/topics, we first consider some of Buffett's background – again, this can be instructive and in Buffett's case, it is especially so.

BACKGROUND

As we will see in the next section, Buffett's approach looks deceptively easy: identify undervalued businesses and buy them. However, Buffett's background and national presence has allowed him to 'walk' corporate America and put his strategy into action. This is not so easy for the normal private investor. Buffett's approach is more akin to turn-around specialists who spot distressed businesses with potential. Essentially, you have to be part of the corporate landscape on a daily basis to be aware of these opportunities. While private investors can apply a 'value strategy' to listed shares, their information set will be a lot less than institutional investors/turn-around specialists. But we are getting ahead of ourselves – we need to understand how Buffett became part of corporate America.

Buffett was born in 1930 in Omaha and graduated from high school in 1947. Even during these early years he showed an uncanny ability to spot business opportunities and create wealth. While there are the usual examples of working in shops, cleaning cars and delivering newspapers, at the age of 15 and at the end of the Second World War, Buffett and his friend spent $25 ($300 in today's money) on a used pinball machine and placed it in a local barber shop. They soon owned several machines in a number of barber shops and sold the 'business' to a war veteran for $1200 (about $15k in today's prices). Not a bad result for a teenager and it demonstrates Buffett's innate understanding of business.

However, such understanding was turbo-charged by his knowledge of the stock market. His father was a stockbroker (and a Congressman) and this gave the young Buffett insights rarely available to most individuals. He spent time in the offices of stockbrokers, made a visit to Wall Street at the age of 10 and bought his first shares at the age of 11. If this is not impressive enough, he bought a 40-acre farm with a tenant farmer at the age of 14 from his savings. As you can see, this is not the usual story of a teenager.

Given his background, it should come as no surprise that his university education is equally impressive with stints at Wharton, the University of Nebraska, Columbia Business School and the New York Institute of Finance, all by the age of 21. However, it was his time at Columbia and attending classes by Benjamin Graham (the father of Value Investing) that were to shape Buffett's natural instinct for value.

After leaving university, Buffett earned his stripes as a stockbroker and by his late twenties (in the late 1950s) he had convinced 10 wealthy clients to invest $10,000 each into his investment partnerships for a nominal investment of $100 by Buffett himself. Essentially, he had raised close on a $1m in today's money. And while there are many aspects of Buffett's investment career, it was the good use of these 'initial' funds that set the stage – 'you need money to make money'.

By taking a 23% stake in the undervalued Sanborn Map Company (he invested 33% of his partnership's funds) and not being afraid to become an activist investor, Buffett made a 50% return on his investment within two years.

The scale of Buffett's acumen can be gauged by the fact that across the 1960s and 1970s he undertook a number of high profile investments (e.g. an investment in *The Washington Post*) that culminated in the $3.5bn purchase of ABC Media. Note, his value investment strategy is coupled with significant and often controlling stakes – this is not your average private investor!

This process of taking significant stakes in companies via his investment vehicle of Berkshire Hathaway continued across the 1980s and 1990s with investments in Salomon Brothers, Coca-Cola (he maintains this is still his best investment) and General Re (not without its problems).

And the story of significant stakes in undervalued companies continues to the present day with investments being taken in Goldman Sachs, Dow Chemical, General Electric, Proctor and Gamble, IBM, etc.

To conclude this section, it is important to note a characteristic that is not normally given emphasis. Buffett couples his value strategy with a significant (and often controlling) stake. This gives him a voice within the company and, in this regard, his strategy is more akin to that of a turn-around specialist. So while private investors may be able to copy his notion of value investing, they will not have the significant stakes needed to gain access and elements of control.

KEY LESSONS

This section will be short because the key lessons of Warren Buffett are very straightforward in principle but, as we will see, are a bit more difficult to apply in a coherent manner.

The first lesson to take from Buffett is to understand the difference between investment and speculation. Investment is buying stocks for less than they are 'fundamentally' worth. Here there is a high probability that the stock market will eventually recognize the undervaluation and the shares will appreciate to their 'true' value. This notion of investment is based on a lot of business understanding and analysis of the potential of the business (see Appendix II, the valuation chapter). In contrast (but only to a degree!), speculation is buying shares on the back of possible future events occurring. However, as value investing also depends on a view of the future, the two are closer than might first seem. The difference seems to be a matter of degree – with investment, the analysis has been done and the value and risks quantified. Speculation is more 'carefree' and less analytical.

A clear difference between investment and speculation emerges when the former is based on past performance and the assumption that the past will continue in the future. But, as seen in Appendix II, it would be strange indeed to base a valuation purely on the past with no recognition of the importance of the future.

Another feature of value investing and Buffett's approach is one of liquidity. While value investors focus on the longer term, and this negates the need for high liquidity in the short term, if the investments of Buffett are considered, they are normally very large companies with liquid stocks – this means that shares can be bought or sold in reasonable quantity without having an undue influence on the price paid.

The final lesson to be taken from Buffett is his eminently sensible margin of safety rule. Given the difficulties associated with drawing up an accurate valuation and making accurate forecasts, it is prudent to build in a margin for error. This is a cushion to tide you over any adverse, unforeseen circumstances. As always, however, there is an issue to reflect on. What scale of safety margin do you decide on: 25%, 50%, etc. and, once you have decided, how many companies meet this criterion? Too large a margin and you may not find the large and liquid stocks you desire. Of course, another and complementary way to manage risk is to diversify. A diversified portfolio of, say, 10 stocks, should allow you to have a reduced margin of safety and a greater range of companies to select from.

APPLYING THE LESSONS

Buffett's lessons appear deceptively simple but, as always, some work needs to be done if his approach is to be applied with rigour. We would suggest an initial screening of companies to come up with a set worthy of more detailed investigation. Here are some initial screening filters:

1. Avoid small companies – Buffett has rarely invested in small companies. They are inherently more risky and have, in general, poorer data. In the UK, the FTSE 350 Index is a good place to start. It combines the FTSE 100 and FTSE 250, with companies in the latter going down to £500m in market capitalization.
2. Avoid recent IPOs if they do not have at least 5 years of trading data pre the IPO.
3. Only select companies with at least 5 years of positive performance – positive EBIT (earnings before interest or taxes, or operating profit), positive cash flow from operations, a return on equity of at least, say, 10% for the majority of the previous 5 years, with a debt/equity ratio of less than 1, with a positive tangible asset value greater than 1.

The above filters will give a group of large companies with good information, solid performance, and strong(ish) balance sheets.

The next step is to apply some ratios to gauge the quality of companies across the various financial dimensions. Ratio analysis can be applied mechanically and this is its benefit in the current context. But as a ratio is made up of at least two components, a level or changes in a ratio can reflect different financial structures. So some care needs to be applied. It also needs to be remembered that each business activity will have its own 'natural' set of ratios that reflect the business and the industry. For example, a chemical company will need a lot of fixed assets, a retail company a lot of stock, a bank a lot of debtors and creditors, etc. Therefore, you need to understand what a sector's ratios should be like and remember that the accounting data underpinning the ratios are likely to be dated.

> **DEFINITIONS**
>
> **Gross profit** is the profit after deducting the costs associated with making and selling its products, or the costs associated with providing its services. **Operating profit** is gross profit minus operating expenses. **Net profit** is operating profit after deduction of interest and taxes.

While there are as many financial ratios as one can almost imagine, there are a number of commonly used ones under the headings of profitability, liquidity, gearing, and stability.

- **Profitability** – let's begin with profit margins: gross, operating and net. For each of these you need to establish what the industry average is and what would count as being in the top quartile and then you select companies within this top band. Some people talk about needing a gross profit margin of at least 40% and a net margin of at least 20% but this makes little sense without some reference to what is achievable in a specific industry. For example, such margins are rarely encountered in the highly competitive packaging industry. In addition to margin, profitability is affected by the ability of the business to generate sales. So some ratio of sales/assets and/or sales growth is normally considered. These measure how well a business uses its assets to generate sales. Finally, we can consider overall profitability ratios – return on assets, return on invested capital, growth of earnings per share, etc. A 10% figure is often stated for these types of ratio. In the current low interest environment, this would be a good, solid but not stellar return. So, in terms of profitability, we need ratios that are consistently in the top quartile of the distribution for that industry. You may, of course, adopt absolute percentages for these various ratios but this is likely to rule out a number of sectors.
- **Liquidity** – this measures the ability of a business to financially run itself on a day-to-day basis. Meeting current liabilities when they fall due from current assets within normal business terms. Again, the textbooks suggest norms for these ratios (which we state) but they need to

reflect the industry and the power of the business within that industry. For example, a major supermarket can run with low liquidity ratios because of the frequency of the turnover of stock and its power over suppliers. Let's start with the current ratio that compares current assets to current liabilities and is supposed to be at least 2 if a business is to be classed as safe. However, as current assets comprise stock, debtors, and cash, it is possible to have a higher than 2 ratio because of obsolete and difficult-to-sell stock and an aged debtor book that might be difficult to collect. This is not to say such matters are likely, just that they need to be borne in mind. This moves us on to the quick ratio that is the same as the current ratio less the stock figure. The idea being that it should be easier and quicker to realize cash from debtors than stock. Here a ratio of at least 1 is normally sought. Finally, we have the interest coverage ratio and this is normally calculated as the EBIT of a business divided by its interest expenses. This is similar to working out if your monthly net income is sufficient to pay the mortgage. A ratio of 5 is often seen as giving reasonable coverage.

- **Gearing (or leverage)** – this aspect of a company's financial profile is supposed to gauge financial exposure but, as already noted, the exact make-up of a company's debt and equity critically affects its exposure. Nonetheless, there are some broad-brush levels regarding gearing ratios. For example, if we take debt divided by equity, you would not historically have wanted a value of more than 1 (and if we took debt divided by total assets, the value should not be more than 0.5). This type of level should ensure a business is able to meet its debt payments when they fall due. However, it needs to be realized that companies can run with higher debt levels, and they are often encouraged to do so, depending on the stability of their income streams and their relationship with the debt providers. Equally, a good cash balance can act as an 'insurance policy' and greater debt levels may be possible.

- **Stability (likelihood of failure)** – when taken together, the above ratios can give an indication of a company's risk of failure – losses combined with poor liquidity and high gearing do not paint a very rosy picture. It will come as no surprise that academics have spent a lot of time coming up with financial models that predict financial failure. The most famous model is the Altman Z-score model that looks as follows:

$$Z - \text{Score} = 1.2A + 1.4B + 3.3C + 0.6D + 1.0E$$
Where:

A = working capital / total assets

B = retained earnings / total assets

C = earnings before interest and tax / total assets

D = market value of equity / total liabilities

E = sales / total assets.

If a company has a Z-score of less than 1.8, then it is seen as being at risk. This model was developed on large US companies and there are other versions of failure prediction models for different countries and sizes of companies. For example, Keasey and Watson spent a lot of the 1980s and 1990s analysing small firm failure prediction for the UK.[1]

Finally, there are some other signs that a company may be entering a period of high risk. For example, if a company has normally been timely with its financial reporting and suddenly there is a significant delay, there is likely to be an explanation based on failing financial performance. Similarly, if a business suddenly starts to lose senior staff, is seen to be expanding head office facilities, is entering overseas markets at a break-neck speed – then, again, care needs to be exercised as these can be signs of managerial hubris. Basically, if a business starts to show signs of instability and/or hubris, start to worry.

EMPIRICAL EVIDENCE

Mainstream academic finance has long held that financial markets are efficient and it is not possible to make money by trading on past information. In other words, it should be impossible to systematically make money from a Buffett-*type* model. The evidence offered by academic finance in support of efficient markets is enormous and while a search on the Web will pull up any number, the paper by Fama in 1991 is not a bad place to start.[2] The essence of the argument and evidence presented by Fama is that while value stocks give

---

[1] K. Keasey and R. Watson, The state of the art of small firm failure prediction: achievements and prognosis. *International Small Business Journal* 9(1) (1991): 11–30.

[2] E.F. Fama, Efficient capital markets: II. *The Journal of Finance* 46 (1991): 1575-1617. doi:10.1111/j.1540-6261.1991.tb04636.x

an excess return in 12 out of 13 international markets, the return is based on not properly controlling for the risk of these value stocks. Once the distress risk of the value stocks is allowed for, then they do not make excess returns. The whole history of mainstream finance is one of it trying to protect its main tenet of efficiency and there are good sociological reasons why this continues to be the case.[3] Nonetheless, there is other academic evidence[4] that suggests markets suffer from behavioural biases and, once these are understood, money can be made.

Buffett defends value investing on the basis of the monies he has made. The response from the efficient market disciples is that this is just dumb luck and in any distribution, somebody will get lucky while, on average, most investors will not be so lucky. Buffett quite rightly has two defences. First, it is quite remarkable that his luck has held out for almost 60 years. Second, and to our mind more powerfully, he argues that if the value approach is just dumb luck, how come so many of its adherents continue to make money on a year-by-year basis? Especially, when the adherents to Benjamin Graham's methods have used slightly different variants of the approach?

Another criticism of the value approach is that a number of the well-known adherents have taken meaningful stakes in companies and have been able to be active in their investments, an approach not available to most investors. However, research by Otuteye and Siddiquee[5] shows that when the value approach is applied methodically to Canadian companies for the period from 2001 to 2011, then it is possible to make excess returns, even after allowing for the excess risk of the investments.

Overall, there seems to be sufficient available evidence to have faith in value investing being able to produce excess returns. At the same time, we should be aware that any approach to investing is not without its ups and downs, and the real trick is to have sufficient capital to withstand the downs and move onto the ups. Basically, no approach is plain sailing, the real question being is whether it produces significant returns in the long run – and, in Buffett's case, it clearly has.

---

[3] K. Keasey, and R. Hudson, Finance theory: A house without windows, *Critical Perspectives on Accounting* 18(8) (2007): 932–951.

[4] C.X. Cai, K. Keasey, P. Li, and Q. Zhang, Nonlinear effects of market development on pricing anomalies (October 26, 2018). Available at SSRN: https://ssrn.com/abstract=2839799 or http://dx.doi.org/10.2139/ssrn.2839

[5] E. Otuteye and M. Siddiquee, examining the performance of a value investing heuristic: Evidence from the S&P/TSX 60 from 2001–2011. *Journal of Business Economics & Finance* 2(4) (2013): 67–81.

QUANTITATIVE EVALUATION

In this section we explore the implementation of Buffett's investment philosophy through a quantitative approach and test its performance using historical data.

Applying Buffett's Method in the UK Market

We set the following criteria in filtering (Table 2.1).

Backtesting set-up: we apply these criteria at the end of June every year from 2004 to 2019 (15 years). We rebalance (rescreening) every year and calculate the portfolio's return.

Cumulated Return

Figure 2.1 reports the total cumulated return of the strategy and the benchmark (FTSE 100). The average annual return for the strategy is 10.77% and on average it beats the market by 3.5%.

It reports the returns in percentages. Active return is the difference between the return of the strategy and the benchmark.

Rebalancing

Figure 2.2 reports the number of securities in the portfolio and decomposes them into a number of securities that are the same as the previous period, new and dropped out in the current period.

It shows that Buffett's value strategy is indeed a long-term strategy with low turnover in the portfolio. It seems there is a structural change in 2010 with more companies meeting the value criteria.

TABLE 2.1   Applying Buffett's method in the UK market

Criteria	Members (as of Sep 2019)
A pool of FTSE 350 constituent stocks	351
Current Market Cap >= £500 Million	346
EBIT in each of the past 5 years > 0	199
FCF in each of the past 5 years >0	149
ROE in each of the past 5 years >10%	76
Debt to Equity < 1	56
Z-score >1.8	50

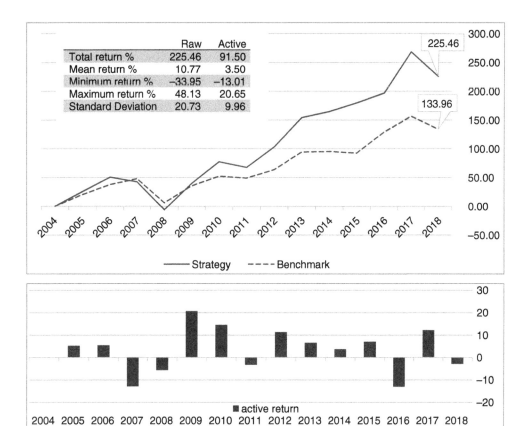

	Raw	Active
Total return %	225.46	91.50
Mean return %	10.77	3.50
Minimum return %	−33.95	−13.01
Maximum return %	48.13	20.65
Standard Deviation	20.73	9.96

FIGURE 2.1 Cumulative return of Buffett's strategy in the UK.
Source: BLOOMBERG PROFESSIONAL®.

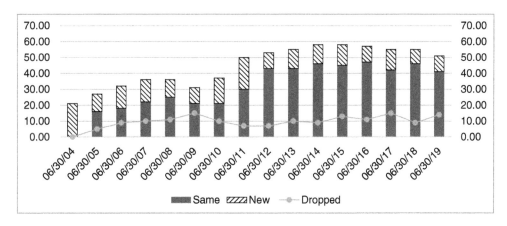

FIGURE 2.2 Security count history.
Source: BLOOMBERG PROFESSIONAL®.

INTERNATIONAL EVIDENCE

The US Market

For the US market, we start our screening with S&P 500 companies and use the S&P 500 as the benchmark. Overall, the strategy also works well in the US although the active return is lower (Figure 2.3).

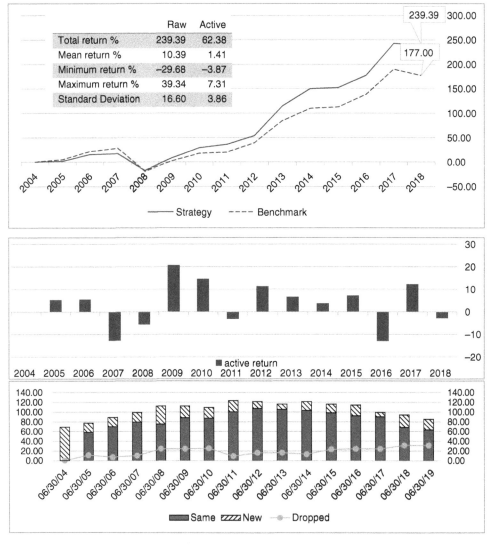

	Raw	Active
Total return %	239.39	62.38
Mean return %	10.39	1.41
Minimum return %	−29.68	−3.87
Maximum return %	39.34	7.31
Standard Deviation	16.60	3.86

FIGURE 2.3 Cumulative return and security count history of Buffett's strategy in the US.
Source: BLOOMBERG PROFESSIONAL®.

The China Market

For the China market, we start our screening with the Shanghai Shenzen 300 index (CSI 300) of companies and use the CSI 300 as the benchmark. The strategy seems to be working better in China with a larger accumulated return but also with larger year-by-year variations (Figure 2.4). This suggests a higher risk in this market, as is to be expected, given the emerging nature of the market.

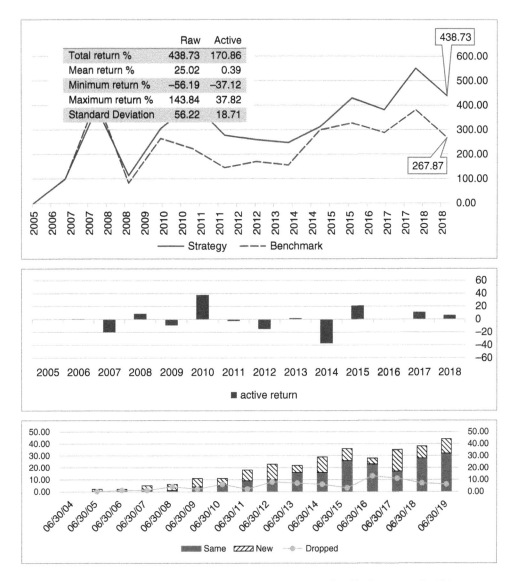

FIGURE 2.4 Cumulative return and security count history of Buffett's strategy in China. Source: BLOOMBERG PROFESSIONAL®.

Overall, the quantitative backtesting shows that Buffett's method is useful in deriving a quantitative investment that can outperform the market in the long run. This serves as a base for the portfolio selection of value stocks. There is, however, room for improvement in this basic set-up. For example, adding a relative value criterion such as a price earnings ratio filter to identify stocks with relative lower pricing (low PE ratio) will improve the performance of the portfolio while reducing the number of holdings (less transaction costs).

THE MISTAKES OF WARREN BUFFETT

In this section we briefly run through a number of Buffett's mistakes and we begin with one of his major mistakes – his investment in Tesco. What is strange about this mistake is that Buffett seems to have broken one of his fundamental tenets – only invest in companies you understand. And while Buffett may have been able to understand the financials of Tesco from the US, it is difficult to see how he could have understood the retail grocery market in the UK from his desk in Omaha. The major retailers in the UK were doing well but there was a slow motion shift taking place – the shift to discount stores and value. Aldi opened its first store in the UK in 1990 and its basic value proposition was dismissed by the large retailers. It, however, gained ground across the 1990s (mainly in the North of England) and started to take off in the 2000s. The financial crisis in 2007 super-charged its model of offering value before the shopping experience.

Against the above background, Buffett bought his first Tesco shares in 2006 and by 2012 had raised his stake to more than 5% of the company. Given what was happening on the high street in the UK, this seemed a strange investment to any interested party. Tesco was a bloated company, offering everything to everybody and was a prime target for retailers such as Aldi and Lidl to take aim at with their value proposition on basic groceries. Across 2013 and 2014, Buffett sold down his stake in Tesco to a total after tax loss of $444m. He concluded that the scale of his loss was amplified because he was indecisive, he took quite some time to sell down his investment – this may have been partly explained by the significant scale of his investment, as well as the fact he was indecisive.

Lesson
When investing, you need to learn from your mistakes, own up to them and move on.

While Tesco looks to have been a significant investment mistake, it is not his only one. Let's start with his investment in Berkshire Hathaway (BH), his investment vehicle. When he bought BH in 1962, it was a failing textile group. He bought a significant stake and then (because of a conflict with the management) bought a controlling stake and tried to keep the group running for nigh on 20 years. Buffett has stated that letting his heart rule his head in this particular instance may have cost him many hundreds of millions. Somewhat surprisingly, he made the same mistake again when he purchased Waumbec Textile Company, 13 years later. It looked a bargain in asset value terms and Buffett seems to have thought he could have gained synergies with Berkshire Hathaway. This seems to be a case of buying a drowning man to save a drowning man. In investing, you need to learn from your mistakes, own up to them, and move on.

Above, we have stated Tesco was a significant investment mistake but when you read Buffett's interviews, he seems to change his mind as to what counts as his worst investment. However, the purchase of Dexster Shoe Company for $433m in 1993 might well be his worst investment – costing his shareholders $3.5bn. The reasons for the scale of this loss are twofold. First, he bought a company, apparently of good value, with no real competitive advantage. Second, he paid for Dexster in BH stock. The value of the purchase price in BH stock had ballooned to $5.7bn in 2014. This looks to have been a case of swapping solid and value-enhancing stock for a company with a less than predictable future.

Similar mistakes were made when he purchased General Re insurance. This eventually became a prize asset in the BH portfolio but not before having to realize $800m of losses. He again made the mistake of paying for the company with BH shares – new shares were issued and BH shareholders were heavily diluted by 22%.

Web resource

See Buffett's 15 investing mistakes he regrets.
`https://www.cnbc.com/2017/12/15/warren-buffetts-`
`failures-15-investing-mistakes-he-regrets.html`

Interestingly, given the above, one of the features of Warren Buffett is his cautious nature. This has served him well but occasionally, it does cost him quite a lot of money. For example, when we were in the midst of compiling this book (end of April 2020, at the height of the Covid-19 crisis), Berkshire Hathaway reported a loss of $50bn – no small amount of money (and about 10% of the value of the fund pre-losses). One of the reasons for the loss seems to have been Buffett's slow response to the crisis, also remember he takes relatively big positions in companies and these are not easy to unwind in a discreet way and will also have a negative impact. Buffett had taken big stakes in a number of US airlines that had catastrophic reductions in revenues of 90% or more. Furthermore, given all the risks of flying in a Covid-19 world, Buffett concluded the business model was unlikely to return to normal for quite some time, if at all. He suffered substantial losses on his airline positions at the end of April – the crisis had been running for approximately six weeks in the West by the time he took action.

In a similar cautious manner, though he admired Google and Amazon, he did not invest because he did not understand their business models. With hindsight (wonderful stuff), he should have taken his time to understand these models and back his admiration. Both of these tech companies have powered ahead during the Covid-19 crisis for obvious reasons.

Overall, even Warren Buffett does not always follow the strictures of his own approach and while a company may look to be good value, there may be solid reasons why a company is marked down. Not searching for such reasons is a mistake, as is using your appreciating stock to buy such companies.

SUMMARY

- The key lesson from Buffett is spotting an investment opportunity that offers long-run value. Although the price you pay is important, you don't mind paying a bit more for a company that offers great long-term value.
- The real question is: how to identify those companies?
- Our evidence shows that applying Buffett's philosophy with a set of screening criteria works in the three test markets – managing to beat the passive investment strategy of investing in the leading index for each market.

- For example, the Buffett strategy with 'our screens' gains 91% more return than the UK benchmark in the 15 years of investment between 2005–2019.
- Such a performance is achieved without looking into the qualitative aspect of the companies, such as governance and CEO track record. It provides a very promising starting point for selecting stocks for long-term investment.

PRACTICAL APPLICATION I: EQUITY SCREENING AND BACKTESTING

Before we look at Equity Screening and Backtesting on the BLOOMBERG PROFESSIONAL® site (this is a useful site to start with), we need to cover a bit of notation to help you progress.

Understanding the Notations of the Book

In general, there are three *forms* of action we normally use when using a software tool: *click*, *type* some inputs, and stroke (*hit*) a specific key on the keyboard.

For example, to load a function in the BLOOMBERG PROFESSIONAL® system we *type* {EQS} in the blue-framed command line on the top of any of the four windows. And *hit* the <Enter> key or on a BLOOMBERG PROFESSIONAL® keyboard the enter key is indicated by <Go>.

We use italic font to indicate the *forms* of action such as *type*, *click*, *hit*. And in the latest stage, some combination actions such as *load* for loading a function which is basically a combination of actions. For example, instead of the instruction given in the above example, we will simply write: *load* {EQS}.

We use { } to indicate function names, strings that needed to be typed in or the option chosen from a list. Only the string inside the brackets need to be typed in, not the brackets themselves.

We use < > to indicate keys on the keyboard and [ ] to indicate on-screen buttons. For example, to save a EQS screen:

Click [98 Actions] , [Save. . .], *type* {my first EQS screen}, *click* [1) Update]

We now introduce one of the most powerful tools of portfolio construction: stock screening. We will provide a detailed discussion of such a function and a review of existing tools available on the Web.

Equity Screening

What is an equity screening tool? 'Screening' originated from medical research where tests are carried out to determine the presence or absence of a disease. It extends to referring to a process of selecting or excluding something after evaluation or investigation. In the investment context, it is a process of determining whether particular stocks should be included in a portfolio; stocks that pass the screen test are those that meet our selection criteria. For example, we may consider stocks that have a positive profit are a good investment. Profit greater than zero will be used as the criterion for this particular screen test. Most of the screen 'engines' go about screening by simply sorting the variable of interest (in this case, profit) in a descending or ascending order, depending on your preference, and finding those observations that meet your criteria.

What are the key considerations when undertaking an equity screening? While the most important aspect of a screen is the core investment idea (such as the value screen with multiple criteria we discussed in this chapter), we focus here on two considerations that are key to starting to use screens:

1. What is the universe of your screening?
2. Should we use absolute or relative criteria?

The first question can be answered by an alternative question: what is the pool of investable securities, given this particular strategy? For example, if a value strategy is being considered – although it can be global – most of the theory applies to relative valuation in a given market and, therefore, it is always a good idea to start with a single market (e.g. the UK market). When including more than one market, issues such as exchange rates and different accounting systems need to be dealt with. Therefore, a pool of fairly homogeneous stocks is a good starting point for testing an idea.

For the second question, most of the investment ideas are not precisely specified. For example, suppose that the higher the profitability the better, but it does not tell us how high is high. In testing, we can use an absolute measure, for example, if we are using return on equity (ROE), we could define a value greater than 15% as being high. The problem of setting criteria in absolute terms is that it does not consider the possible time variations in the average of the measures that may be driven by macro events and, therefore, apply to all stocks. Practically, it is also less used as a strategy to test because we will not know how many stocks we will end up with ex ante; it could be that 50 or 200 stocks meet such a criterion at different points in time. Alternatively, we can use a relative criterion such as selecting the top 10 companies or the top 10% of the stocks. In this way, we have a better control of the number of selected stocks. The relative criteria, especially the percentile approach, is the most popular one in academic testing since most of the theory is interested in relative mispricing. Once you can separate overpriced from underpriced stocks, you can then short and long the two different types of stocks to lock in the arbitrage profit. Box 2.1 explains the detailed criteria that can be set when adding a new variable into your screen.

Box 2.1   Setting Screening Criteria

List of options
No Condition, display only
> Greater than
>= Greater than or equal to
< Less

When adding a new variable, there are 12 options for setting your criteria.

1. You can test this variable for its relationship to a fixed value or another variable. This uses the top 7 options in the drop-down lists.

2. For selecting stocks based on their relative ranking you can choose 'R Rank' to specify the number of top or bottom observations to be selected. Alternatively selecting '% Percentile' to specify the segment of stocks from the list you like to include.

3. The difference between % and PT can be illustrated in an example. Let's say the variable of interest is Sales and the pool of securities is the FTSE 350. Specifying the top 10% will produce a list of 35 stocks which is 10% of the total number of stocks. 10PT will produce a list of stocks that makes up the first 10% of the total sales in the 350 companies when companies are ordered in high to low sales. The number of securities that met this criteria will change from one month to another.

Worked Example: Applying Buffett's Lessons

In this example we work through a step-by-step construction of Buffett's criteria using the BLOOMBERG PROFESSIONAL® terminal.

Step 1 Loading EQS

Type {EQS} and *hit* <Enter> in the command line on the top of any of the four BLOOMBERG PROFESSIONAL® windows.

Step 2 Add Criteria

	Criteria	Members (as of Sep 2019)
1	A pool FTSE 350 constituent stocks	351
2	Current Market Cap >= £500 million	346
3	EBIT in each of the past 5 years > 0	199
4	FCF in each of the past 5 years >0	149
5	ROE in each of the past 5 years >10%	76
6	Debt to Equity < 1	56
7	Z-score >1.8	50

Criteria 1 – Selecting Only FTSE 350 Companies in the List

Type {FTSE 350} in the orange strip underneath the Add Criteria then wait for the autofill dropdown list to appear and select from the list {FTSE 350 Index} and *hit* <Enter>.

Criteria 2 – Selecting Only Companies that Are Larger than £500 Million from the List

Type {Market Cap} in the orange strip underneath the Add Criteria then select {Greater than or equal to} and *type* {500} in the value box and *hit* <Enter>.

Criteria 3 – EBIT in Each of the Past 5 Years > 0

We add the following criteria one-by-one

> Field, period, operator, criteria, with previous criterion
> EBIT, latest year, Greater than, 0, AND

EBIT, Y-1, Greater than, 0, AND

. . .

EBIT, Y-5, Greater than, 0, AND

Criteria 4 – FCF in Each of the Past 5 Years > 0

Criteria 5 – ROE in Each of the Past 5 Years >10%

Similarly, we add criteria for each of the past five years as in criteria 3 above by replacing EBIT by Free Cash Flow.

And for ROE each of the past five years one-by-one:

Field, period, operator, criteria, with previous criterion
Return on Common Equity, latest year, Greater than, 10%, AND
Return on Common Equity, Y-1, Greater than, 10%, AND
. . .
Return on Common Equity, Y-4, Greater than, 10%, AND

Criteria 6 – Debt to Equity < 1

Field, period, operator, criteria, with previous criterion
Total Debt to Total Equity, latest year, less than, 100%, AND

Criteria 7 – Z-Score >1.8

Field, operator, criteria, with previous criterion
Altman's Z-score, Greater than, 1.8, AND

Step 3 Save the Screen

Click [98 Actions] , [Save. . .], *type* {Buffett_01_UK}, *click* [1) Update]

Step 4 Backtest

We will then study the historical performance of this screening. The basic idea is that if we select stocks according to the above criteria historically every year, we can ask the question 'what would have been the performance in the following year?'

Click on the [99) Backtest] at the top red strip after you save the screen. Or if you like to backtest previously saved screens, you should upload them up first by clicking into the saved screen from the list on the left.

Setting Backtesting Parameters

How Many Years and How Often Should You Rebalance?

Rebalancing involves redoing the screening with up-to-date data, selling the stocks in the existing portfolio and buying new stocks from the screening result. We set these parameters by

Clicking on [3) ✎ Analysis Period]

In this example, we chose 15 years with an annual rebalance. This is done with the following inputs:

Start Date, Relative, {15}, {years}
End Date, Relative, {Last Year End}
Rebalance Frequency, {Annually}
Then Clicking [1) Update]

Portfolio Weighting and Benchmark

In this example, we chose to equally weight all the stocks. In other words, we divided our total investment equally to invest in each stock. We can also choose a benchmark that will be used to compare our portfolio return. In this example, we chose the FTSE100 index and specify the currency to be GDP.

We set these parameters by

Clicking on [4) ✎ Analytic Parameters]
We then enter the followings:

Weighting schema: {Equal}
☑ Use Benchmark: {UKX Index}
Currency: {GDP}
Then clicking [1) Update]

Run the Model

After finishing the set-up, we run the backtesting by

Clicking [1) Run Model]

It will ask to save the model. We can enter the following

Name: {Buffett}
Then clicking [1) Save & Run]

It will display a window indicating that

Your EQBT run is now processing, please see RPT for progress. You will receive a message when the run is finished.
Clicking [1) OK] to close this notification.

Step 5 Review the Result in EQBT

When the model is finished running by BLOOMBERG PROFESSIONAL® , you will receive a notification through the Message in the BLOOMBERG

Tips
To obtain more information about each function or screen, after loading the function, click the green [HELP] button on the top menu or F1 on the BLOOMBERG PROFESSIONAL® keyboard to load the help page . It often also contains examples for you to understand the usage of the function in real life.

PROFESSIONAL® terminal.

Click the Attached: [97 BLOOMBERG PROFESSIONAL® Function (EQBT)] link will take you to the EQBT function.

Alternatively, you can just *type* {EQBT} then <Enter> and *click* the magnify icon for a given model to see the result.

The standard EQBT function reports the strategy return in three tabs; most of the elements we have discussed in our main text. For the detail of these functions, you can access the function's help page by clicking the green [HELP] button on the top menu or F1 on the BLOOMBERG PROFESSIONAL® keyboard.

SUMMARY

The above example demonstrates the power of using data to test an investment idea. With just a few steps we can answer the many 'what if' questions that take investors years to practise and reach conclusions. In the following chapters, we are going to learn more insights from these successful investors' lessons and see how to test them with data and see their relevance for your own investment decisions.

EXERCISES

Replicate the quantitative strategies we discussed in the main text in a different market of your choice with the {EQS} and {EQBT} functions.

CHAPTER 3

Philip Fisher

Growth Investor

INTRODUCTION

We began the book by learning the lessons of Warren Buffett because he is, possibly, the investor best known to the man on the street. In many ways, we should have focused on Benjamin Graham, the 'father' of value investing but this would have been less immediate. Another, on the face of it, reason for looking at Graham is that he followed a purist value strategy, whereas Buffett is slightly more nuanced – according to Buffett, he is 85% 'Graham' and 15% 'Fisher'. However, Buffett was also chosen for this very reason – while value and growth investing are often seen as entirely separable approaches, they have to share a number of characteristics. Essentially, it is not sensible to ignore a company's growth potential when looking at value, although the immediate value can be ignored when looking at growth potential. We will look more deeply into this interface of the two approaches at the end of this chapter but for the moment and for most of the chapter we will see the growth approach as a separate approach to investing. And in the way investment is approached, it has indeed a very different mindset.

Before we look at the background of Philip Fisher (the recognized father of growth investing), we need to agree on a definition of what constitutes growth investing.

Somewhat unhelpfully to our minds, growth investing is often portrayed as high price to earnings or high price to book value stocks. The logic being that the 'market' is seeing something in these stocks (growth) that goes beyond earnings or asset values. The notion of growth is derived and implicit rather than being explicit, the high price could simply be an error and/or the case of market hubris. A more explicit and direct definition of growth investing is one where an investor believes the market is undervaluing the future growth potential of a company. Interestingly (and somewhat obviously on reflection), both value and growth investors are trying to pinpoint undervalued companies (and why would you be trying to spot an overvalued stock unless you have the ability to short?). The difference between the two types of investors is the perceived source of the undervaluation. With the growth investor, the source is that the market does not understand the future growth potential of the business. With the value investor, the mis-valuation comes from the value in profits/assets not being properly appreciated. The interesting difference between the two sources of mis-valuation is one of scale. With profit and asset values, it is unlikely that the error will exceed 50% (of course, it could be more), whereas, with growth, long-term value can be 10 to 100 times the current value – consider the past valuations of Apple, Amazon, Google, etc.

How Good Is the PE Ratio at Measuring Growth?

We illustrate the use of PE ratio to measure the market's expectation about the company's ability to grow with a set of well-known companies (Table 3.1).

TABLE 3.1   PE ratio changes and stock returns

Year end	Amazon	Facebook	GE	Walmart	Apple	S&P 500
2013	687.57	92.63	20.07	15.19	13.92	16.52
2014	846.89	70.93	19.56	17.31	14.92	21.74
2015	543.22	81.77	30.40	13.08	11.22	20.54
2016	152.52	32.97	26.89	16.00	13.86	18.78
2017	256.50	28.65	742.47	22.55	17.59	18.37
2018	79.31	17.32	13.07	19.25	12.99	17.41
Difference (2018 - 2013)	-608.26	-75.31	-7.00	4.06	-0.93	0.89
Five-year total investment return (invested between ends of 2013 and 2018) (%)	276.63	139.88	-68.31	34.74	115.47	50.27

Source: BLOOMBERG PROFESSIONAL®.

Looking back to 2013, Amazon had the highest PE ratio, while Apple had the lowest. We then look at the returns generated by investing in these companies. It shows that, in general, higher PE ratios are indeed earning higher returns with two exceptions in our sample: GE and Apple. GE, despite its high PE ratio, earns a negative return in this five-year period, while Apple with a modest PE ratio earns more than double the index.

This illustrates the importance of looking beyond the market's expectation in identifying the growth potential of a company.

Value vs Growth

The range of variation provides a good illustration of the difference between the value and growth approaches. For growth investing, as the growth potential is realized and reflected in the earnings, the PE ratio will decrease. Amazon and Facebook are both on a growth trajectory during this period. For value investing, the growth of value in your investment is driven by fundamental value creation (net cash flow generation), and this does not affect the growth perspective dramatically and, therefore, there is less movement in the PE ratio. This is applied to Apple and Walmart. It is still a puzzle as to why Walmart and GE should have higher PE ratios than Apple for all of the period from 2013 to 2018.

BACKGROUND

Philip Fisher was born at the beginning of the twentieth century in San Francisco and, a bit like Buffett, he attended one of the best US universities – the newly founded Stanford Business School. He left, however, before finishing his degree and joined a stockbroking house in 1928. Given the looming Great Depression (normally seen as starting in 1929 and finishing in 1939), this was not the best time to enter the US stock market and we do wonder how much this early experience (the difficulty of timing the stock market) led to his focus on a long-term growth strategy – a form of investing that largely ignores/avoids the short-term vagaries of the stock market. Two years into the Great Depression, Fisher founded 'Fisher and Company', a wealth management company in 1931 and he continued to run the company for the rest of the century. We also need to bear in mind that this decade before the Second World War was the period of the New Deal and the US government was increasingly involved in the economy and companies were facing ever tighter regulations – not the best of times for US capitalism. This, of course, all changed with the war when the US government had to turn to the industrialists to power the war machine via their production of tanks, trucks, planes, ships, etc.

Fisher was an intensely private man and gave very few interviews. This is a pity because his career spanned so many macro ups and downs (the Great Depression, the Second World War, the 1950s and 1960s boom years, etc.) that his insights would have been worth listening to. We are, however, lucky in that Fisher wrote a small number of very insightful books, the best known being *Common Stocks and Uncommon Profits*, published in 1958 and still regarded as one of the true classics on investment;[1] this was followed in 1960 with *Paths to Wealth through Common Stocks*.[2]

In addition to being an author of classic investment books, Fisher's career included management of venture capital and private equity companies, adviser to chief executives, and teacher of investment classes at Stanford Business School! These activities obviously fit in with his focus on long-term investment, but they are also an active part of his investment technique. While we will cover his investment lessons in detail later, it is worth discussing one key aspect of his approach. Fisher stated on many occasions that his approach depended on 'scuttlebutt'. This is a process of gathering information beyond that publicly available in the financial statements and via news. It involves conversations with people who actively know a company – management, workers, customers, suppliers, competitors, etc. This takes a lot of time but these are the type of people who are able to go beyond the financials – to comment on the day-to-day activities of a business. With this process you can start to understand the principles that guide the company, the quality of the business across its various dimensions. A business is a complex web of activities and if one dimension is being 'treated badly', then it is more than likely that other dimensions will also be suffering. For example, a company that treats its staff as mere units of production may be able to manage short-term costs but is unlikely to be getting the most out of its staff in terms of motivation, innovation, commitment, etc. These are important qualities to help a company cope with the vagaries of business life. Such an attitude towards staff is likely to spill over to customers (disgruntled staff won't help in this regard) and suppliers.

In essence, if the approach to investing is a long-term growth strategy, then understanding the principles and attitudes that guide the business is

---

[1] P.A. Fisher, *Common Stocks and Uncommon Profits* (New York: Harper, 1958).
[2] P.A. Fisher, *Paths to Wealth through Common Stocks*. (2nd edn) (Englewood Cliffs, NJ: Prentice-Hall, 1960).

absolutely key – for it is these that will create the environment that enables long-term success. However, it needs to be realized that this level of understanding will rarely be available to most investors – you need access and this only comes with the type of fame that Fisher and the likes of Buffett had/have. Nonetheless, the connected world we now live in does make matters somewhat easier (even allowing for 'fake' news). There are a number of online news services and social media commentary sites that give greater insight. For example, the Glassdoor dataset tables the views of past and current employees of a company. In addition to the usual questionnaire-type structure, there are boxes where employees can offer free flow textual commentary (there are procedures to deal with the disgruntled ex-employee problem). So, while most investors will not be able to replicate the type of access that Fisher had to 'finer' sources of company information, modern sources go some way to filling the gap. However, even in the information-rich modern world, investors would do well to follow another of Fisher's approaches – stay focused and don't diversify too widely.

Web resource
The Glassdoor data offers the views of past and current employees of a company: www.Glassdoor.com

This section is supposed to cover the background of Philip Fisher and its relative brevity reflects his intense privacy. While we know quite a lot about his approach to investing, we do not know a lot about the man. What we do know is that he was generous, unassuming, ran his business from a plain office with little technology, was a gifted teacher and that his son, Ken Fisher, was also a gifted investor – achieving approximately double the returns of the market. Essentially, the limited picture we have of the man is one that is almost monk-like in its simplicity. Perhaps, this is what is needed to make the most of a long-term investment strategy – you need to be free of the noise and fads of everyday life.

At its heart, Philip Fisher's strategy is based on a belief in capitalism; in the long term, quality and a market focus will shine through and be rewarded by the markets. The cut and thrust of markets, and innovation, can only be benefited from if a company has the appropriate qualities of management, etc.

And it is this focus on the qualitative aspects of a company that differentiates Fisher from the quantitative value investors. He looks beyond the numbers to the characteristics that will enable a company to compete and innovate. However, in addition to carefully understanding the strengths of a company, the growth investor strategy also needs to reflect on the long-term macro trends within an economy. There would have been little point in investing in a superbly managed typewriter company at the start of the word processing revolution, unless the company had the ability to innovate in this new space. It is a similar argument regarding Kodak – once, one of the world's biggest suppliers of cameras and films, which proved itself unable to innovate in the digital space.

KEY LESSONS

While Philip Fisher's approach to investment is a detailed understanding of a company's potential, he has boiled his approach down to a number of key lessons. These are effectively signals that a company is doing the right or wrong things and they been covered a number of times in the investment literature; we will list them and discuss how they should be seen together and/or in their entirety. As we will see, they cover a lot of Porter's Five Forces that we discuss in detail in Appendix II, on valuation – remember that value must be derived from future potential.

Good Products and Future Development

1. **Products with market potential** – first and foremost for a company to have growth potential, it must have products/services that are attractive to a sizeable audience within, hopefully, a growing market. Think Apple iPhone in its early days.
2. **Good leadership** – does the company have the management to continue to develop the product to enable growth to be sustained? Think Steve Jobs and Apple. Does the company have the management to sustain and improve the profit margin through price and cost avenues? Does the company have a principled and trustworthy management?
3. **Investing for growth** – does the company have sufficient R&D activities to continue to develop the product? Again, think Apple. Without its significant investment in product development, it would have been picked off by competitors, i.e. Samsung. In such a competitive market, the only means of defence is offense and this comes through the constant and continued development of the product(s).

4. **Competitive advantage** – are there aspects specific to the industry that the company excels at and will it convey ongoing competitive advantage? For example, in mining, the ability to complete test drills efficiently is very important. A company that has a slick geological and test drilling facility may well have an important competitive advantage.

Healthy Accounts and Finance

1. **The sales machine** – there is little point in having a world-beating product design, if the company does not have the sales organization to take the product to market. While the iPhone may have the characteristics to 'sell itself', there can be little doubt that the Apple sales machine is impressive. Its shops and online facilities have definitely complemented its products in terms of look and feel, and customer service.

Sales Growth: A Better Measure of Growth

Continuing with the previous example, we illustrate the use of three-year average sales growth to measure the market's expectation about the company's ability to grow with a set of well-known companies (Figure 3.1).

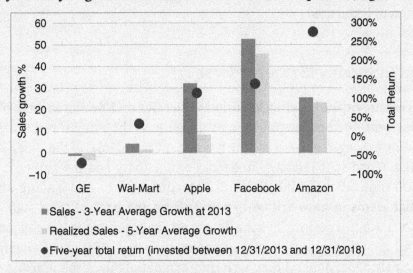

FIGURE 3.1 Three-year average sales growth of well-known companies.

(continued)

(continued)

A simple examination of the average growth rate seems to be able to provide a better explanation of the return than the PE ratio. The ordering of growth rate is a closer match to that of the return than the PE ratio in the earlier illustration. Amazon is an exception in that its sales growth is high but its stock return is much higher. This could be partly reflecting its dominant size in the industry and this increases the expectation about its future growth.

The negative growth in GE would have provided a good warning of its lack of potential.

Source: BLOOMBERG PROFESSIONAL®.

2. **Profit margin** – while the focus so far has been on products and sales, these are both pointless unless they can be turned into a profit margin that will eventually enable dividends to be paid and future investment undertaken. Does the company have a long-range outlook on profits, or is it too focused on the short term?

3. **Sufficient liquidity and access to borrowing** – does the company have sufficient liquidity and access to borrowings to fund long-term growth? Or are existing shareholders going to be heavily diluted as growth is pursued?

A Good Company (Stakeholders)

1. **Human capital** – after looking at the sales and profits aspects of the business, the next steps are to establish how the human resources are being managed – these are the resources that enable all the other activities. Good staff relations underpin productivity and the ability to sustain innovation. Think about British Airways – once a leading airline that seems to have drifted downwards on the back of poor staff relations. Another example is the debate on the gig economy. The valuation and growth perspective of companies such as UBER and Deliveroo is heavily dependent on how well they can handle their relationship with their 'employees' in a sustainable and legally compliant way.

2. **Good governance** – similarly, does the company have good relationships at the board level? The board of a company 'sets the tone and aspirations' and this has effects across many dimensions, e.g. relationships

with the city, the regulators, etc. Think about Sports Direct and Mike Ashley to reflect on how important this might be.[3]

3. **Depth of management** – staying with the Sports Direct example, a company needs a depth of management to maintain progress and to deal with unforeseen circumstances. All companies will have to deal with difficult circumstances (e.g. a fraudulent financial director) and if they are reliant on a thin top management team, they may not have 'sufficient bandwidth' to deal with the issue fully and properly.

Limited Downside Risk

1. **Fraud** – is an extreme issue to deal with but all companies need good internal accounting systems to track costs and activities. If a company does not have good internal accounting systems, it will be difficult for it to be efficient. While it seems obvious from a rational point of view that the things which need tracking will be tracked, anyone who has worked in an organization will know that some of the most basic facts are not always to hand. This is because when organizations are small, a lot of the key items can be 'eye-balled' and as the business grows, nobody thinks fit to put in place formal tracking systems until it is too late. Then we have the opposite situation of everything being tracked and staff becoming lost in a morass of data. In one of its many cost efficiency drives the NHS once tracked the usage of bed pans!! Not sure what outcome they hoped to achieve with this data. The problem facing most investors is that such internal activities are hard to access.

2. **Performance** – is the company candid about its performance (good and bad)?

The above is a quite a long list to remember, so let's focus down on what Fisher is trying to find.

First and foremost, Fisher is trying to find good businesses with the potential to offer huge future multiples, the current valuation is almost irrelevant. In this regard, the questions are simple: does a company have goods or services with long-term potential that it is able to protect and does it have the management to deliver this potential?

---

[3] An overpowering CEO and large shareholder, such as Mike Ashley, makes many of the important corporate decisions, such as large M&A deals, unchecked. When things turn bad, minority shareholders can do little but complain or leave with a loss. https://www.bbc.co.uk/news/business-49660675

Second, ignore current valuations. If the company delivers its potential, it will produce way above what the market expects.

Third, it is difficult to find mature companies with the potential to produce many times their current price. It is the young and small companies at the start of their life cycle that have the potential to deliver massive multiples. However, to find a prince, many frogs have to be kissed – and, we are sure Neil Woodford will attest to this conclusion.

APPLYING THE LESSONS

Being a true growth investor involves a lot of work and a lot of patience – both of which can be a struggle for most of us. Remembering that growth investing is identifying those companies with long-term potential and this should indicate that significant analysis of companies and their markets needs to be undertaken. We have been here and the work involved is a full-time occupation, not something that can be achieved in the odd hour, here and there.

It is not surprising, therefore, that investors try to identify short-cuts and there are three that spring to mind, given the overall ethos of growth investing:

1. An investor could focus on **small cap companies** because this is where the serious multiples can be achieved.
2. Similarly, and moving along the life-cycle path, **initial public offerings** (IPOs) could be the target of focus. These are companies that have grown sufficiently and have enough potential to attract the attention of a public funding market. In many ways, these should be ideal candidates for growth investors.
3. Lastly, and in many ways these go against the ethos of growth investing, **quantitative filters** could be applied, e.g., the Price Earnings Growth rate and the Price to Sales Ratio.

Rather than going through each of these 'applications' now, we will discuss them as we present the empirical evidence.

Growth Investing via Small Caps

This is the simplest and easiest means of 'growth investing'. In the UK, the private investor would look at the AIM market and try to identify those companies with considerable potential. Investment in these small cap listed companies is relatively straightforward, as we will see, but not for the faint-hearted. Trying to identify and gain an equity stake in unlisted, private companies is considerably more difficult and almost impossible for the private investor.

AIM Investment, Not for the Faint-Hearted?Simply investing in small companies does not produce growth. Figure 3.2 compares the total return of the FTSE AIM 50 index and the FTSE 100 index. It clearly shows a strategy of investing in AIM companies is not a good one to take.

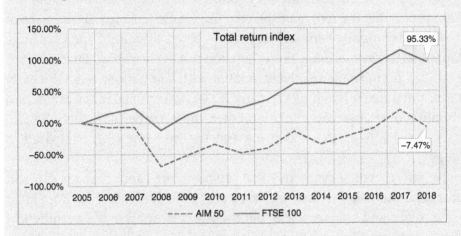

FIGURE 3.2 Total return index of FTSE 100 index and the AIM 50 index.

This illustrates the importance of looking beyond the market's expectation in identifying the growth potential of the company.

Source: BLOOMBERG PROFESSIONAL®.

The private investor could pick a number of sectors (our advice is, not too many) and understand the basic drivers of a sector and its performance. Once the macro understanding is established, the analysis can go a step down and high growth companies with all the appropriate characteristics can be identified. As noted above, this is not a quick job because it involves a lot of understanding of a range of qualitative factors. The danger here is to see a sector as having high potential and then not undertaking sufficient analysis of the individual companies. We have fallen foul of this very mistake. At the start of the shale gas revolution in the US, we were offered quite a substantial share of a new entrant with seemingly experienced management. We could not have been more wrong. Right sector call, wrong company call!!! This one cost us quite a lot.

There is quite a lot of but somewhat mixed evidence that small cap companies earn returns in excess of larger cap companies. But remember 'averages' in each category are being compared and what we are really interested in are growth companies and it is unclear whether the usual metrics of relatively short period excess returns are an entirely appropriate form of measurement – remember, growth investment is normally seen as being for the medium to long term. Nonetheless, let's now turn to the available empirical evidence.

If we look at the returns made by different size classes of companies, then across the past hundred years the very smallest class of listed companies has made almost double the return of the very largest class. Note that the risks of failure vary substantially between very small (prone to failure) and very large companies (with obvious exceptions these are relatively stable). Furthermore, the small cap premium is relatively volatile with hot periods (e.g., the early 1960s and the dotcom boom of the early 2000s) when small caps can earn a 50% premium over large cap stocks, and then there are periods when the premium is negative (e.g., the mid-1970s and the mid-1990s) as compared to large caps.

Essentially, there are cycles in small cap premiums and these are difficult to predict and the volatility has increased since the 1980s. It is far from clear that real funds based on a small cap philosophy can replicate the hypothetical returns of academic studies. This is because the risk modelling in the academic studies may not reflect the true costs and risks involved with investing in small cap stocks. The costs of investing in small caps involve higher search costs because of the relatively limited available data and the higher costs of trading because of lower levels of trading liquidity and the higher bid-ask spreads. The risks are greater because of the higher probabilities of distress that are difficult to estimate. At a single point in time, two small firms can have very similar financial profiles (fast growth, relatively limited financial resources, etc.) and one manages to keep the balls in the air and push onto greater things, while the other just can't manage all the stresses and strains, and eventually fails. This issue of predicting small cap success/failure is amplified by the relative lack of information on the activities of small cap businesses, for example, while large caps will be followed by any number of analysts, small caps will often have no analysts following whatsoever.

So, using a small cap approach to growth investing is not without its difficulties. Nonetheless, evidence points to a small number of factors that can aid success. First, there is no substitute for doing your homework with small caps, the lack of information makes this difficult but even more important if you are to avoid the large number of failures. Second, while individual small caps are inherently more risky than large caps, a broad portfolio of small caps is no riskier than a portfolio of large caps – so long as the small cap portfolio is well diversified. But this involves more costs of search, etc. Third, there is evidence that small cap stocks have to be held for a longer period if the return premiums are to be achieved.

Liquidity and Small Company Investment

For many investors, small stocks have quite an appeal. They have seen some of the stellar successes and if they had just bought early on, they too could have made a fortune. Sadly, for every one success, there are legions of small company failures – never forget this. The small company 'effect' even had a number of famous finance academics fooled. Banz[1] and Reinganum[2] found evidence for the period from 1926 to 1979 that small stocks earned a higher return than large stocks. On the back of this, a new fund (Dimensional Funds Advisors) was formed in the late 1980s with the great and the good of academic finance (Ibbotson, Fama, Miller, Scholes, Banz, etc.) on its board. By 1996, DFA had $11bn under management (impressive marketing!). However, and this is a lesson to us all, the great and the good, combined with computer power, still managed to underperform the S&P 500 by 54% across the period from 1981 and 1997.

So what went wrong with the above strategy and what can we learn from it more generally? When considering the results of academic studies, always try to work out how far they can be achieved in practice. And here we have the problem of liquidity. While smaller stocks look to have impressive returns, such returns are often difficult to achieve, given the size of the bid-ask spreads that reflect the relative illiquidity. In addition, there is the problem of the higher probability of failure of such stocks.

Overall, if you are interested in small stock investing (and some can earn stellar returns), be extra vigilant and turbo-charge the 'rules of safety' discussed above: go for very strong financial performance, a high dividend yield, high earnings growth rates, diversify widely, and be patient.

---

[1] R.W. Banz, The relationship between return and market value of common stocks, *Journal of Financial Economics* 9 (1981): 3–18.

[2] M.R. Reinganum, Misspecification of capital asset pricing: Empirical anomalies based on earnings' yields and market values, *Journal of Financial Economics* 9 (1981): 19–46.

Essentially, we are back to Fisher, do your homework, pick wisely, and hold for long periods. The only difference being that Fisher argues for focused portfolios, while this would be highly risky with small cap stocks.

Growth Investing via IPOs

IPOs can offer excellent returns (averaging 16% during the first year) on the face of it but these may be somewhat illusory for the private investor. Institutional investors often get first 'dibs' on IPOs as the underwriter builds the book for the IPO (noting that there are different processes for taking a company to market) and that means private investors may only get access to the less attractive offerings. Be wary when the initial pricing is revised downwards as this signals a lack of appetite in the market.

The returns from IPOs come from them being initially underpriced, the underpricing being necessary to entice investors to the new shares. The degree of underpricing varies, depending on the nature of the company, the sector, and the 'hotness' of the market. For example, during the dotcom boom, a number of the IPOs made stellar initial returns (often without any trading history) and looked to be hugely underpriced. In retrospect, they may have been overpriced because large numbers eventually failed. Also at the same time, in such hot markets, the shares being offered to the market can be limited in number – the initial rationing driving up prices post the IPO and this is then followed by further offerings to the market. In other words, the process of the IPO is being staged to give the impression of underpricing that eventually leads to higher prices being achieved. This type of IPO process is difficult to achieve in normal times but in periods of hot markets, when the pressure is on not to miss out (and the analysis being undertaken is at best cursory), investors are open to manipulation by the professionals.

So, there may be a bit of winner's curse for the private investor with IPOs, i.e. you only get access to the IPOs that the professionals don't really want. This amplifies a key issue with IPOs – while most look to be underpriced at the time of the listing, most underperform (compared to the market) for up to 5 years later. What is going on here is that companies are marketed strongly and underpriced and this gives impressive initial returns (remember it pays the company and its advisers to give away some initial value to ensure the flotation is a success – advisers definitely don't want a failed IPO), but once the initial excitement fades and reality kicks in, companies fade from the limelight of the market and the companies struggle to meet all the promises made to the market. At the time of writing, Aston Martin seems to be a perfect example – huge excitement on the back of the brand, huge promises on volumes to be achieved and all slowly falling away – 1 year after the IPO, its shares were trading at approximately 40% of the float price. As of May 2020, it is trading at less than 10% of the float price.

The issues we discussed with small caps apply here, just with the added complication of dealing with a process that leans against the private investor. Just as for small caps, the trick will be to identify those IPOs with true long-term potential – ignoring all the promotional hype (easier said than done).

Growth Investing via Growth Filters

While this approach runs counter to the expressly qualitative emphasis of Philip Fisher, it may be one way to spot potential companies before doing further analysis. In fact, Ken Fisher, the son of Philip, argued strongly for the use of the **price to sales ratio (PSR)**. This is similar to the price to earnings ratio with sales being swapped for earnings, the argument being that earnings are too open to accounting manipulation, while sales are not. This ratio is calculated by dividing a company's share price by its sales (normally over a year) per share. The problem we have is what might be a reasonable figure for this ratio – should it be below 2, 3 or 4? There is no correct answer and the best guide is to look at values historically within a given sector. Some of the tech companies have achieved PSRs well in excess of 4.

The more usual growth filter is the price earnings growth (PEG) ratio. This is the PE ratio scaled by the growth of a company and it is supposed to enable greater comparability of companies with different growth rates. It is defined as the price earnings ratio divided by annual earnings per share (EPS) growth. So if we had a PE ratio of 50 and an earnings growth of 50%, we would have a PEG ratio of 1 (we will discuss shortly whether this is good or bad).

As with all financial ratios, care needs to be taken to ensure like is being compared with like. If the PE ratio is for the past year, then the EPS should be for the past year. If the PE is based on prospective numbers, then so should the EPS ratio.

A lower PEG means that a company is undervalued more, given its stated growth per share rate. Normally, a PEG of 1 is seen as fair value (not sure why) and companies with a PEG lower than 1 are seen as good value.

While the PEG ratio has the appeal of simplicity, it has the usual problems of any ratio. The PEG could be low because the PE is low and reflective of short-term volatility issues. The PEG could be low because the EPS growth rate is high because of unsustainable growth in earnings per share.

Essentially, growth filters have issues but so long as the limitations are appreciated, they can act as an initial step in identifying potential companies. The question is whether they will work. We do know that earnings growth is volatile (sales growth is more stable – hence Ken Fisher's focus) and that there is a tendency to revert to the mean. In other words, a period of high growth will often be followed by low growth because it is difficult for companies to maintain high levels of growth.

In conclusion, use the filters with caution and remember they are not a replacement for doing the hard yards of comprehensive business analysis.

QUANTITATIVE EVALUATION

Small Firm Effects: UK

As we discuss in this and Chapter 2, market liquidity of a stock can significantly affect the valuation of a stock and has a direct impact on the strategy return through transaction costs and price impact. Therefore, when we study the small firm effect, for practical reasons, we should still focus on the more liquid stocks. We, therefore, focus our universe on the FTSE 350.

Update Online
Updates of the selective strategies can be found on the companion website: investinstyle.org.

We start our screening with FTSE 350 companies and selecting the bottom 10% of companies in terms of market capitalization. We rebalance this annually at the end of June.

The results show that such a strategy will beat the market index (Figure 3.3). And in this particular market and time period, it performs better than the value strategy we studied in Chapter 2 on Buffett. But this comes with a higher variation as indicated in the standard deviation of the return. It reports the returns in percentages. Active return is the difference between the return of a strategy and the benchmark.

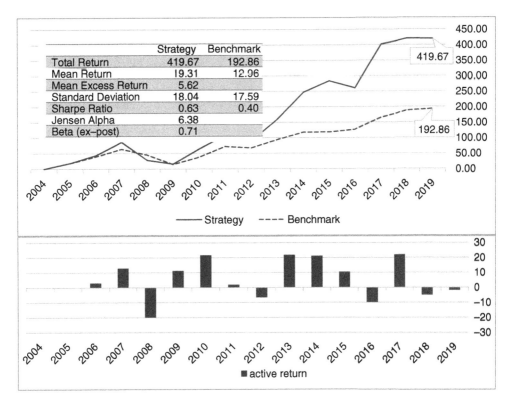

	Strategy	Benchmark
Total Return	419.67	192.86
Mean Return	19.31	12.96
Mean Excess Return	5.62	
Standard Deviation	18.04	17.59
Sharpe Ratio	0.63	0.40
Jensen Alpha	6.38	
Beta (ex-post)	0.71	

FIGURE 3.3 Cumulative return of the small size strategy in the UK.
Source: BLOOMBERG PROFESSIONAL®.

Other Filters

We also report the performance of other selected filters.

Table 3.2 shows that a portfolio of relatively low PEG stocks outperforms the benchmark by 3.75% a year on average. While investing in high PE ratio companies does not provide the expected growth that is implied in the valuation; a further filtering, taking into consideration sales growth, provides a strong portfolio return. Table 3.2 reports the backtesting of the strategy in the universe of FTSE 350 stocks in the 15-year period between June 2004 and June 2019.

It seems that multiple filters using both the PE and Price to Sales ratios produce very good results in our backtest. Companies that the market thinks highly of (ranked top 20 by their PE ratio) and that also have strong sales growth history to back up this 'potential' will continue to do well in the next year.

TABLE 3.2   Backtesting the FTSE 350 stocks, June 2004–June 2019

Criteria	Low PEG	High PE	High PE and high sales growth	FTSE 100
	Low 10 percentile PEG	Top 10 high PE stocks	Top 10 5-year high sales growth stocks among the top 20 high PE stocks	Benchmark
Total Return	309.87	131.58	417.91	192.86
Mean Return (Annualized)	17.20	11.22	20.33	12.96
Mean Excess Return (Annualized)	3.75	-1.55	6.52	
Standard Deviation (Annualized)	19.67	19.99	21.27	17.59
Sharpe Ratio	0.51	0.29	0.57	0.40
Jensen Alpha	3.54	-0.43	5.67	
Beta (ex-post)	0.91	0.89	0.91	

Source: BLOOMBERG PROFESSIONAL®.

MISTAKES

In other chapters we have discussed the mistakes made by a specific investor. This is not possible given the essential privacy of Philip Fisher. So, we are going to return to the issue of the false dichotomy of growth versus value.

Growth stocks are normally seen as those trading on higher than average valuations and value stocks are seen as trading on lower than average valuations.

The critical question, and one not easy to answer without a lot of analysis, is whether the relative valuations tell us anything, or are they just the consequence of haphazard valuations by the market? The idea these basic notions can be used is that the market is incorrectly valuing a company, given its potential. In the case of value stocks, the valuation is too low because the inherent value of the company (including its growth potential) is being downplayed. In terms of growth stocks, they will only be worth buying if the overvaluation as compared to averages is still an underestimate of the long-term potential of the business. Effectively, the market is unable to fix on the true value of a stock at a current moment in time but with the passage of time, 'it' will learn the errors of its ways and the stock price will properly reveal true underlying values.

In other words, both strategies work on the premise that the market is inefficient at any one point in time but will be efficient across the longer term. This takes some thinking about but it contains a kernel of truth and if we believe in this kernel, then we should approach all companies with a valuation/business model in mind.

The question we have to address is that, given everything we know about the business model of a company (including growth) and its financial structure, is it being fairly valued by the market? Given this simple conclusion, the difference between growth and value investing is one of focus. With growth investing, it is the long-term potential of a business to secure competitive advantage and the consequent rewards. With value investing, it is more to do with short-term profits and balance sheet strengths. So, you pick your focus (depending on patience) and follow with diligence, remembering that any form of stock investing involves a strong stomach.

Finally, instead of discussing the mistakes Fisher made, we review a few mistakes to avoid which he points out in his book (in Chapters 8 and 9 of *Common Stocks and Uncommon Profit*) that are relevant to retail investors in today's environment.

1. **Buying promotional (start-up) companies** – start-up vs established companies. Young promotional companies are often dominated by one or two individuals who are highly talented in a couple of areas, but have no expertise in other operational areas. The lack of information on these young companies makes it very risky to invest. Being on the safe side, one should invest in established companies since there are enough opportunities in these companies. There is more information for you to research and a less dramatic downside. He suggests that start-up investments should be left to the professional and not individual investors.

2. **Buying based on the 'tone' of the report** – investors should not be fooled by the presentation of the annual report.

3. **Being misled by the price-earning ratio** – as our analysis shows, this is indeed a dangerous path of growth investment.

4. **Do not be too concerned about transaction costs** – investors who identified a growth stock may miss the opportunity of holding the stock because they try to save transaction costs. This happens when putting a limit order in with a price just a fraction lower than the market price; and the price runs away from it and the order is never executed. The lesson is that once you decided to buy the stock, use a market order to avoid regret.

5. **Do not over-stretch diversification** – the limited attention and ability
    of individual investors suggest they should not hold too many stocks in
    their portfolios. He points out that wrong investments can be more det-
    rimental to the performance than insufficient diversification. Ten to 15
    stocks is a reasonable number, especially if you are investing in large
    companies, given their operations are already diversified in product
    lines, markets or regional segments.

SUMMARY

- Growth investing is an exciting and fundamental investment philosophy
  that is consistent with the core function of the capital market: providing
  risk capital for innovation. By bearing the risk of new development that
  others do not, growth investors earn large returns in those successful
  picks but can lose all of their capital in others.
- A successful growth investor is able to get it right more often than not
  and has the ability to learn from earlier mistakes.
- Fisher's approach, similar to that of Buffett's, is difficult for ordinary
  investors to strictly replicate. The closest alternative is the screening
  approach with key indicators that are in line with Fisher's philosophy.
- We demonstrate that combining the market assessment of growth
  opportunity (PE ratio) with their earnings (PEG) or sales growth provides a good starting point to identify stocks with long-term growth
  potential.

PRACTICAL APPLICATION II: UNDERSTANDING A COMPANY'S REALIZED AND POTENTIAL GROWTH

In this Practical Application section we look into the data and functions that
allow us to assess a company's past growth and its future growth potential.

There are two key functions providing comprehensive coverage of a company's financial analysis and a summary of analysts' estimates. We will introduce both of them with special emphasis on understanding the growth aspect
of a company and its valuation.

Tips
To Load a Security   Start typing the name of the security in the blue-framed box on the top of any of the four terminal windows. A dropdown list of Functions and Securities will appear. Click on the security from the list or [More securities] to search further.

Financial Analysis {FA} Go

The FA function provides financial information for a company or equity index. It includes not only historical fundamental data but also future estimates.

After loading a security, for example, AAPL US, *type* {FA} to load the FA screen. The presentation of information is organized in different templates grouped in tabs. Depending on the security you select and the availability of data, different sub-tabs may appear. The first level of tabs covers nine categories (Table 3.3).

TABLE 3.3   First level of tabs in the FA function

Tab	Definition
Key Stats	Displays a summary view of the most important information on underlying financial performance and economic impact
Income Statement	Displays income statement analysis that is included as reported statements and comparisons against company's peers
Balance Sheet	Displays a breakdown of the reported and standardized balance sheets
Cash Flow	Displays a breakdown both as reported and standardized cash flow analysis
Ratios	Displays derived financial ratios such as profitability, margins, growth rates, and credit ratios
Segments	Displays the company-provided mandatory breakdown of revenue by operating segment. A segment is defined by its ability to provide the company with at least 10% of the total firm revenue
Additional	Displays additional industry-specific data, such as pensions, dividends, and obligations
ESG	Displays environmental, social, and governance statistics. It also includes executive compensation
Custom	Displays the templates you have created and customized

Source: BLOOMBERG PROFESSIONAL®.

Growth

The financial statements (income statement, balance sheet, cash flow) contain important information on a firm's operations. However, if they are read on their own, it is very difficult to assess their value relevance. Most financial analyses are undertaken on the basis of ratio analysis, as ratios are more comparable across companies. In the Ratios tab there is a specific Growth sub tab.

Tip
Getting Historical Data from Excel @BDH (BLOOMBERG PROFESSIONAL® Data History) function returns the historical data for a selected security in Excel.

Here is how one can find the growth ratio for Apple Inc.

- After *loading* {AAPL US Equity},
- Then *type* {FA}<Go> to load the FA function,
- *Click* [5) Ratios], then [12) Growth],
- To export this view to excel *Click* [97) Export], [Excel], [73) Current template].

This will generate an Excel spreadsheet that will dynamically update the data through the @BDH function. A partial view of this table will be similar to Table 3.4.

TABLE 3.4 Apple Inc (AAPL US): growth

In millions of USD except for per share measures	FY 2016	FY 2017	FY 2018	FY 2019	FY 2020
12 months ending	09/24/2016	09/30/2017	09/29/2018	09/28/2019	09/26/2020
1-Year Growth					
Revenue	-7.73	6.30	15.86	-2.04	5.51
EBITDA	-14.50	1.38	14.41	-6.51	3.10
Operating Income	-15.73	2.20	15.57	-9.83	3.69
Net Income to Common	-14.43	5.83	23.12	-7.18	3.90
EPS Diluted	-9.87	10.83	29.32	-0.17	10.34
EPS Diluted before XO	-9.87	10.83	29.32	-0.17	10.34
EPS Diluted before Abnormal	-10.56	10.45	30.19	0.20	10.17
Dividend per Share	10.10	10.09	13.33	10.29	6.00

Source: BLOOMBERG PROFESSIONAL®.

Table 3.4 displays five years of data. The growth template reports 1- and 5-year growth of all the major relevant financial data from the three financial statements. The first group contains key measures from the income statement including Revenue (Sales) and Net Income to Common (equity).

In the BLOOMBERG PROFESSIONAL® terminal window, we can also change the table format into a chart presentation by clicking the chart icon similar to this 📊 which is to the left of the measurement heading.

Segments

To understand a company's performance and potential, it is important to understand its strength and weakness of its product lines and regional operations. For example, in the decade from 2010, the sales of iPhones (and particularly in China in the latter half) have been the dominant contribution to Apple's sales outside the US. Therefore, understanding their proportion to the overall sales and trends is important to assessing its growth. We find such information under the segments tab.

- After *loading* {AAPL US Equity},
- Then *type* {FA}<Go> to load the FA function,
- *Click* [6) Segment], then [11) By measure],
- Then expand the products under the Revenue heading.

A partial view of the table would look like Table 3.5.

Table 3.5 shows that the iPhone still dominates Apple's sales. However, the source of growth in recent years is from other products such as the Apple watch and especially services (such as the App store, and home entertainment) reflecting the company's change of strategy to enter into the 'content business'.

To study the geographical distribution of business

- After *loading* {AAPL US Equity},
- Then *type* {FA}<Go> to load the FA function,
- *Click* [6) Segment], then [12) By Geography],

A partial view of the table focusing on the revenue would look like Table 3.6.

TABLE 3.5   Apple Inc (AAPL US): by measure

In millions of USD except for per share measures	FY 2016	(%)	FY 2017	(%)	FY 2018	(%)	FY 2019	(%)	FY 2020	(%)
12 months ending	09/24/2016	(%)	09/30/2017	(%)	09/29/2018	(%)	09/28/2019	(%)	09/26/2020	(%)
Revenue	215,639.0	100.0	229,234.0	100.0	265,595.0	100.0	260,174.0	100.0	274,515.0	100.0
Products	—		196,534.0	85.7	225,847.0	85.0	213,883.0	82.2	220,747.0	80.4
iPhone	136,700.0	63.4	139,337.0	60.8	164,888.0	62.1	142,381.0	54.7	137,781.0	50.2
Wearables, Home and Accessories	11,132.0	5.2	12,826.0	5.6	17,381.0	6.5	24,482.0	9.4	30,620.0	11.2
Mac	22,831.0	10.6	25,569.0	11.2	25,198.0	9.5	25,740.0	9.9	28,622.0	10.4
iPad	20,628.0	9.6	18,802.0	8.2	18,380.0	6.9	21,280.0	8.2	23,724.0	8.6
Services	24,348.0	11.3	32,700.0	14.3	39,748.0	15.0	46,291.0	17.8	53,768.0	19.6
Accessories	—		—		—		—		—	
iTunes, Software and Services	—		—		—		—		—	
iPod	—		—		—		—		—	
Revenue growth %										
Wearables, Home and Accessories	11.00		16.00		36.00		41.00		25.00	
Services	23.00		23.00		22.00		16.00		16.00	
Mac	-10.00		13.00		-1.00		2.00		11.00	
Portables	—		—		—		—		—	

In millions of USD except for per share measures	FY 2016		FY 2017		FY 2018		FY 2019		FY 2020	
12 months ending	09/24/2016	(%)	09/30/2017	(%)	09/29/2018	(%)	09/28/2019	(%)	09/26/2020	(%)
Desktops		—		—		—		—		—
iPad		11.00		-7.00		-2.00		16.00		11.00
iPhone		12.00		3.00		18.00		-14.00		-3.00
Other music-related products and services		—		—		—		—		—
Software, Service and Other Sales		—		—		—		—		—
iPad and related products and services		—		—		—		—		—
iPod		—		—		—		—		—
Peripherals and other hardware		—		—		—		—		—
iPhone and related products and services		—		—		—		—		—

Source: BLOOMBERG PROFESSIONAL®.

TABLE 3.6 Apple Inc (AAPL US): by geography

In millions of USD except for per share measures	FY 2016	(%)	FY 2017	(%)	FY 2018	(%)	FY 2019	(%)	FY 2020	(%)
12 months ending	09/24/2016	(%)	09/30/2017	(%)	09/29/2018	(%)	09/28/2019	(%)	09/26/2020	(%)
Revenue	215,639.0	100.0	229,234.0	100.	265,595.0	100.0	260,174.0	100.0	274,515.0	100.0
Americas	86,613.0	40.2	96,600.0	42.1	112,093.0	42.2	116,914.0	44.9	124,556.0	45.4
Europe	49,952.0	23.2	54,938.0	24.0	62,420.0	23.5	60,288.0	23.2	68,640.0	25.0
Greater China	48,492.0	22.5	44,764.0	19.5	51,942.0	19.6	43,678.0	16.8	40,308.0	14.7
Japan	16,928.0	7.9	17,733.0	7.7	21,733.0	8.2	21,506.0	8.3	21,418.0	7.8
Rest of Asia Pacific	13,654.0	6.3	15,199.0	6.6	17,407.0	6.6	17,788.0	6.8	19,593.0	7.1
Rest of Asia Pacific	—		—		—		—		—	
Greater China	—		—		—		—		—	
Japan	—		—		—		—		—	
Europe	—		—		—		—		—	
Americas	—		—		—		—		—	
Retail	—		—		—		—		—	
Revenue growth %	—									
Europe	-1.00		10.00		14.00		-3.00		14.00	
Rest of Asia Pacific	-10.00		11.00		15.00		2.00		10.00	
Americas	-8.00		12.00		16.00		4.00		7.00	
Japan	8.00		5.00		23.00		-1.00		0.00	
Greater China	-17.00		-8.00		16.00		-16.00		-8.00	
Rest of Asia Pacific	—		—		—		—		—	
Japan	—		—		—		—		—	
Europe	—		—		—		—		—	
Americas	—		—		—		—		—	
Retail	—		—		—		—		—	

Source: BLOOMBERG PROFESSIONAL®.

The Americas are the main market for Apple Inc., while the China market makes up about one-fifth of it sales. The US-China trade war has had a visible, negative effect on Apple's 2019 sales in China and this has been the main contributor to the overall reduction of sales. The recent growth is from Europe and the rest of Asia Pacific.

Environmental, Social and Governance (ESG)

Among the tabs, the ESG is the one that contains the non-financial measurement of firms. It reports the quality and extent of a company's reporting on these three aspects, as well as some of the quantifiable reporting statistics. It contains subsections for each of the ESG aspects and executive compensation.

Table 3.7 shows that the environmental scores have been improving (with less waste) slowly over time, while the social disclosure score is decreasing. The governance aspect of the company is relatively stable as a mature company.

One of the main global risks that has increasing importance to investors is climate risk. The Carbon Disclosure Project (CDP) and the Energy ESG provide some data in this regard.[4] These types of data still lack structure and a standard format. However, as regulation improves with more standard disclosure, they will enter into investors' quantitative evaluation model.

Earnings & Estimates {EE}

Another way to understand the growth prospects of a company is to learn from the professional financial analysts. To this end, the {EE} function provides a summary of aggregated broker earnings projections, surprise earnings data, and a summary of earnings history. Especially, this function contains BLOOMBERG PROFESSIONAL®'s customizable consensus estimates.

To view the main window of the EE function, we do the following with the example of Apple Inc.:

- After *loading* {AAPL US Equity},
- Then *type* {EE}<Go> to load the EE function,

This brings the main display with several subpanels of information. Each of the panels includes a link to a sub-function that produces much more detailed analyses. The key panels and functions information can be summarized as shown in Table 3.8.

---

[4] The Carbon Disclosure Project (CDP) focus investors, companies and cities on taking urgent action to build a truly sustainable economy by measuring and understanding their environmental impact. It encourages companies to disclose ESG-related information. https://www.cdp.net/en

TABLE 3.7　Apple Inc (AAPL US): ES overview

In millions of USD except for per share measures	FY 2016	FY 2017	FY 2018	FY 2019	FY 2020
12 months ending	09/24/2016	09/30/2017	09/29/2018	09/28/2019	09/26/2020
ESG disclosure score	53.11	53.11	54.55	51.67	—
Environmental					
Environmental disclosure score	62.50	62.50	65.63	65.63	—
Total GHG emissions	633.8	696.0	831.1	912.7	—
Direct CO_2 emissions	—	—	54.5	50.3	—
Total energy consumption	1,736.5	2,192.2	2,598.3	2,832.4	—
Total water use	8,684.9	3,876.4	5,008.3	4,989.4	—
Hazardous waste	1.0	1.5	2.8	2.8	—
Total waste	29.9	53.8	73.9	58.4	—
Paper consumption	1.1	1.1	1.3	1.4	—
Social					
Social disclosure score	29.82	29.82	29.82	19.30	—
Number of employees	116,000.00	123,000.00	132,000.00	137,000.00	—
% women in workforce	32.00	32.00	33.00	—	—
% women in management	28.00	29.00	29.00	—	—
Governance					
Governance disclosure score	60.71	60.71	60.71	60.71	—
Size of the Board	8.00	8.00	8.00	7.00	7.00
Independent directors	7.00	7.00	7.00	6.00	6.00
% independent directors	87.50	87.50	87.50	85.71	85.71
Board duration (years)	1.00	1.00	1.00	1.00	1.00
# Board meetings	4.00	4.00	4.00	5.00	4.00
Board management attendance	75.00	75.00	75.00	75.00	75.00

Source: BLOOMBERG PROFESSIONAL®.

TABLE 3.8 Key earnings forecast functions

Earnings	ERN	The Earnings History section displays estimate announcement dates and pricing information
Consensus Overview	EEO	The Consensus Overview section provides analysts' consensus for the current and previous period. It shows how well the company bettered, met, or missed the analysts' consensus estimates historically. The EEO function will display detailed information from all analysts
Analyst Coverage	ANR	The Analyst Coverage in the Earnings Summary panel provides information about the number of analysts recommending buy, hold, or sell along with their average target price and the evolution of recommendations over time
Earnings Trends	EM	The Earnings Trends section displays a snapshot of the chart that plots the estimated and actual earnings values
BI Review	BI	The BLOOMBERG PROFESSIONAL® Intelligence Review section displays BLOOMBERG PROFESSIONAL® Intelligence (BI) analysis on the selected security. It covers discussion of both past and upcoming earnings
Estimate Revisions	EEG	The Estimate Revision Graph section displays a chart of price and earnings values over a period of time

Source: Authors' summary using information from BLOOMBERG PROFESSIONAL®.

The EE screen displays a control panel for many functions that are related to analysts' estimates with a focus on earnings estimates. *Click* on each of the elements to drill down and obtain further details for each of the sub-functions.

The most relevant to growth is possibly the Earnings trend. We enter this function - either *click* on [5) Earnings Trends] or type {EM} <Go> (see Table 3.9).

Table 3.9 shows that the analysts' consensus for Apple Inc. The figures in italic font are estimated numbers while the non-italics are reported numbers. It suggests that, on average, analysts are expecting consistent growth in Apple. Especially it will have significant growth in 2021 continuing from the positive growth in 2020 during the pandemic period. Nevertheless, the medium-term growth is expected to be lower compared to Apple's historical records.

Relative Valuation {RV}

Once you have a detailed understanding of a company's growth history and analysts' consensus, one way to link them to valuation is to make a comparison with its peers – an approach known as relative valuation (RV) or valuation with multiples. The RV function in the terminal is a good example of such a tool. It allows you to perform relative valuation analysis on selected equity. For valuation peer groups, there are handpicked peers by the BLOOMBERG

TABLE 3.9 Apple Inc (AAPL US): earnings trends overview

	EPS, GAAP+						YoY % growth					
	2018	2019	2020	2021	2022	2023	2018	2019	2020	2021	2022	2023
Q1 Dec	0.97	1.05	1.25	1.68	1.78	1.89	15.8	7.5	19.4	34.7	5.9	6.0
Q2 Mar	0.68	0.62	0.64	1.4	1.22	1.24	30.0	-9.9	3.7	119.6	-13.1	1.7
Q3 Jun	0.59	0.55	0.65	1	1.06	1.11	40.1	-6.8	18.4	54.6	6.0	4.5
Q4 Sep	0.73	0.76	0.73	1.1	1.21	1.29	40.6	4.1	-3.6	50.7	10.2	6.0
Year	2.98	2.97	3.28	5.17	5.33	5.57	29.3	-0.2	10.3	57.6	3.0	4.6
Cal Yr	3.04	3.17	3.69	5.28	5.37	5.63	25.0	4.1	16.7	42.9	1.8	4.8

Source: BLOOMBERG PROFESSIONAL® (accessed 11 June 2021).

PROFESSIONAL® Intelligence unit or peers identified by the BLOOMBERG PROFESSIONAL® Industry Classification Standard (BICS) best-fit algorithm. You can also create your own benchmark securities. You can also choose the scope of your peer group such as the regions of the companies to choose from (e.g., Global developed).

There are two main functions for relative valuations: RV and EQRV. The RV will provide an overview of the relative valuation of the company with its peers in terms of financial information such as price, ROE, EPS, ownership, and credit. It also has a summary of pricing ratios which is produced from the Equity Relative Valuation function {EQRV}<Go>. A summary of the key relative valuations is provided in Table 3.10 with a definition of enterprise value.

For the above valuation matrix, a simple interpretation is that the higher this value, then the stock is potentially 'expensive' compared to its fundamentals such as earnings, sales or book value. However, the alternative view is that a high valuation ratio could be justified by a high future growth ratio. The challenge is how to differentiate these two.

The following information is produced from EQRV for Apple Inc. in June 2021 (Table 3.11).

TABLE 3.10 Definition of key valuation measures

Price to Earnings	BF P/E	Calculated as price per share divided by EPS consensus estimate. BF stands for blended forward in the sense that the metric is a time-weighted average of fiscal year 1 and fiscal year 2 forward estimates.
Enterprise Value	EV	The sum of a company's Market Capitalization, Preferred Equity, and short- and long-term interest-bearing debt, less cash and equivalents. It measures the total firm value that is owned by both equity and debt holders. This is used as a proxy for the takeover value of a firm
Enterprise Value to EBIT	BF EV/ EBIT	Calculated as enterprise value divided by earnings before interest and taxes - consensus estimate
Enterprise Value to EBITDA	BF EV/ EBITDA	Calculated as enterprise value divided by earnings before interest, taxes, depreciation, and amortization - consensus estimate
Enterprise Value to Sales	BF EV/ Rev	Calculated as enterprise value divided by revenue estimate
Price to Book	LF P/BV	Current share price divided by book value per share in the latest filing (LF)

TABLE 3.11 Apple Inc (AAPL US): equity relative value

Name	Ticker	2Y Corr	Mkt Cap (billion USD)	BF P/E	BF EV/ EBITDA	BF EV/ EBIT	BF EV/ Rev	LF P/ BV
Apple Inc	AAPL US		2117.33	24.0	17.9	19.9	5.6	30.6
Current premium to comps mean (%)				31	42	40	71	–
Mean (Including AAPL US)			252.64	18.4	12.6	14.2	3.3	5.9
Median			27.83	18.0	11.5	12.7	2.3	5.7
Low			4.37	8.5	4.4	6.6	0.6	1.8
High			2117.33	33.7	21.9	22.6	8.6	10.5
Peers								
Ciena Corp	CIEN US	0.53	9.11	19.2	11.6	12.8	2.3	3.4
Dell Technologies Inc	DELL US	0.52	77.92	11.7	8.6	10.9	1.2	19.3
Arista Networks Inc	ANET US	0.52	27.83	33.7	21.9	22.6	8.6	8.1
Motorola Solutions Inc	MSI US	0.52	36.00	23.1	15.8	17.9	4.9	–
HP Inc	HPQ US	0.47	36.17	8.5	6.7	7.8	0.6	–
F5 Networks Inc	FFIV US	0.47	11.38	16.9	11.5	12.5	4.2	5.7
Ubiquiti Inc	UI US	0.42	20.04	29.7	–	–	9.8	–
CommScope Holding Co Inc	COMM US	0.36	4.37	10.1	10.6	12.3	1.7	21.0
Samsung Electronics Co Ltd	005930 KS	0.21	432.96	13.0	4.4	6.6	1.4	1.8
Accton Technology Corp	2345 TT	0.17	5.98	23.6	17.0	18.4	2.4	10.5

Source: BLOOMBERG PROFESSIONAL®.

Table 3.11 shows that Apple's valuation is high (value at a premium) compared to its peers. It suggests that the market is still betting on Apple being able to have a higher than average growth in its earnings compared to its peers. Its early strong competitor, Samsung, has experienced various troubles and is lagging behind in recent years. Its valuation ratio looks very attractive at the time of the analysis.

Traditionally, the biggest challenge of relative valuation is to identify comparable peers. Although no two companies are the same, the benefit of using data-driven criteria (e.g. as in BLOOMBERG PROFESSIONAL®) is to achieve a closer match not only at the company level but also at the segment level.

An Example Worked Through: Will Tesla Inc Have Electrified Growth?

Let's look at Tesla Inc. We start with the earnings trend {EM} (Table 3.12).

The short answer to our question is YES. Tesla has had strong growth since 2018 and the growth exploded in 2020. However, the earnings number can be misleading as Tesla only starts to make positive earnings in the financial year 2019. Sales growth is a much more important and meaningful gauge for a growth company in its early stage. We get the revenue growth trend by changing the Measure from {EPS, GAAP+} to {Revenue}.

Tesla has some healthy growth in sales in the last few years with a slowdown in 2019, which was a very volatile year for this company. The consensus is that it will pick up growth again from 2021 and so far the realized growth is strong (Table 3.13).

To see what are the analysts' recommendations for the stock we *load* {TSLA US Equity}, then type {ANR}. An example of information is presented in Table 3.14.

On average, the analysts think that the company is undervalued by 3.1% at the moment. But there is a potentially large long-term return of 210.84%. Some 43.2% of the analysts recommend buying the stock at this time.

The analysts' caution is understandable if they take the auto industry group as the benchmark for Tesla. The valuation metrics of Tesla are much higher than this traditionally low-multiple industry. The following information is abstracted using the {EQRV} we introduced earlier.

TABLE 3.12   TSLA US: earnings trend overview

	EPS, GAAP+						YoY % Growth					
	2018	2019	2020	2021	2022	2023	2018	2019	2020	2021	2022	2023
Q1 Mar	-0.67	-0.58	0.23	0.93	1.48	2.3	-151.9	13.4	139.3	307.9	59.4	54.8
Q2 Jun	-0.61	-0.22	0.44	0.95	1.65	2.57	-130.1	63.4	294.6	116.7	74.2	56.0
Q3 Sep	0.58	0.37	0.76	1.18	1.9	2.79	199.3	-35.9	104.3	55.1	61.5	46.3
Q4 Dec	0.39	0.43	0.8	1.42	2.11	3.1	163.5	10.9	86.9	78.0	48.4	46.6
Year	-0.27	0.04	2.24	4.49	6.5	8.39	84.6	115.0	5500.0	100.4	44.8	29.1
Cal Yr	-0.27	0.04	2.24	4.49	6.5	8.39	84.6	115.0	5500.0	100.4	44.8	29.1

Source: BLOOMBERG PROFESSIONAL® (accessed 11 June 2021).

TABLE 3.13 TSLA US: revalue trends overview

	Revenue						YoY % Growth					
	2018	2019	2020	2021	2022	2023	2018	2019	2020	2021	2022	2023
Q1 Mar	3.41	4.54	5.99	10.39	14.24	18.94	26.4	33.2	31.8	73.6	37.1	33.0
Q2 Jun	4.00	6.35	6.04	11.33	15.39	21.10	43.5	58.7	-4.9	87.7	35.9	37.1
Q3 Sep	6.82	6.30	8.77	12.78	17.04	22.63	128.7	-7.6	39.2	45.7	33.3	32.9
Q4 Dec	7.23	7.38	10.74	14.28	18.36	24.51	119.8	2.2	45.5	32.9	28.6	33.5
Year	21.46	24.58	31.54	49.57	67.27	83.78	82.5%	14.5%	28.3%	57.2%	35.7%	24.6%
Cal Yr	21.46	24.58	31.54	49.57	67.27	83.78	82.5%	14.5%	28.3%	57.2%	35.7%	24.6%

Source: BLOOMBERG PROFESSIONAL® (accessed 11 June 2021).

TABLE 3.14   TSLA US: analysts' recommendation overview

Ticker	TSLA US Equity	Date	11/06/2021
Buys (%)	43.2	Consensus Rating	3.30
Holds (%)	29.5	Total Buy Recs	19
Sells (%)	27.3	Total Hold Recs	13
Last price	604.79	Total Sell Recs	12
Pricing currency	USD	Best Target Price	623.31
Return potential (%)	3.1		
LTM return (%)	210.84		

Source: BLOOMBERG PROFESSIONAL®.

Since Tesla only just started to make a profit about one year ago, most of the valuation metrics comparing to earnings would not be informative. All of the multiples are extremely high with its market capitalization being bigger than the next three car companies combined (Table 3.15). Given these valuation ratios, Tesla would need very strong and persistent growth to deliver the value.

According to the analysts' growth forecast and their target price, on average, they are convinced at the moment. However, this was not the case just one year ago in early 2020. Then we had large disagreements and, on average, sell recommendations for Tesla.

If, however, Tesla is seen as a leading technology company that happens to be working in the auto industry, then it can be benchmarked against a group of tech-companies. We can do this by changing the Comp source from GICS to our own custom list (Table 3.16).

The relative valuation still looks very stretched. This is because most of the other companies are a firm or in an industry that are in a later cycle than Tesla.

Amazon and Facebook experienced an above 1000 PE ratio in 2012 and 2013.

All in all, Tesla's current valuation is closer to the early stage of those successful technology companies. While there is a risk, the growth potential is large. Given the global focus on climate change, being a leader in the electric car industry is a very compelling position to gain investors' trust.

TABLE 3.15 TSLA US: relative value

Name	Ticker	2Y Corr	Mkt Cap (billion USD)	BF EV/ EBITDA	BF P/E	BF EV/ EBIT	BF EV/ Rev	LF P/BV
Tesla Inc	TSLA US		587.53	54.1	113.4	100.1	10.2	25.5
Current premium to comps mean				–	–	–	42870%	–
Mean (Including TSLA US)			0.00	10.8	12.3	18.5	1.9	17
Peers								
Ferrari NV	RACE US	0.40	39.08	21.1	39.7	31.1	7.6	17.4
NIO Inc	NIO US	0.34	74.85	–	–	–	10.2	14.1
Porsche Automobil Holding SE	PAH3 GR	0.33	36.45	–	6.9	–	247.0	0.8
Daimler AG	DAI GR	0.32	103.13	2.5	7.5	3.9	0.4	1.3
Stellantis NV	STLA US	0.32	64.94	2.7	6.6	4.7	0.3	1.0
Volkswagen AG	VOW GR	0.32	164.71	2.9	10.5	6.5	0.5	1.3
Bayerische Motoren Werke AG	BMW GR	0.31	74.51	6.5	7.9	10.2	1.0	1.0
General Motors Co	GM US	0.30	89.20	5.7	10.2	8.0	0.7	1.8
Ford Motor Co	F US	0.29	60.99	4.9	11.4	6.8	0.4	1.8
Great Wall Motor Co Ltd	2333 HK	0.17	52.02	23.3	19.8	35.4	2.5	3.3
BYD Co Ltd	1211 HK	0.16	93.29	28.1	87.7	59.9	3.0	6.3
Hyundai Motor Co	005380 KS	0.16	45.61	10.7	9.8	17.4	1.0	0.7
Honda Motor Co Ltd	7267 JP	0.15	59.20	9.5	9.0	14.1	0.8	0.7
SAIC Motor Corp Ltd	600104 CH	0.10	36.35	8.8177	8.6981	11.5827	0.4263	0.8672
Toyota Motor Corp	7203 JP	0.09	293.34	14.2624	10.8439	18.6448	1.7533	1.2039

Source: BLOOMBERG PROFESSIONAL®.

TABLE 3.16   TSLA US: relative value: custom list

Name	Ticker	2Y Corr	Mkt Cap (USD)	BF EV/ EBITDA	BF P/E	BF EV/ EBIT	BF EV/ Rev	LF P/ BV
Tesla Inc	TSLA US		587.53	54.1	113.4	100.1	10.2	25.5
Current premium to comps mean				–	–	–	7280%	–
Mean (Including TSLA US)			1065.61	17.2	29.5	20.3	5.9	6.1
Peers								
Apple Inc	AAPL US	0.47	2125.17	17.9	24.1	20.0	5.6	30.7
Amazon.com Inc	AMZN US	0.45	1687.89	20.1	44.6	41.5	3.2	16.3
Alphabet Inc	GOOGL US	0.41	1657.64	15.6	23.9	21.3	7.4	7.1
Facebook Inc	FB US	0.39	939.28	13.3	21.7	17.8	7.0	7.0
Netflix Inc	NFLX US	0.37	216.72	29.9	41.8	32.7	7.1	16.8
Alibaba Group Holding Ltd	BABA US	0.34	573.78	2.3	20.0	3.5	3.3	3.9
Tencent Holdings Ltd	700 HK	0.17	736.88	21.1	30.0	26.3	7.5	6.2

Source: BLOOMBERG PROFESSIONAL®.

SUMMARY

In our main text, we have illustrated some quantitative sorting using combinations of PE and sales growth to identify potential growth companies. In this practical application section, we have illustrated how we can assess these companies' past growth and potential growth through financial statement analysis and analysts' reports. These types of analysis can help us to narrow down our search list. Also, these analyses will form the basis of our inputs into the valuation model discussed in our Valuation Appendix II (where we illustrate how to use a dividend discount model with multiple stages of growth estimates).

EXERCISES

- Conduct a similar growth analysis as we did for Tesla with a company of your choice.
- Study Zoom and compare it to Microsoft.
- Replicate the quantitative strategies we discussed in the main text with the {EQS} and {EQBT} function we discussed in Chapter 2.

CHAPTER 4

David Dreman

The Master Contrarian?

INTRODUCTION

Contrarian investors make their money by backing their own judgement and going against the herd. As we will see as we progress through the chapter, this takes a lot of self-belief and an understanding of the psychology that drives the investment herd. Such understanding is earned through watching the market and learning from the mistakes of others and your own. None of us is free from the psychological traits that power the market up and down but with understanding and a strong sense of restraint, we can profit from the overreaction of the herd.

David Dreman is a Canadian investor who has built his career on taking contrarian positions and, more importantly, he has spent a lot of time reflecting on market sentiment, its make-up, and how to profit from it. As with all the other chapters, this all seems deceptively easy but, in practice, it is devilishly difficult.

BACKGROUND

David Dreman graduated in 1958 from the University of Manitoba and started working for investment companies such Rauscher Pierce, and Seligman, and was editor of the Value Line Investment Service. During this early part of his career he lost money (a lot of his wealth) by buying popular shares, i.e. following the herd. Learning from his mistakes, 10 years later, he was running his own fund (he founded Dreman Value Management Inc. in 1977 and has served as its chairman and president), based on investing against the herd, his fund eventually peaked at $22bn. Following the likes of Graham and Buffett, Dreman learned to look for value and not seek profits from glamour stocks; the important question being how to identify real value stocks. Stocks may look cheap because the market has correctly seen the weaknesses in a company, or they may look cheap because a stock has been wrongly downgraded, given the market is turning against a sector or a segment of a sector.

Over the decades since he founded Value Management, Dreman has consistently shown that out-of-favour stocks, as measured by the price/earnings ratio, outperform stocks with a supposedly more positive outlook (as measured by standard metrics such as the PE ratio, etc.).

As well as being a stellar investor, Dreman has been a very successful author of investment books. He published a very influential book in 1979, *Contrarian Investment Strategy: The Psychology of Stock Market Success*,[1] that has been reprinted many times and his latest book, published in 2012, *Contrarian Investment Strategies: The Psychological Edge* continues the theme.[2] He is also a regular columnist in *Forbes*.

KEY LESSONS

Dreman uses simple ratios (such as price to earnings, price to book, and price to cash flow) and metrics to compare the price of a business to its underlying value.

A high dividend yield is also a good signal of a company being out of favour with the market. This metric can be a signal of things going wrong (if the market is correct) or equally, it may be a sign of value.

To ensure value is being identified, Dreman only considers the bottom 20% of stocks under each metric. In addition, to avoid problems of liquidity, etc., he also only looks at businesses with strong fundamental characteristics – he

---

[1] D.N. Dreman, *Contrarian Investment Strategy: The Psychology Of Stock Market Success* (New York: Vintage Books, 1981).

[2] D.N. Dreman, *Contrarian Investment Strategies: The Psychological Edge* (New York: Simon & Schuster, 2012).

avoids small companies and only invests in businesses with strong earnings growth and other signs of financial strength.

He is realistic about the potential downside of a share, promotes patience, and avoids over-priced businesses. A typical Dreman-type portfolio will hold 20–30 shares across 15-plus sectors.

Knowing when to sell a share is equally as important as knowing when to buy. Here Dreman has some similarly strict rules – sell when the PE ratio moves above the average of a market/sector and when a share shows weak/declining price momentum and/or falling fundamentals.

Searching the whole market for contrarian value can be hard work but some simple screens may ease the burden, for example, a good place to start might be high dividend yield stocks or low PE stocks.

Applying the Lessons

Betting against the herd is not for the faint-hearted, as contrarian investing can be destructive of value before its starts to create value. In addition, betting on companies that are out of favour may lead to the worst case of losing all your investment in a given stock. This type of investment strategy needs a strong stomach and any investor needs to reflect on the inherent risks. It is really quite simple, could you stand the stress of watching an investment hit the floor and staying there for quite some time? An investor needs to reflect on his/her risk appetite and the appetite to live with such losses for long periods.

Contrarian investing is best suited to investors with the necessary wealth to withstand substantial losses and holding loss positions across time.

A bit of reflection will indicate that contrarian investing is not a million miles away from value investing. There are two factors that separate these two types of investment strategy. First, with contrarian investing, there is the risk associated with buying shares that are 'at the bottom' and out of favour with the market. Second, contrarian investing tends to buy shares that have recently fallen – this may be an individual stock being out of favour and/or a whole sector. These two factors suggest that, in contrast to value investing, contrarian investing needs a very deep understanding of the underlying business and the exact nature of the market sentiment driving prices lower.

Essentially, a contrarian investment strategy is for the experienced investor with the time to undertake the necessary analysis. Once you believe you have understood why a stock is being driven down, you need to be comfortable with the possibility that it will continue to be driven down – essentially, your bet has proved wrong. For the amateur investor, such a strategy may form part of a wider, safer approach to investment. The contrarian bets may be seen as the wild cards and only form a small proportion of the overall portfolio.

Nonetheless, even if contrarian investing only forms a small part of the overall investment, it is still wise to minimize the risk as far as possible – this is supposed to be investment, not speculation. With this in mind, Dreman's investment philosophy is to buy companies with strong fundamentals, above-market dividend yields and strong/persistent earnings growth. He also wishes to avoid speculative stocks and ones that have a high risk of failure.

In applying Dreman's approach, the following metrics can act as a guide

- P/E (earnings) bottom 20% of the market
- P/CF (cash flow) bottom 20% of the market
- P/B (book value) bottom 20% of the market
- P/D (dividends) bottom 20% of the market
- Large companies (in the UK context, it will be the FTSE 350)
- Earnings growth
- For non-cyclical companies, EPS (earnings per share) growth should be higher than the market
- Payout ratio should be between 40% and 80%
- ROE should be in the top 30% of stocks
- Pre-tax margin should be above 8% but this depends on the nature of the sector
- Debt should not exceed equity
- It should be liquid with a current ratio of more than 2.

All of the above seems very sensible and should help to weed out potentially disastrous investments. However, as noted above, a key part of making successful contrarian investments is to understand what is driving the market against a particular stock – in other words, understanding market sentiment. Behavioural finance has identified five means of measuring/tracking market sentiment: (1) financial market measures; (2) survey measures of sentiment; (3) textual sentiment; (4) internet search behaviour; and (5) non-economic factors.

Financial Market Measures

The first place to start to consider sentiment is by the actions of the stock market. If a stock's price has suddenly dropped, then something is clearly happening. What is interesting, of course, is how much volume has been needed to drop the price. If a large volume has been needed, then this tells you there has been resistance but a head of steam is gathering, whereas only a small volume tells you the opposite. Comparing recent movements in volume contains information, as do the number and the size of the trades. So comparisons of relative volume, number of trades, and the size of trades need reflecting on. A given volume is achieved by the number of trades times the size of trades and different profiles can be telling you different 'stories'. Similarly, the speed and consistency of the changes in prices and volumes of a stock can be equally informative.

Turning to market sentiment, measures of volatility (VIX – volatility index) and the average closed end fund discount (price is below the net asset value) can give indications of how the market is feeling about risk and overall value. Increases in both are signals that market sentiment is weakening.

Of course, while these market measures of sentiment have the advantage of being readily available, they have the disadvantage of resulting from many different forces and how far they accurately capture pure sentiment is open to question.

Survey-Based Sentiment Index

When assembling or exiting an investment portfolio, market-based sentiment can play a role in determining overall returns. At the time of writing (October 2019) market sentiment is all over the place as the winds of Brexit, Trump, and recession in a number of EU countries buffet the markets. While a daily read of the financial news will give a feel for these issues, keeping an eye on a number of indices (and being aware when they are due to be published) can be helpful in gauging the timing of such actions. For example, the UK has quarterly consumer and business confidence indices. The relative infrequency of these surveys is not overly helpful but an ongoing, watching brief can be informative of overall trends.

Other indices (while not directly measuring sentiment) can have a significant effect on sentiment. To illustrate this point we will use an example. At the beginning of October 2019, we were looking at the FTSE 100 that had stabilized for a few days at about 7400. Considering all the factors, there seemed to be a lot more downside than upside. So we assembled an instrument where we would profit on downside movements and lose money on any upside. We stopped the gain side at 7500 and we would let the downside run. Through bad luck, one of us developed a stomach upset during this process just after lunch and we decided to leave 'actioning' the instrument until the following morning, forgetting that the US Purchasing Managers Index (PMI) was due to announce that afternoon. The PMI is seen as a leading indicator of what is going on in the US economy and the announcement was not good. The FTSE started to plummet after the announcement (the UK market often follows the US markets) and we decided not to try to catch the 'falling knife'. We just watched until it almost hit 7000 and then it slowly recovered. This may have been the most 'expensive' lunch we have ever had.

In summary, the markets do respond to sentiment surveys and indices, and it is worth spending time understanding the key ones and the dates they are released.

Textual Sentiment

Newspapers, financial magazines, and their internet equivalents (e.g. the Motley Fool) can have a dramatic impact on sentiment, especially the sentiment of retail investors. The Money section of the *Daily Mail* is very widely read and while we do not have concrete proof, decades of anecdotal evidence suggests a negative column in the Money section can have a significant impact on retail investor sentiment. While tools are developing that allow individuals to assess the sentiment of texts about a stock (through counting the number of negative words and negative sentences, as compared to positive comments), the retail investor can quickly search through a number of key, news outlets to gain a flavour of the sentiment facing a company.

Internet Search Behaviour

The world of Big Data has brought further tools to track market and company sentiment. The best known of these is Google Trends that allows investors to track the search volumes on individual companies. There is some initial evidence that internet search volumes have predictive power in terms of the trading volumes and volatility of stocks.[3] Google Trends also allow analysis of

---

[3] I. Bordino, S. Battiston, G. Caldarelli, M. Cristelli, A. Ukkonen, and I. Weber, Web search queries can predict stock market volumes. *PLoS ONE* 7(7) (2012): e40014. https://doi.org/10.1371/journal.pone.0040014

trends on given topics, and the seasonality and geography of trends. This is a relatively new area for tracking volume and in time there will be further developments as Big Data continues to be harnessed.

Non-Economic Factors

The final set of factors that can influence sentiment are a bit ephemeral. There is evidence[4] that the mood of the nation and investors can be affected by major sporting events – for example, success (relative) in a World Cup (cricket, rugby, football), the Tour de France, the Olympics, etc. Major disasters, such as an air crash, and natural disasters can dampen the mood of the investment market. There are other factors such as the weather that have also been found to have an effect. However, while all of these factors have been found to affect sentiment, the effects are often short-lived and variable. Nonetheless, they are worth bearing in mind if you are adopting a contrarian strategy.

EMPIRICAL EVIDENCE: INDIRECT

It is difficult to find empirical evidence on the success of contrarian investment. This is not surprising because it is very much an individual-based strategy. At a more general level, we already know investing in 'losers' can offer better gains than investing in winners but this is not a direct test of contrarian investing per se. Contrarian investing is concerned with doing the analysis to see which of the losers is worth investing in because the herd is mistaken in its views.

Lesson
Investors suffer from many behavioural biases and crowd effects, the consequence of which is that stocks can move a long way from their underlying values.

---

[4] A. Edmans, D. García, and Ø. Norli, Sports sentiment and stock returns. *Journal of Finance* 62(4) (2007): 1967–1998.

What we do know is that Dreman has been very successful as a contrarian investor and his arguments against more conventional approaches are worth discussing.

In his many books, he has been highly critical of portfolio theory and efficient markets. His basic argument is that investors suffer from many behavioural biases and crowd effects, the consequence of which is that stocks can move a long way from their underlying values.

In addition to being critical of mainstream theories, Dreman is not a great fan of experts. The basis of his criticism is that in financial markets it is difficult to work with the mass of data in any meaningful and coherent manner. The future changes in unpredictable ways and past correlations/investment methods based on past data offer only illusory certainties. In essence, the market data can tell us little about the way to invest – in one way, this result could be seen as supporting efficient markets (no profits can be made from modelling existing data) but Dreman sees it differently, the data are just too voluminous to make sense of and there is too much change to model in a predictive way. Complex systems are difficult to model and financial markets are a very complex system made up of many different actors acting in very unpredictable ways. Given all of this, Dreman argues, with some conviction, that the so-called experts are more often wrong than right. One ray of hope is that the experts seem to be making predictable errors (based on psychological biases) and the contrarian can use his/her insights to make profits.

As a simple rule, you should be highly sceptical of experts' predictions (including analysts) – they consistently make large errors. Perhaps this is not fair but the UK investor just needs to keep in mind Neil Woodford, the sacked financial analyst, before trusting any money to advisers.

In addition to the issues with predicting stock price changes in a reliable manner, given the complexity of the system, advisors have built-in biases, given their reward structures. First, companies do not like seeing a 'sell note' against them and advising firms naturally shy away from upsetting clients/potential clients. There is, therefore, an understandable asymmetry towards buy notes. Easterwood and Nutt[5] report that financial analysts under-react to negative information but over-react to positive information, which could be caused by systematic optimism regarding earnings information among analysts.

---

[5] J.C. Easterwood and S.R. Nutt, Inefficiency in analysts' earnings forecasts: Systematic misreaction or systematic optimism? *Journal of Finance* 54(5) (1999): 1777–1797.

Advisers gain commission on activity and buy activity is their preferred route. In gaining buy orders, the advisers just need to make up a convincing story as to why a particular stock is worth investing in – to be able to convince punters this stock is indeed different and this time real money will be made. Essentially, they need to be able to convince investors that the opportunity on offer is unique and different from past experiences and mistakes. As an investor you just need to ask the question – what evidence do I have to suggest this stock is any different from all the others?

In addition to analysts suffering from behavioural biases, so do investors, one of the most common biases being over-confidence. This bias is caused by three factors: (1) optimism about the future; (2) an overly positive evaluation of self-skills; and (3) too strong a belief in being able to control situations. Being aware of this bias should allow an investor to recalibrate his/her view of the upside and, equally importantly, the downside of an investment. Be realistic about the downside and you should not suffer too much pain.

The over-confidence bias also has an impact on growth stocks. Through over-confidence about their ability to see the future, investors are willing to pay a premium for already expensive stocks based on measures such as the price-earnings ratio. What they don't think through is what happens when there is news (e.g. an earnings surprise). From a lot of evidence, there is a very simple (and obvious after a bit of thought) conclusion. High-priced stocks suffer heavily from negative news (confidence is badly dented) and do not get much upside from positive news. Low-priced stocks have a completely opposite response – gaining significantly on positive news and not losing much on negative news.

In addition to contrarian stocks benefiting from aggregate news flow, such a strategy has the benefit of avoiding the costs of overtrading. In general, contrarian stocks take time to catch up and for the market to realize their true value – as a consequence, holding times can be quite long and trading costs low.

We now come to the point of deciding what type of contrarian investor you want to be: aggressive or defensive? Let's take the example of a defensive contrarian. This is an individual who will forsake some of the upside for avoiding the worst of the downside. In terms of which ratios to focus on, the dividend yield is more defensive than the price earnings ratio. While the former does not give the upside boost of the latter, it tends to give a reasonable upside across the long term and is best at avoiding the downside, it also has the benefit of a healthy ongoing dividend stream.

As mentioned previously, a defensive contrarian should only invest in large companies that are fundamentally sound from a financial perspective (you need to do your analysis!). You are looking for a strong financial position with as many positive operating and financial ratios as possible. You also need a picture of recent earnings growth and some assurance it is not going to plummet in the near future (you need to look at the dynamics of the industry and competitors). Also build in a margin of safety as discussed in Chapter 1.

Furthermore, a diversified portfolio of up to 20 stocks across different sectors is also sensible. While an industry-diversified contrarian strategy does not give quite the same returns as a strategy based purely on stocks, it has the benefits of avoiding being too exposed to a sector in decline and of feeling the warm glow of being part of a sector on the up.

We also need to consider when to exit a position. The simple answer is to sell when the PE has reached the average for the sector; don't be greedy and remember the Rothschilds' dictum: 'I never lost money by selling too early.' To get to this point you may need to hold on for up to three years (John Templeton had even more patience and suggested up to six years).

REMEMBER – all of the above is essentially to do with regression to the mean, few stocks can continue to perform at a high level for any length of time and regress back down to the mean. And the 'dogs' can eventually be turned around so long as they avoid failure.

The principle of reversion to the mean also applies to the market reaction to crisis events. The market normally massively over-reacts and the smart contrarian knows this and can profit on the bounce-back: the defensive contrarian will take advantage of this reversion by holding a portfolio of stocks to minimize the risk of being too exposed to 'sinkers'.

And this moves us on to the final topic in this section: what do we mean by risk? Dreman is, correctly (in the main), highly critical of risk being measured via the volatility of a stock price. The volatility of a share price is just that – investors changing their minds about a stock. A company has some level of volatility but the stock volatility is many times the company volatility. Some of the volatility will reflect news but a lot will reflect rumour, changing attitudes, and the herd thundering around the park.

So, if we accept volatility does not capture the fundamental risk of a company (and here we mean poor performance and possible failure) but the market movement of a stock, how can we use this measure, if at all? If the volatility of a stock is understood to a reasonable degree, then the volatility, both the upside and downside, can be used to make money. However, to play this game, there is a real need to understand the volatility and what is driving it. However, this is moving us away from risk and into the realms of technical analysis.

So far, we have discussed risk without the notion of time being mentioned, and this is the case in mainstream academic finance. If we take what risk means to the man in the street, it is the loss of wealth and this should help to guide us in thinking more clearly about risk. If an investor is concerned about risk on a daily basis, then the downside volatility (the semi-variance) of a stock price is not a bad measure (see further evidence in Chapter 6). If one stock has only a daily downside variance of 1%, while another has 5%, then it would be wise to focus on the former and stay away from the latter. However, such a short-term perspective does not capture the time frame of a lot of investors, which can be many years (especially pension funds). From a longer term perspective, volatility does not tell us a lot about the risk of stock. What is important is the probability over the long term of whether your wealth is increased/decreased, taking into account trading costs, inflation, and taxes. In trying to benchmark the risk of a stock (or stocks in general), you will note that inflation and taxes tend to dent bonds and cash. Holding a stock (and hopefully one with potential, given a contrarian position) avoids trading costs and annual taxes (ongoing paper gains are not taxed), and stocks tend to move (to a degree) in line with inflation.

SUCCESSES AND MISTAKES OF DAVID DREMAN AND QUANTITATIVE EVALUATION

As for so much with David Dreman, it is not easy to get a handle on his successes and failures. He says that his best investments have been the tobacco stocks of Philip Morris and R.J. Reynolds, whose prices collapsed in the early 2000s because of the liabilities brought about by class actions. However, Dreman placed a bet on the Supreme Court capping the scale of the punitive damages – his bet proved correct and the prices recovered hugely. His biggest mistakes were Fannie Mae and Freddie Mac, both of which suffered massive losses in the wake of the Global Financial Crisis.

Given the difficulties of gaining insights into Dreman's highlights/lowlights, the rest of this section focuses on the quantitative evaluation of a contrarian approach to investing; this has also not been easy!

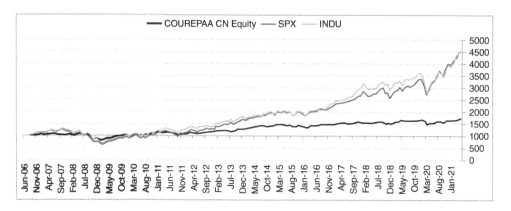

FIGURE 4.1   COUNSEL REGUL fund performance.
Source: Bloomberg

The recent performance of Dreman doesn't look to have been so great. From the Bio in BLOOMBERG PROFESSIONAL®, he looks to have $2.4 billion under management.

The largest one is a fund of funds, COUNSEL REGUL PAY PORTF-A FE, that also has a reported return (Figure 4.1). It does not compare too highly among its peers and significantly underperforms the S&P 500 and Dow Jones Industrial Average. This raises the question of whether he is finding it difficult to maintain top performance.

Applying Dreman's Method in the UK Market

We start with the simplest relative value filter: the price to earnings ratio (PE). We focus on PE stocks where the market is placing a lower earnings multiple. To avoid investing in very small and illiquid stock, we set our pool of investments as the FTSE 350 stocks.

We can see that the strategy produces an impressive average annual return of 20.33%. Beating the market 12 out of 15 years, having a negative active return only in 2007, 2008, and 2016, it demonstrates the contrarian nature of such a strategy. It is most likely that investors who experienced the losses in 2007–2008 would have pulled their money out and watched from the sidelines. Such investors would have missed the largest gain of this strategy during this sample period. Such a value strategy needs both patience and a strong gut to see it through.

Examining the holdings, it shows this portfolio holds about 25 stocks and rebalances more than half of them every year (Figure 4.2).

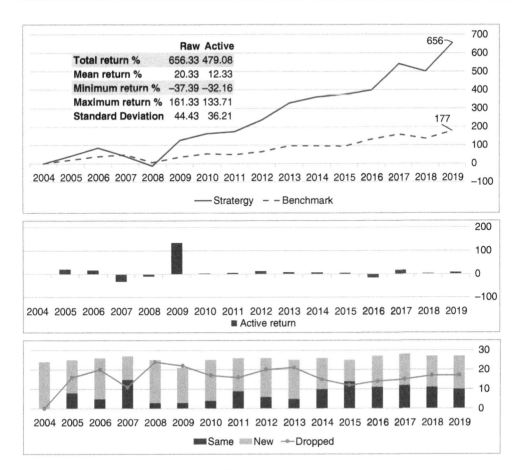

FIGURE 4.2 Cumulative return of the low PE strategy.
Source: BLOOMBERG PROFESSIONAL®.

Alternative Filters

Among the other value filters, the price to cash flow criterion performs at a similar level to the price to earnings ratio, while the price to book and dividend yield (dividend to price) filters give a much weaker performance in the UK market (Table 4.1).

International Evidence

We study the value strategies for the US and China markets during the same period. The simple value filter does not work as well in the US market. Since 2000, there has been a significant decrease in these value anomaly returns documented in this market. This is partly due to more smart money

TABLE 4.1 Comparison of value investment strategies, UK market

	Low PE	Low price to cash flow	Low price to book	High dividend yield	FTSE 100
Total return	656.33	702.10	310.90	374.77	177.38
Mean return (annualized)	24.77	25.94	18.69	18.66	12.41
Mean excess return (annualized)	11.00	12.04	5.59	5.56	
Standard deviation (annualized)	21.58	22.83	23.79	19.20	17.66
Sharpe ratio	0.71	0.70	0.47	0.58	0.39
Jensen alpha	9.01	8.95	4.26	4.95	
Beta (ex-post)	0.91	1.04	1.01	0.90	

Source: BLOOMBERG PROFESSIONAL®.

(hedge funds) using such strategies and, therefore, the 'mispricing' has been reduced. This may provide an explanation as to why Dreman's portfolio may be struggling to beat the market in recent years if he applies a similar strategy in the US.

For less-developed markets, e.g. China, it works relatively better. When considering the mean return, the low PE strategy in China produces the highest annualized return of 29.32%. However, this is also associated with a higher level of risk. This strategy's Sharpe ratio (0.64) is lower than that of the same strategy in the UK market (0.71). The fact that the UK market performs the best for this type of semi-strong efficient market anomaly is not a coincidence. Our research paper published in the *Journal of Financial and Quantitative Analysis*, shows that market return anomalies and market development have a humped shape relationship.[6] The return is low for the least developed (emerging) and most developed markets and peaks in the countries that are in between (Table 4.2).

---

[6] C.X. Cai, K. Keasey, P. Li, and Q. Zhang (2021). Market development, information diffusion and the global anomaly puzzle. *Journal of Financial and Quantitative Analysis*. Available at SSRN: https://ssrn.com/abstract=2839799 or http://dx.doi.org/10.2139/ssrn.2839799

TABLE 4.2 Comparison of value investment strategies – US and China

	US			China		
	Low PE	Low PC	SP 500	Low PE	Low PC	CSI 300
Total return	268.98	259.13	264.23	745.66	486.44	347.53
Mean return (annualized)	19.06	18.92	15.52	29.32	24.84	21.00
Mean excess return (annualized)	3.06	2.94		5.43	3.17	
Standard deviation (annualized)	27.36	27.74	18.39	28.71	28.43	26.92
Sharpe ratio	0.44	0.43	0.52	0.64	0.54	0.47
Jensen alpha	-0.87	-0.92		4.71	2.91	
Beta (ex-post)	1.34	1.34		0.98	0.97	

Source: BLOOMBERG PROFESSIONAL®.

SUMMARY

- It is almost a truism that great investors see value where others don't. They have insights about businesses and investors that elude the vast majority.
- Contrarian investing is just this insight taken to its logical extreme. Here we recap some of the key features of contrarian investing.
- But before we turn to these lessons, it is important to remember that a lot of the players in financial markets have their own game to play and things to sell – if you do want to follow others, work out what they are selling.
- Of course, if you have bought into the contrarian way of doing things, you will not be doing much following.
- It must be remembered that contrarian investing has features that can create huge gains, at the same time, unless care is exercised, huge losses can also be incurred.
- There are a number of ways of executing contrarian investing:
  - Buying into the biggest losers on the presumption they will survive and revert to the mean.
  - Looking for companies that have suffered a price drop because they are the 'collateral damage' of issues with other companies in the sector.

- Finally, there is the 'long odds' bet. A company has collapsed because of good reasons but it may have value because of patents, proprietary technology, etc. These could form the basis of a revitalization of the company in the longer term or the purchase of the company.
- Make sure your contrarian decisions are based on solid analysis and you are not going against the crowd for the sake of it – this can be costly. When everyone is running out of a building, it is normally for a good reason.
- Be patient – it can often take a long time for the market to realize its mistake and come round to your way of thinking.
- Equally, money is made through rigorous analysis. Lots of other individuals and institutions will be seeing the data in a very different way from you, work out why your view is correct and theirs is incorrect.
- When your views are isolated and against the crowd, your position can be very lonely and it is only natural to seek out confirmatory evidence. Remember, we all suffer from confirmation bias (seeking evidence, no matter how flaky, that supports our view) and you need to be aware of twisting the evidence to suit your perspective.
- Finally, to be successful, you need to believe in your honest analysis and be brave enough to hold your nerve – often easier said than done.

PRACTICAL APPLICATION III: A CLOSER LOOK AT PORTFOLIO PERFORMANCE

To understand why and how a strategy works, it is useful to look into the individual stocks that make it into the selection and how they contribute. The PORT function provides great functionality in this regard. Combining this function with other company-specific functions, such as the FA and EEM functions discussed in previous chapters, can help us understand more about the strategy constituents.

In the following, we are going to look into the low PE strategy. Particularly, we are interested in the following questions:

- What different aspects of the portfolio information are relevant to performance evaluations?
- What is the industry diversification of the strategy and how does it affect performance?

- What drives the low PE strategy during and after the financial crisis?
- How did the strategy pick these stocks?
- Can we improve the strategy?

What Different Aspects of the Portfolio Information Are Relevant to Performance Evaluations?

In this section, we will work through an analysis of the low PE strategy in the UK market that we reported in the main text. Please see Practical Application I in Chapter 2 for more instruction on how to conduct the screening using equity screening (EQS) and backtesting through EQBT. Once these two steps are done, the portfolio (holdings generated by the EQBT function) will be available to the PORT function. To load the EQBT into the PORT function, we have two methods.

Method 1 from EQBT:

- *Type* {EQBT}<Go> to load the function.
- *Click* the 'view results' icon (a magnifying glass icon) on the backtest model that you want to see the results for.
- *Click* [Analyze in PORT] on the red menu bar.

Method 2 from PORT:

- *Type* {PORT}<Go> to load the function.
- *Click* the dropdown icon on the portfolio field at the top left
- *Click* [More Sources. . .]
- Use the <SEARCH> to find the EQBT portfolio you have created. The portfolio name will be the model name you gave during the backtesting prefixed with 'EQBT-'. For example, we name the backtesting 'Low PE UK' in the EQBT function. The portfolio will be named 'EQBT-Low PE UK'.
- *Click* on [EQBT- Low PE UK], then [1) Select] to load the portfolio.

We can see that the PORT function has a large collection of sub-functions which are organized into tabs and subtabs. This indicates what is considered to be important information for performance evaluation by financial professionals. The starting point of a performance evaluation is to define your

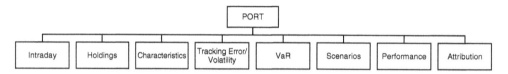

FIGURE 4.3   Key tabs in the PORT function.

benchmark. For example, for the UK stock market investment, we often use the FTSE 100 index as the benchmark. The PORT function then allows users to compare their portfolio holdings, returns, risk, or other fundamental characteristics to those of the benchmark. The key tabs are listed in Figure 4.3.

In this application, we focus mainly on the *Performance, Holding, Characteristics*, and *Attribution* tabs of this function.

The *Performance* tab provides a report of the time series return and the key realized risk statistics such as standard deviation, beta, and the Sharpe ratio.

To understand the fundamental characteristics (e.g. financial ratios, valuation ratios) of the portfolio, the *Characteristics* tab can produce the portfolio's average statistics by sectors at a specific date or as a time series trend.

The *Holdings* tab allows users to view their portfolio's positions and sector weights. In particular, it can analyse over-/under-weights relative to a benchmark.

Performance attribution is a way to understand where the active return is coming from. It allows users to decompose the sources of a portfolio's active return into sector bets (Allocation Effect), security bets (Selection Effect), and FX rate bets (Currency Effect).

What Is the Industry Diversification of the Strategy and How Does It Affect Performance?

To see the average weight of the portfolio by sectors and their performance compared to the benchmark, the *Attribution* tab is the best place for such information. To view the information, we need to undertake some specifications after loading the EQBT portfolio into the Port function:

- *Click* [Attribution] tab to load the attribution tab main view.
- To set a benchmark index we *click* the dropdown icon on the benchmark field at the top left on the right of the portfolio name. *Click* [More Sources. . .], then [Indices. . .], on the right side of the window *type* {FTSE 350} and select from the suggested dropdown list 'NMX index FTSE 350 Index', *click* [1) Select] to load this

- To set the period of study, click on the start and end date fields to edit. In this example, it is from 12/31/2014 to 12/31/2019.
- Then *hit* <GO> to run the analysis.

A partial view of the results is summarized in Table 4.3.

A low PE strategy seems to favour real estate, financials and consumer discretionary (CD) in the UK during these 15 years. Especially when compared to the benchmark, it is significantly overweight in real estate and CD. It underweights consumer staples and energy. The overweight in real estate is especially detrimental to the overall performance. It contributes to the largest negative return of the portfolio in absolute terms (-70.59%) and relative terms (-73.16%). By contrast, the portfolio's overall outperformance is driven by the overweighting of the CD sector.

The financial sector is an interesting one to demonstrate the ability of the analysis to reveal the source of portfolio performance. From the holding comparison, we see there is very little difference between the portfolio and benchmark in terms of its proportional allocation to this sector. However, the low PE portfolio outperforms the benchmark significantly. When we study where the alpha comes from, it confirms that it is mainly driven by the selection effect. In other words, the strategy is able to select the better-performing stocks within the financial sectors than those stocks in the benchmark.

What Drives the Low PE Strategy During and After the Financial Crisis?

In our earlier discussion, we noticed that the low PE strategy significantly underperformed during the financial crisis (2007–2008) and has the highest return subsequently (2009). What has contributed to this performance? In this section, we look at what types of company are in the portfolio and their contribution to the total performance during the financial crisis of 2007–2008 and the recovery in 2009. We do that by examing the characteristics of the portfolio in the *Characteristics* tab:

- *Click* the [Characteristics] tab to load the tab's main view.
- To study the portfolio's characteristics at a specific time point, we specify this in the 'As of' field on the top right of the view. For example, we are interested in the characteristics at the end of 2007 (Table 4.4). We *type* {12/31/07} and *hit* <GO> to run the analysis.

TABLE 4.3   Attribution summary, PE strategy UK

	% Average weight			Contribution to return (%)			Total attribution (alpha) (%)	Allocation effect (%)	Selection effect (%)	Currency effect (%)
	Port	Bench	+/-	Port	Bench	+/-				
EQBT-Dreman_ PE_UK	100.00	100.00	0.00	654.71	199.45	455.26	455.26	-114.18	569.45	-0.01
Real estate	27.00	1.96	25.04	-70.59	2.56	-73.16	-127.95	-159.75	31.80	0.00
Financials	19.39	19.08	0.31	174.78	14.65	160.13	251.15	-5.40	256.55	0.00
Consumer discretionary	16.20	6.01	10.19	217.05	14.21	202.84	189.91	35.15	154.76	0.00
Not classified	9.96	6.08	3.88	68.15	16.29	51.86	14.98	32.22	-17.23	-0.01
Industrials	9.41	8.05	1.36	105.88	20.62	85.26	72.79	18.39	54.40	0.00
Materials	6.73	8.77	-2.04	105.83	19.03	86.80	77.60	25.59	52.01	0.00
Energy	3.76	15.40	-11.64	-12.61	25.15	-37.76	-36.36	-22.52	-13.84	0.00
Utilities	3.56	3.53	0.03	30.62	7.32	23.30	35.93	14.82	21.11	0.00
Consumer staples	1.35	13.37	-12.02	11.63	35.88	-24.24	-20.34	-27.54	7.20	0.00
Health care	1.23	8.29	-7.06	13.46	22.99	-9.54	-12.30	-27.75	15.45	0.00
Communication services	1.06	7.94	-6.88	11.48	14.97	-3.49	8.86	5.66	3.20	0.00
Information technology	0.36	1.52	-1.17	-0.95	5.78	-6.73	1.00	-3.05	4.05	0.00

Source: BLOOMBERG PROFESSIONAL®.

TABLE 4.4 Portfolio characteristics: PE strategy UK on 12/31/2007

	Wgt			Dividend yield			Price to earnings ratio (P/E)			Price to cash flow ratio (P/CF)		
	Port	Bench	+/-	Port	Bench	+/-	Port	Bench	+/-	Port	Bench	+/-
EQBT-Dreman_PE_UK	100.00	100.00	0.00	7.50	4.53	2.97	2.77	12.69	-9.92	2.30	10.67	-8.38
Communication services		9.15	-9.15		4.36	-4.36		20.36	-20.36		8.93	-8.93
Consumer discretionary	18.52	4.44	14.08	5.82	6.19	-0.37	4.45	10.89	-6.44	11.07	9.76	1.31
Consumer staples		11.38	-11.38		2.63	-2.63		21.11	-21.11		15.68	-15.68
Energy		17.44	-17.44		3.49	-3.49		11.40	-11.40		9.24	-9.24
Financials	18.52	19.13	-0.61	7.03	9.19	-2.16	3.63	8.44	-4.81	14.86	8.71	6.15
Health care		6.49	-6.49		3.87	-3.87		15.41	-15.41		11.44	-11.44
Industrials		6.54	-6.54		3.00	-3.00		17.62	-17.62		11.00	-11.00
Information technology	3.70	0.87	2.84		2.34	-2.34	5.57	21.61	-16.04	9.59	15.29	-5.70
Materials		8.98	-8.98		1.70	-1.70		14.66	-14.66		11.45	-11.45
Real estate	44.44	1.61	42.84	3.93	3.86	0.07	2.44	2.62	-0.18	42.68	354.59	-311.91
Utilities	3.70	3.58	0.12	2.28	4.60	-2.32	4.69	13.15	-8.46	5.23	8.79	-3.56
Not classified	11.11	10.40	0.71		15.65	-15.65	1.55	11.71	-10.16	0.32	10.74	-10.42

Source: BLOOMBERG PROFESSIONAL®.

The above shows the holding at the end of 2007 which would have been held during 2008. The over-weighting of real estate is obviously detrimental in hindsight. But alarm bells would have been ringing at the end of 2007 if developments in the US had been followed/noted. Looking at the price to cash flow ratio also suggests this sector should have been avoided.

To study the performance in 2008, we go back to the attribution tab and specify the date:

- *Click* the [Attribution] tab to load the tab's main view.
- Set the benchmark to be 'NMX index FTSE 350 Index' as we did earlier.
- To set the period of study, *click* on the start and end date fields to edit. In this example, it is from 12/31/2007 to 12/31/2008 (Table 4.5).
- Then *hit* <GO> to run the analysis.

The above confirms that real estate was the driver of the last crisis and CD is a cyclical industry that follows the ups and downs of an economy. This is true when we study the recovery in 2009 by setting the date range to be from 12/31/2008 to 12/31/2009 (see Table 4.6).

The over-weight of CD, materials, industrials and financials is the correct decision, given that these are all the right sectors to be in when an economy is recovering.

Overall, the above analysis shows that the strategy picks the lowest PE in the pool and, therefore, those with a relatively low PE ratio in each of these industries. The fact that the strategy performs well is because it realizes two relative gains. First, by comparing the benchmark's performance in the sectors picked by the strategy and those not selected, we can see that the low PE strategy seems to also work at the industry level, especially during a transition period of the business cycle. Second, the performance of the stocks selected by the strategy in each of these sectors is even stronger than the sector pick.

The real estate companies completely drop out of our selection because their earnings are negative and, therefore, they do not have a PE ratio.

Tips
You can export the data from the function to Excel or PDF by *clicking* on [12 actions], [Create/Edit Templates ...], [Current Tabl (xls)] or other templates of your choice.

TABLE 4.5 Portfolio performance, PE strategy UK from 12/31/2007 to 12/31/2008

	% Average weight			Contribution to return (%)			Total attribution (alpha) (%)	Allocation effect (%)	Selection effect (%)	Currency effect (%)
	Port	Bench	+/-	Port	Bench	+/-				
EQBT-Dreman_PE_UK	100.00	100.00	0.00	-37.39	-29.44	-7.95	-7.95	-13.26	5.31	-0.01
Real estate	45.44	1.60	43.84	-23.34	-0.80	-22.54	-8.17	-6.54	-1.63	0.00
Financials	21.05	18.66	2.39	-1.65	-9.82	8.18	6.37	-0.39	6.76	0.00
Consumer discretionary	14.10	3.75	10.35	-10.12	-1.80	-8.33	-4.93	-1.85	-3.08	0.00
Not classified	8.96	8.71	0.25	-1.60	-4.64	3.03	2.44	-0.07	2.52	-0.01
Information technology	5.32	0.97	4.35	-0.23	-0.19	-0.04	0.97	0.42	0.55	0.00
Utilities	5.14	3.75	1.40	-0.44	-0.56	0.12	0.57	0.37	0.20	0.00
Energy	0.00	18.59	-18.59		-1.80	1.80	-2.89	-2.89	0.00	0.00
Materials	0.00	9.51	-9.51		-5.03	5.03	1.68	1.68	0.00	0.00
Industrials	0.00	6.38	-6.38		-2.07	2.07	0.16	0.16	0.00	0.00
Consumer staples	0.00	12.09	-12.09		-1.36	1.36	-1.55	-1.55	0.00	0.00
Health care	0.00	7.51	-7.51		0.81	-0.81	-2.39	-2.39	0.00	0.00
Communication services	0.00	8.49	-8.49		-2.18	2.18	-0.21	-0.21	0.00	0.00

Source: BLOOMBERG PROFESSIONAL®.

TABLE 4.6   Portfolio performance, PE strategy UK from 12/31/2008 to 12/31/2009

	% Average weight			Contribution to return (%)			Total attribution (alpha) (%)	Allocation effect (%)	Selection effect (%)	Currency effect (%)
	Port	Bench	+/-	Port	Bench	+/-				
EQBT-Dreman_PE_UK	100.00	100.00	0.00	161.33	29.95	131.38	131.38	40.54	91.79	-0.95
Consumer discretionary	34.40	4.23	30.17	58.75	2.22	56.54	45.76	9.61	36.15	0.00
Materials	31.53	8.78	22.75	69.95	7.19	62.76	55.61	18.15	37.46	0.00
Industrials	14.23	6.35	7.88	18.49	1.78	16.71	13.93	0.03	13.90	0.00
Financials	10.20	17.48	-7.28	12.74	6.15	6.59	9.22	1.45	8.73	-0.96
Not classified	9.63	6.21	3.43	1.39	3.30	-1.90	-2.20	2.23	-4.45	0.01
Energy	0.00	19.89	-19.89		3.87	-3.87	2.48	2.48	0.00	0.00
Consumer staples	0.00	14.01	-14.01		3.04	-3.04	0.88	0.88	0.00	0.00
Health care	0.00	8.63	-8.63		0.64	-0.64	2.32	2.32	0.00	0.00
Information technology	0.00	1.16	-1.16		0.44	-0.44	-0.13	-0.13	0.00	0.00
Communication services	0.00	8.28	-8.28		1.10	-1.10	1.75	1.75	0.00	0.00
Utilities	0.00	3.64	-3.64		-0.12	0.12	1.52	1.52	0.00	0.00
Real estate	0.00	1.34	-1.34		0.34	-0.34	0.25	0.25	0.00	0.00

Source: BLOOMBERG PROFESSIONAL®.

Can We Improve the Strategy?

There is a difference between data mining and strategy testing. To improve this strategy, we cannot just exclude the real estate industry from our strategy after seeing their poor performance during the crisis. The fact that this industry underperformed during the 2007–2008 financial crisis would not be available to us when forming a strategy before the crisis. This is one of the mistakes that can be made in a backtesting strategy. It is important to note that when we change a criterion for a strategy after seeing the backtesting results, we may be suffering from 'look-back bias'. The last crisis was caused by subprime mortgages and that is why the real estate industry was hit hard but it is not saying that real estate should always be avoided going forward. Removing real estate will improve our backtesting results but not necessarily the future performance of the strategy. Instead of trying to remove one industry, we may try to see if we can improve our screen with the information available at the rebalancing. For example, we can try combining the PE ratio filter with the price to cash flow as an additional filter.

Specifically, within the bottom 10% of PE stocks, we select the bottom half of the stocks with a lower price to cash ratio. The criteria for the EQS will be as follows in Table 4.7.

Examining the return in the PORT function, we can see a summary of the return between 2004 and 2019 in the following. Adding the price to cash flow would reduce the number of stocks held, but the remaining holdings are of better quality than the original strategy. We can see that the total return has increased to 898% from 655%. When we examine the yearly return, the strategy beat the market every year in these 15 years (Table 4.8). The weighting information shows that while the real estate sector is still featured in the portfolio, it is with a much lower overall weight – thus causing less damage.

TABLE 4.7　Criteria for the EQS

Criteria	Matches (as of Dec 2019)
A pool of FTSE 350 constituent stocks	350
Bottom 10 sequential percentile rank - higher is better (current price earnings ratio (P/E))	27
Bottom 50 sequential percentile rank - higher is better (current price/cash flow)	11

TABLE 4.8 Portfolio performance, PE-PC strategy UK, 2004 to 2019

	% Average weight			Contribution to return (%)			Total attribution (alpha) (%)	Allocation effect (%)	Selection effect (%)	Currency effect (%)
	Port	Bench	+/-	Port	Bench	+/-				
EQBT-Dreman_PE_PC_UK	100.00	100.00	0.00	898.54	199.45	699.09	699.09	-95.85	787.38	7.57
Financials	21.28	19.08	2.20	265.14	14.65	250.49	344.45	-12.61	349.48	7.58
Consumer discretionary	20.44	5.96	14.48	261.04	13.78	247.25	238.27	27.84	210.43	0.00
Materials	11.72	8.77	2.95	211.60	19.03	192.57	175.92	19.56	156.35	0.00
Industrials	11.62	8.05	3.57	90.89	20.62	70.26	25.71	30.75	-5.04	0.00
Not classified	10.68	6.08	4.60	118.33	16.29	102.04	91.43	21.64	69.81	-0.02
Real estate	7.97	1.96	6.01	-62.88	2.56	-65.45	-129.33	-129.10	-0.23	0.00
Utilities	6.84	3.53	3.32	66.64	7.32	59.33	109.99	58.06	51.93	0.00
Energy	5.74	15.40	-9.65	-84.67	25.15	-109.81	-151.53	-57.09	-94.44	0.00
Consumer staples	1.32	13.43	-12.10	21.51	36.30	-14.79	-20.00	-33.76	13.75	0.00
Information technology	1.14	1.52	-0.38	-5.21	5.78	-10.99	20.82	6.90	13.92	0.00
Health care	0.65	8.29	-7.64	19.23	22.99	-3.77	-3.51	-28.26	24.75	0.00
Communication services	0.58	7.94	-7.36	-3.06	14.97	-18.03	-3.13	0.21	-3.35	0.00

Source: BLOOMBERG PROFESSIONAL®.

EXERCISES

1. Look into the low PE strategy's performance closely around the 2020
   Covid-19 crisis (make sure the backtesting includes this period). Answer
   the following questions:
   (a) Which industry leads the crisis?
   (b) Which is the most affected industry in the index?
   (c) Which industry in our portfolio contributes most to the downturn?
   (d) Can we improve the strategy further?
2. Do a similar analysis into the growth strategy we discussed in Chapter 3.

CHAPTER 5

Harry Markowitz

The Father of Portfolio Theory

INTRODUCTION

This chapter reviews and discusses the core of modern academic finance – portfolio theory. It is no exaggeration to say that portfolio theory changed the way we think about investing and it has also changed the way, to a degree, large, institutional investors manage their investments. The idea behind portfolio theory is deceptively simple and deeply embedded in our common sense way of seeing investments – 'don't put all your eggs in one basket'. Essentially, you will reduce your risk if you diversify your investment into a number of different assets. This simple idea can be traced back to the Bible and principles of Roman banking, and even Shakespeare makes mention of the concept in a couple of his plays.

While the concept of portfolio management is deceptively simple, it is hideously complicated in both theoretical and empirical terms, and, as we will see, theoretically it only makes any sense if the market has a collective wisdom – if not, it is just compounding guess after guess, no matter how fancy the mathematics and empirical methods.

Harry Markowitz began the debate in academic terms and developed some of the applications. He is rightly seen as the father of portfolio theory, in spite of James Tobin being awarded the Nobel Prize in Economics in 1981 for his work on monetary theory and portfolio theory. Markowitz did not receive the Nobel Prize until 1990 for his work on portfolio theory!

While we will follow approximately the same structure as other chapters, the balance will differ, with more emphasis being given to some of the issues in applying the 'detail' of the Markowitz approach – this especially applies to smaller investors. Nonetheless, the basic principle of holding uncorrelated assets to reduce risk still holds.

BACKGROUND

Harry Markowitz is still working at the age of 94 (2021) and he intends to do so until he drops. He was born in Chicago to parents running a grocery store and was an only child. By his own admission, he was a bit of a 'swot' and this aptitude for academic work (he was attracted to the philosophers at high school and this interest continues to the present day) propelled him to the University of Chicago were he was fortunate to be taught by some of the great economists of the twentieth century – Friedman, Savage, Koopmans, Marschak, etc. From this experience he developed an interest in decision-making under uncertainty, a solid foundation for his later path-breaking work which came out of his doctoral thesis.

Under the supervision of Marschak, he decided to try to apply statistical techniques to stock investment. The story goes that his ideas of portfolio theory came to him one afternoon while reading John Burr Williams' *Theory of Investment Value* (1938).[1] From the perspective of this text, the value of a stock comes from the future value of expected dividends. Markowitz realized that if the sole concern of an investor was expected value, then he/she would only invest in a single stock, the one with the highest expected return. This, he noted, did not square with what investors actually did – they hold a diverse portfolio to reduce risk. In other words, they are concerned with risk and return, and Markowitz used his training in economics and analytics to model how they might do so efficiently. His ground-breaking paper 'Portfolio Selection' that came out of his doctoral thesis was published in *The Journal of Finance* in 1952.[2]

In many ways, the rest of Markowitz's career was involved in operationalizing the insights of his doctoral thesis. He moved to the RAND Corporation in 1952 and worked on the optimization techniques that underpinned his later work on the fast estimation of mean-variance frontiers. Across the 1950s and 1960s he worked at RAND and other investment-focused companies and eventually became a full-time academic in the early 1970s at the Rady School of

---

[1] J.B. Williams, *The Theory of Investment Value* (Cambridge, MA: Harvard University Press, 1938).
[2] H. Markowitz, Portfolio selection. *The Journal of Finance* 7(1) (1952): 77–91. https://doi.org/10.2307/2975974.

Management at the University of California, San Diego. It is worth noting for the small investor that Markowitz sees himself as an operations researcher who applied standard computer techniques to the estimation of the efficient frontier of risk/return portfolios. IIe is not an economist by nature and Milton Friedman 'joked' whether he should award Markowitz a doctorate in economics, given its mathematical/operational research focus. As we will see, this subtle distinction is important in considering some of the limitations of his approach to portfolio theory.

While the next section delves into some of the detail of Markowitz's portfolio selection, the one lesson we should not forget is that when investing in stocks, the associated risks are as important as the returns, and Markowitz gives us one means of computing risk – whether it is entirely appropriate is an ongoing debate, but we are getting ahead of ourselves, yet again!

KEY LESSONS

The core of the Markowitz approach is conceptually simple – work out the expected return and the expected risk of an asset (or a portfolio of assets) and choose the one which best matches your preference for risk and return. This simplicity soon disappears, however, when one tries to operationalize and apply the idea in a practical manner. We will not go into the mathematical detail of the approach (this can be found very easily via a web search) but we will highlight the practical issues in applying the key lessons. What will become apparent is that while the approach might be a useful filter for institutions assembling large portfolios, it is of limited use to small investors and their advisers unless they have computing power (not too difficult nowadays) and access to quite a lot of quantitative data (a bit more difficult). We will walk through the approach step by step.

Expected Returns

Stocks are bought to generate expected returns. The expected return of an investment is the expected value of the probability distribution of future returns. So the first question we have to ask is how to form the set of future returns. In theory, in an efficient market, the expected returns of a stock should reflect future values and their probabilities of occurring and these will depend on the operation of the business. So we have unknown future values and unknown future probabilities. Academics have drawn up models to try to overcome the problem of the unknown. For example, they have used dividends to proxy for value.[3] Nonetheless, we should not kid ourselves we are dealing with 'knowns'.

Another trick used by academics is to use the past as a guide to the future. This makes some sense when the economy is in a stable state but just consider how much change we are going through at the moment (Spring 2021).

Nonetheless, if we assume the past is a good guide to the future, then historical data could be gone through to assess the past returns and their probabilities. As an example, consider an investment that has achieved the following returns in the past 10 years: three of the years with 15%, three with 10% and four with 8%; this gives the probabilities of 30%, 30% and 40% for those returns respectively. You may wish to reflect on the types of past data you might use to derive these returns and probabilities. If these past returns are a reasonable indicator of future returns, then the expected return will be:

$$0.3\,(15\%) + 0.3\,(10\%) + 0.4\,(8\%) = 10.7\%.$$

So, if we can assume that the past represents the future, then this would be a good indicator. BUT we need to consider how these numbers came to be formed before we go marching on. Let's take the 15% return. If this was achieved by a stock for a given year, then it reflects how the market of investors sees the potential of the company. THINK. So while past returns have been achieved, they are really past 'expected returns' and, therefore, our current expected return is just the aggregation of prior expected returns. AND here we come to the core issue. If the market is efficient and has collective wisdom, none of this should really concern us because on average the expectations will have to mirror 'true values' as errors of valuation will be spotted and reworked. However, where all of this comes unstuck is if the market is not efficient and there are bubbles in expectations. It also comes unstuck if the past returns have not been able to adapt to major changes in the economic environment. There is only so much we can learn from the history.

It is worth emphasizing that while the returns have the seeming truth-value of numbers, they are just the aggregation of guesses about the future.

---

[3] M.J. Gordon, Dividends, earnings and stock prices. *Review of Economics and Statistics* 41(2) (1959): 99–105. doi:10.2307/1927792. JSTOR 1927792.

Expected Return

Historical return is backward-looking. To improve our estimate of expected value, rather than use the past returns and simply average them (taking expectation), economists try to identify the fundamental factors that drive those historical returns and the expectation about the expected return based on the relationship between the stock and those pricing factors. In this regard, while market conditions (factors) are changing, the pricing relationship is assumed to be stable and can be estimated from historical data. We move away from guessing the specifics of each company to guessing their relationship with the macro factors. We will start our discussion with the most obvious factor used in asset pricing: the market factor in our introduction to the capital asset pricing model (CAPM) later in this chapter.

Before we move on to consider risk, we need to note that the expected return of a portfolio follows the same logic with the added notion that the return will reflect the balance of the weights across the various assets in the portfolio.[4]

In summary, the first step in applying the Markowitz approach is to estimate from past data the expected returns of stocks and then aggregate them into different portfolios.

Expected Risk

As noted above, Markowitz's main insight was that investors are concerned with risk and this can be tackled in a methodical way via diversified portfolios. In choosing between portfolios, investors need to be able to compare them on the basis of expected return and expected risk. And expected risk in this context is relatively simple in concept but again somewhat questionable.

Risk in this setting equates, in the first instance, to the standard deviation of the expected returns. This measures risk as a notion of distance from the mean expected return and it equates distance below the mean in exactly the same way as distance above. In other words, risk is seen symmetrically. Here, an asset with a greater dispersion will be seen as being more risky subject to a simple caveat; namely, the covariation between the assets also affects the risk of a portfolio – and this goes back to the notion of a diversified portfolio. Imagine two portfolios with exactly the same expected means and expected

---

[4] In a portfolio setting we also have to assume we have the same faith in the probabilities of different asset classes. For example, would we have the same faith in the probabilities of returns in thickly traded stocks as compared to thinly traded stocks?

standard deviations (risk). But with one of the portfolios, the assets are not correlated in the slightest, while in the second portfolio the assets are perfectly correlated (effectively, they all look the same). The first portfolio would be seen as being less risky by most people because when one asset is doing poorly, another may be doing well – the portfolio feels diversified. Whereas with the second portfolio, if one asset is doing badly, they will all be doing badly and this will feel painful. It is debatable if people would feel the same if all the assets were doing well. This is part of the debate over whether people see the probabilities of gains and losses as both being equally risky. We will discuss some of this later in Chapter 6 on behavioural finance.

So, once we have the past data on returns, we can compute the expected returns and the expected risk of assets and portfolios.

From the set of all return and risk combinations, for any level of risk, we will be able to identify the portfolio with the highest expected return – from this, we will be able to construct the 'efficient frontier' of portfolios (see Figure 5.1). And from all the portfolios that make up the frontier, an investor will choose the one that matches their preference trade-off between risk and return. Some individuals will prefer a higher return and they will have to accept a high risk, etc. This trade-off is based on the notion that the efficient frontier is upward sloping, i.e. to gain a higher return, you need to accept a higher risk. But what would happen if lower risk portfolios gave higher returns?

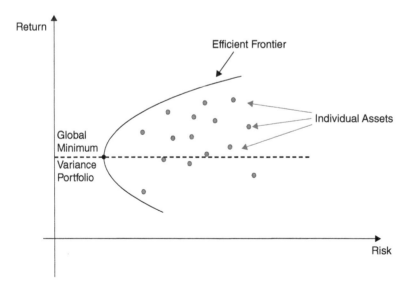

FIGURE 5.1   Efficient frontier.

Investor Preferences between Risk and Return

The above has constructed the efficient frontier of expected returns and expected risks on the back of some fairly strong assumptions, the future reflects the past, and the shape of past returns follows some nice conditions – one being that average returns have a higher probability than extreme returns.

Once the efficient frontier has been computed, it is up to the investor to decide how he/she feels about the trade-off between risk and return; this is his/her preference for risk.

Asking an individual to detail his/her preference for risk in terms of means and variances is far from straightforward. There is the issue of how far these statistical constructs make any sense to the person in the street and even if they did, whether they could be used to express an individual's attitudes to risk, etc.

Nonetheless, an individual needs to be able to express his/her risk preferences if a specific portfolio is to be chosen, unless a random portfolio is chosen from the efficient frontier. For this to occur, the preferences have to have certain properties – an aversion to risk and an aversion to increasing risk. These seem to be reasonable conditions but they do not capture a fundamental feature of most individuals' attitudes to risk – they feel the pain of losses far more keenly than the joy from gains. This asymmetry in losses/gains runs counter to the modelling of preferences in a Markowitz portfolio model and as a consequence investors may be unable to choose a unique portfolio.

APPLYING THE LESSONS AND THE EMPIRICAL EVIDENCE

There can be little doubt that the Markowitz efficient frontier is conceptually strong but it has elements that limit its practical appeal. While it may be used by very large institutions as a filter, it has failed to gain traction among retail investors and the investment community in general. One explanation of this state of affairs is that it is difficult for most individuals/advisers to apply the approach in any truly meaningful sense. Another, equally concerning explanation is that the portfolios offered by such an approach do not perform any better than an equal weighting of assets in many situations. As we have spent quite a lot of time on the former explanation, we will focus here on the latter.

One of the fundamental issues with the portfolio approach is that it is prone to estimation error maximization. By its own definition, the Markowitz technique over-weights the assets with the highest expected returns and as these are normally based on past actual returns, those with the highest positive errors will be over-weighted.

A further issue is one of liquidity. The portfolio approach assumes all stocks are equally liquid and that buying/selling a stock will not affect its price. Clearly, some smaller stocks are not overly liquid and the sale of a significant stake by an institution can impact the share price and, therefore, the expected return.

This notion of different stocks having different liquidity is similar to the notion that the level of uncertainty over the return and variance estimates will vary across assets. For example, investors may have faith in their estimates for mature stocks but less so for relatively new and small stocks. In many ways, the faith in the estimates depends on the quality and quantity of data underpinning the estimates. With small stocks there may be a long times-series of past returns on which to build but the problem is how good the information has been on which the expected returns have been built. Small firms have more limited accounts and are subject to less oversight, both of which may limit the quality of the information set. New firms (and these can be large in some circumstances) may have a rich set of data but only available for a short time.

Effectively, what is being questioned here is the quality of the inputs into the optimization process. There is a suspicion among investors that the robustness of the input estimates does not match up to the rigour of the mathematical approach – basically, garbage in/garbage out. The scepticism of practical investors is in many ways supported by the available evidence – which is, at best, mixed.

While Markowitz's efficient frontier is the main contribution of his work to modern portfolio theory and the foundation of subsequent asset pricing and investment research in the academic finance world, the truly useful lesson from Markowitz for the ordinary investor is that diversification, if done properly, can always reduce risk. And taking this diversification to a greater extreme, investing in the market portfolio is probably the best bet for ordinary investors. In other words, passive investment in index tracking funds is not a bad choice in this regard.

Relatedly, as we will see later, Markowitz's work led to the development of the Capital Asset Pricing Model, which predicts that all investors will hold an identical portfolio, the market portfolio. The difference among individual investors being their allocation of investment between this portfolio and 'the risk-free asset' depending on their attitude to risk.

THE ISSUE OF RISK

Markowitz is seen as bringing the importance of risk to the attention of the academic community, professional investors having already understood that having diversified portfolios brings benefits. In many ways, however, Markowitz did the investment community a disservice in the way he modelled risk. If the future just reflects the past, then all we need to concern ourselves with is the variance and covariance of the expected returns of assets. In the Markowitz world, we don't have to worry about where the risk is coming from or how it might change. But the world does change and it is changing a lot at the time of writing, and understanding how risk impacts assets is the key to making good investment decisions. In the Markowitz world, we can reduce risk by diversifying away the 'idiosyncratic risk' of individual stocks but we can't reduce systemic risk. However, the variance of individual assets is not static, nor is the covariance between them, nor is the systemic risk. The portfolio model lulls investors into a passive sense of security by freeing them from analysing the sources of risk – DON'T WORRY, THE MODEL WILL SORT IT OUT. Nothing could be further from the truth in a changing world. The rest of this section discusses some of the types of risk that might affect a business, and, therefore, its share price. Of course, the share price will only be affected if the investors see the consequences of these risks and here we have a strange thought; if all investors became 'passive' and solely based their buying/selling decisions on past expected returns, etc., then none of the following risks would matter – because investors are only buying shares not the shares of businesses. While there has been a movement to passive index investing, there is still a large cohort of investors concerned with the underlying businesses. And we have to be thankful to such active investors for taking the time to understand the underlying businesses and driving share prices to their fundamental values.

Here are some of the main risks that investors should be aware of:

- **Headline risk**: With the move to 24-hour news and the ever-present social media, companies are at risk from headline news. While such news is difficult to predict, some companies are more newsworthy and seem to be never out of the press, others you rarely hear of. It is worth being aware of this risk. In addition, some sectors attract news coverage and if you want a quiet life, they might best be avoided. A good example is travel companies – the press likes nothing better than writing about the woes of fellow human beings being stranded or let down by a travel company. As we are writing this paragraph, the news is being bombarded by the demise of Thomas Cook.

- **Rating risk**: It will come as no surprise in our very busy, news-(noise)-filled world that the ratings of analysts can have a significant impact on the share price of a company. In a similar fashion to headline risk, companies vary in how far they are tracked by analysts – some have quite a few following them, others, only a single analyst. Being aware of the analysts following a particular stock may help one avoid the vagaries of a single analyst.

- **Commodity price risk**: Nobody can have failed to notice the risk associated with changes in the oil price. While some stocks are obviously affected by an oil price hike (airlines being just one example) in a globalized world where transport costs are important, a range of products can be affected – foodstuffs, clothes, etc. Of course, if we stick to the example of oil, a price hike can have wider consequences through consumers reining in their spending on a whole range of activities. So, while an oil price hike can have immediate effects on some stocks, it can feed into many other stocks on the back of its general economic influence.

- **Obsolescence risk**: While many of the risks being discussed here can affect your wealth, this one can create a very serious dent. Think Kodak. The company was founded in 1888 and was synonymous with photography for almost 100 years, many families took their holiday snaps on the cheap and ubiquitous Box Brownie. Then came the digital camera revolution. It is difficult to date the start of the revolution (and this is the case of most revolutions – they tend to be evolutions rather than revolutions) with digital imaging going back to the 1950s. However, it is accepted that the 'revolution' took hold around the time of the Dotcom boom in the late 1990s/early 2000s and it was supercharged with the advent of smart phones.

  While some camera companies (Nikon, Fuji, Canon, etc.) embraced this fundamental change to the way we take photographs, Kodak did not. The great irony of this situation is that Kodak developed the first fully digital, hand-held camera in 1975! Since the onset of the revolution, it has been a slow decline for the mighty Kodak company. In the early 2000s, it sold a number (500 plus) of its patents to the emerging tech giants, raising cash to survive but signing its eventual death warrant. The current share price is approximately $2.5, declining from $25 over the past five years – it was $95 in 1997. The story of Kodak is one of obsolescence and a bumbling entry into a range of sectors – photocopiers, video recorders, batteries – rather than focusing on its key sector, photography. And even here it made a number of fundamental mistakes – entering instant photography and being sued by Polaroid, a cassette system of tiny negative photography that gave hopeless images, etc. However, Kodak is not alone in failing to understand the importance of developments. Xerox developed the first viable personal computer and never understood its potential – but at least it maintained its focus on copiers.

And development never stops. The companies that embraced digital photography have done well over the past couple of decades with some exceptions – Olympus being one of them. However, they too are now under threat as smart phones and online services such as Instagram become the way to take and share photographs.

- **Legislative risk**: None of us live in pure, free markets – governments always have a role to play, be it with the institutions they manage or with the legislation they pass. In the UK, there are many examples of the ways sectors and companies have been buffeted by the moves of government. There are so many examples it is difficult knowing where to start. Let's take a couple of examples close to home (in every sense). The UK government gave quite large subsidies to solar panels and the industry boomed, those subsidies are now being phased out, fewer consumers are fitting panels and the firms in the sector are suffering. In a similar fashion, diesel engines in cars were encouraged through favourable tax treatment, this has now been reversed with manufacturers and consumers bearing the cost of this *volte face*.

- **Inflation and interest rate risk**: In addition to the government directly affecting companies and sectors, its influence on inflation and interest rates can have a profound effect. Western economies have 'benefited' from low interest rates and quantitative easing (the injection of money) since the crash of 2007. The wall of money and the cheap cost of borrowing have led to many sectors being underpinned and pushed forward – the UK housing sector being just one example. It also has benefited from the ludicrous Help to Buy scheme where the taxpayer essentially passes cash to the house builders via subsidies. However, these policies cannot last forever and the return to more normal times cannot be far away, when and how this reversal will impact on different sectors is one of the current imponderables. (Note: this sentence was written before Covid-19 descended on the world! Just shows how difficult predicting the future can be. Similarly, can you imagine how 'sick' you would be feeling if you had bought a luggage company in February 2020 just before the pandemic 'was released'?)

- **Detection risk**: Staying with the diesel example, some manufacturers jumped on the 'diesel bandwagon' by cheating the declared MPG statistics. The Volkswagen group has suffered hugely through its behaviour and it is unclear how long it will take to revive its brand. In the meantime it has left the field open to new entrants to the electric car sector. The cost to the investor of such detection scandals can be huge and some companies never recover – Enron being a good example.

The above has discussed some of the risks that can directly affect an individual company (idiosyncratic risks) and those that can feed through to a company via more general effects (systemic risks). All companies and individuals face risks on a daily basis, and in terms of stocks there are two important and complementary ways of managing the risks: (1) diversifying (no matter how simply); and (2) understanding the basic shape of where the key risks are coming from. On the back of these mechanisms, portfolios can be assessed and rebalanced on a planned basis, noting that too much rebalancing can be costly.

THE CAPITAL ASSET PRICING MODEL

While the focus of this chapter has been on portfolio theory, it would be remiss not to at least touch upon the capital asset pricing model (CAPM). Many of the constructs in modern finance were developed within and from the CAPM and readers should have at least a nodding acquaintance with them. We should note at the outset, that while the CAPM builds on the portfolio theory of Markowitz, the latter stands independent of the former – we do not need the CAPM to apply the broad lessons of portfolio theory.

While portfolio theory focuses on the behaviour of an individual investor, the CAPM considers how a capital market will operate if investors follow the tenets of portfolio theory and a range of strict assumptions. More specifically, to achieve an equilibrium the model assumes:

1. all investors have the same expectations regarding the future returns of assets;
2. they have the same expectations regarding risk;
3. they experience the same net returns – the same tax treatment, etc.;
4. they are no constraints on borrowing and/or short selling;
5. all investors can access the same risk-free rate;
6. they have the same utility function defined over risk and returns;
7. they only experience risk from the assets they invest in;
8. markets are perfect and clear – there are no constraints (i.e. transaction costs and costs of information).

Give some thought to any of the above, and it does not portray the market we are used to. However, these assumptions lead to a market portfolio that cannot be bettered and the needs of the identical investors are met fully. The problem we have in moving from this theoretical model is that it is unclear why a market would exist in the first place – markets exist because of asymmetries in information and values. In the CAPM world, there would be no active management and no need for research – the prices are set by some unknown process and all investor expectations are met. Effectively, the whole purpose of markets, i.e. the ongoing search for a balance between supply and demand, is negated.

Not surprisingly, academics have tried over the past decades to relax the assumptions, one by one, of the original CAPM with varying degrees of success. However, at its heart, it cannot get around the fundamental issue that markets are dynamic and do not clear, they are constantly changing and moving forwards; this is the insight of the Austrian economists such as Hayek. So, we do not believe the CAPM has much to tell investors in terms of markets and we have to turn to some of the constructs it has added to the discussion of modern finance.

In one sense, the CAPM has given investors a single but important insight – that is, the returns achieved from an asset, in part at least, reflect how the market is doing. How important the market is for an individual stock varies, but all stocks are influenced by the market to some degree and this is measured by a stock's beta. If a stock directly mirrors movements in the market, then its beta is equal to 1, if its response is a dampened version, then its beta is less than 1, whereas if it amplifies the market, its beta is more than 1.

Given the market portfolio has an important impact on the returns of individual stocks, we need to consider the factors that are likely to impact on the return of the market portfolio (which is the aggregation of all asset returns in the market). There are a range of factors that may impact on the return of the market, the more obvious being how far does the market respond to external risks, to information and transaction costs, and to tax effects?

In the rest of this section, we will consider some of the key factors that might impact on the current application of modern portfolio theory (MPT). To guide our discussion, we use three of the major assumptions in MPT, namely, (1) risk is quantified by reference to the volatility of returns; (2) asset correlations are static; and (3) asset returns can be captured by the normal distribution. In terms of the latter, we do not see the fat tails that seem to characterize stock returns and, therefore, we underestimate the possibility of significant losses.

Let's go back to risk. The market is being buffeted currently (autumn of 2019) by a number of factors – Trump's minute-by-minute Twitter tirades that are impossible to predict, the trade war between the USA and China that seems to be escalating but switches up and down on a daily basis, the Brexit saga, the ongoing injection of cash into the western economies by central banks. The last policy intervention has driven asset prices ever higher and the stock markets bull run has charged on. These policy effects are not part of the MPT framework but their influence seems ever more strident.

If we were trying to understand the risks facing a portfolio at the current time (September 2019), we would be watching how the FTSE 100 is being blown around by the debates (rows) within the UK Parliament. We would also be wondering how far the rise of populism in the West will go and how this will affect the stock market. In the context of the UK, it is hard to predict an outcome with many scenarios being equally likely. For example, Brexit might be 'forced' through with a weak deal, there may be no deal, there may a Labour government with a very left-leaning policy agenda. All of these will impact significantly on the economy (and by derivation the stock market) but they will impact in many different ways, but they all are difficult to forecast. In addition to these immediate and parochial effects, one has to overlay the more global factors, as an example, consider the impact of the crisis with Iran and the way in which oil production is being affected.

The second assumption is that the correlations between asset classes are static (this is needed to estimate the risk of portfolios). Consider, however, how the correlation between real asset values and financial assets has changed over recent decades. It could be argued that the increase in financial asset values reflects the booming nature of the business economy. But this would be far from the truth as productivity is at best static and even declining. A better explanation has been the wall of cash created by the central banks had to find a home somewhere and this is especially the case, given the interest rates on savings has been slashed to zero in many cases. This interest rate effect also feeds into a lower discount rate on the future values of financial assets and, therefore, increases their present values.

The third assumption is that returns can be captured by the normal distribution. In normal competitive times, this would not be a bad assumption – with the extremes being competed away and the diseconomies of scale limiting winner-take-all conclusions. This has all changed in our digital, network economy where ever-expanding networks create value and are not limited by physical constraints. We are seeing the likes of Amazon, Google, and even Ebay, forcing strangleholds on their sectors. In this type of world, the normal distribution does not capture returns – we have a relatively flat distribution with a huge fat tail. In this kind of world, a passive, diversified portfolio may be the last thing we should invest in.

Finally, we should never forget that we are living in a very different financial market. We have highly connected global markets, where an effect in one geography swiftly washes across the markets. We have algorithmic trading and high-speed trading that can create and amplify shocks in the markets. In other words, the market that underpinned the thinking of Markowitz is long gone and we need to be aware of these new structures and processes if we are to manage our portfolios in an intelligent manner.

QUANTITATIVE EVALUATION

In this section we examine two important implications of Markowitz's work: (1) the expected risk and return relationship; and (2) diversification.

Expected Risk and Return Relationship

Figure 5.2 shows the annualized return of 10 different portfolios based on their past one-year volatility and being rebalanced annually between June 2004 and June 2019 in the UK market. Annualized active return is the average of the decile portfolio daily return minus the benchmark return (FTSE 350) multiplied by the number of rebalancing dates in a year.

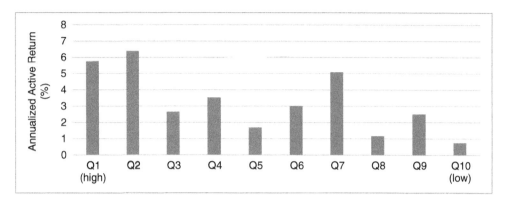

FIGURE 5.2   Annualized active returns of portfolios sorted by last year's volatility.
Source: BLOOMBERG PROFESSIONAL®.

If we use historical return variance as a measure of expected risk, we will see that the future return, in general, compensates for bearing higher total risk. Although the relationship is not linear, as suggested by the theory. If we take the lesson of CAPM about the importance of systematic risk, we can repeat the analysis replacing volatility with the beta from the last year's 'daily regressions'. Figure 5.3 presents this result for the UK market. The relationship between beta and expected return seems to be more in line with the theory; the highest beta stocks (decile 1) earn higher expected returns than the lowest beta stocks (decile 10).

We further consider the correlations with the ups and downs of the market separately. If investors are loss-averse, instead of risk-averse, we should see downside risk being compensated more. Figure 5.4 presents the portfolio's active returns sorted by these two types of betas (see the Practical Application IV for more details about the estimations). It shows that for the highest Bear beta, the portfolio earns the highest active annual return.

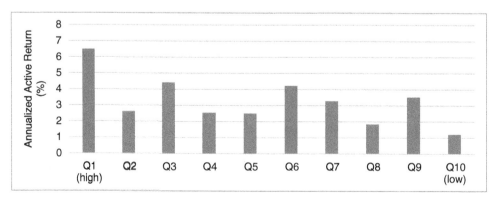

FIGURE 5.3   Return of portfolio sorted by last year's CAPM beta.
Source: BLOOMBERG PROFESSIONAL®.

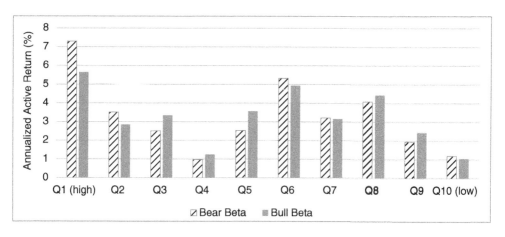

FIGURE 5.4   Annualized active returns of portfolios sorted by last year's Bull/Bear betas.
Source: BLOOMBERG PROFESSIONAL®.

It may be tempting to conclude that CAPM is a useful model to direct our investment. However, it is important to know that the above illustration only covers 15 years of data in one market. Academic studies have shown this beta and return relationship does not hold in large samples and multiple markets. For example, as an illustration, we present the same period analysis for the US and China in the following section.

INTERNATIONAL EVIDENCE

We report the active returns of the volatility and beta-sorted portfolio for the US and China. The results show that the risk and return trade-off relationship we found in the UK is an exception. For the US, it seems that investing in the middle group provides a relatively higher return than the two extremes (Figure 5.5).

In the academic literature, the finding we presented here is known as the beta anomaly. There are many subsequent theoretical attempts to explain this contradiction to the CAPM's prediction. Black (1972)[5] proposes that relaxing one of the CAPM assumptions of borrowing at the risk-free rate would make the risk and return relationship less positively correlated. Hong and Sraer (2016)[6] point out that high beta stocks are inherently more speculative since they have greater exposure to macro uncertainty. The exposure to the high

---

[5] F. Black, Capital market equilibrium with restricted borrowing. *The Journal of Business* 45(3) (1972): 444–455. http://www.jstor.org/stable/2351499.

[6] H. Hong and D.A. Sraer, Speculative betas. *The Journal of Finance* 71 (2016): 2095–2144. https://doi.org/10.1111/jofi.12431

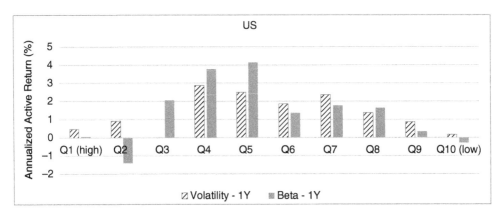

FIGURE 5.5   Annualized active returns of portfolios sorted by last year's Bull/Bear betas – US.
Source: BLOOMBERG PROFESSIONAL®.

macro uncertainty will induce more disagreement in these high beta securities and with the short-sale constraint, these stocks will be more likely to be held by optimists. This leads to high beta stocks earning lower returns in the future. While this is one possible explanation, it seems to be more specifically in line with the US market. There seems to be a negative volatility and return relationship in China, while beta and return seem to be randomly matched (Figure 5.6). Therefore, this evidence shows there is not a universal risk factor that will be compensated in all the markets in all periods. It may well be that as markets evolve, the relationship between risk and return for a given risk measure changes.

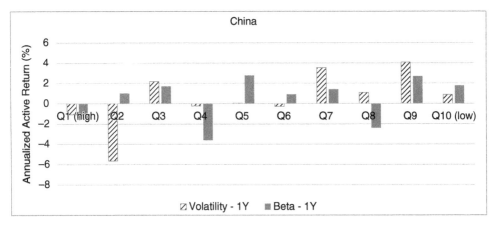

FIGURE 5.6   Annualized active returns of portfolios sorted by last year's Bull/Bear betas – China.
Source: BLOOMBERG PROFESSIONAL®.

SUMMARY

- Maybe we should take this opportunity to conclude that going passive by investing in the market index is not such a bad idea after all.
- Although the risk-return trade-off is theoretically elegant and the importance of systematic risk seems rational, the empirical evidence does not support one constant 'risk' measure that can always explain the cross-sectional variation of the expected return.
- The recent finance literature has been trying to solve this problem by adding more 'risk' factors. However, it seems the academic literature is much better at explaining the market in the past than identifying fundamental factors that can sustain predictions over time.
- This is partly because of the endogenous nature of social science research; the research findings are taught to finance students who then become practitioners and their behaviour enhances the prediction of the theory initially.
- However, there is an eventual overreaction to the factors identified as the 'herd' chases the price.
- As an ordinary investor, you can try to be part of the group of early participants in a market when the factor is still working.
- Alternatively, if you are not confident you have the resources to research and select stocks from a pool, investing in a passive indexing fund is a good choice. Although whether the market is efficient is an ongoing debate, the market being competitive (no free lunch) is a much less debatable fact.
- Over the longer term, trying to outsmart the market needs a lot of resources and luck.

Buffett's Bet with the Hedge Funds: And the Winner Is . . .

In 2008, Warren Buffett issued a challenge to the hedge fund industry, which, in his view, charged exorbitant fees that the funds' performances could not justify. Protégé Partners LLC accepted, and the two parties placed a million-dollar bet; namely (including fees, costs and expenses) an S&P 500 index fund would outperform a hand-picked portfolio of hedge funds over 10 years. The bet pitched two basic investing philosophies against each other: passive against active investing. Buffett won the bet in the end.

(continued)

(*continued*)

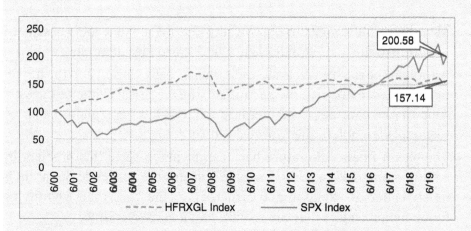

FIGURE 5.7　Comparison of performance ofo HFRX against the S&P 500.
Source: BLOOMBERG PROFESSIONAL®.

Although the bet was not directly focused on indexes, comparing the performance of the 'Hedge Fund Research HFRX Global Hedge Fund Index' (Figure 5.7), we can see that hedge funds had been performing very well in early 2000. After that their performance is either tracking the S&P 500 or flat.

Source: https://www.investopedia.com/articles/investing/030916/buffetts-bet-hedge-funds-year-eight-brka-brkb.asp

Tips
The beta used in the BLOOMBERG PROFESSIONAL® system to calculate the cost of capital is the adjusted beta instead of the raw beta.

PRACTICAL APPLICATION IV: BETA ESTIMATION AND FACTOR BACKTESTING (FTST)

Beta Estimation (BETA)

One of the main conclusions of the CAPM is that an individual security's systematic risk can be quantified by its correlation with the market portfolio. In practice, this can be estimated using historical time series data of the stock's return and the market portfolio return. In BLOOMBERG PROFESSIONAL®, there is a function to run this regression analysis and visually examine the relationship {BETA}<Go>. This function is basically a regression function. One can use it to determine the sensitivity of any security to other statistics (e.g. an index or an economic indicator). For example, you can use regression analysis to determine how commodity prices or interest rates influence changes in the price of a security.

Here is an example when we have loaded Apple Inc and then *typed* {BETA}<Go> to load this function.

By default, it reports the regression of the security and its main market index. In this case, the market index is the S&P 500. It reports the regression using the last two years (2Y) of weekly data. It also plots the return of the stock (Y) and the market index (X).

The right panel in the screen reports the beta statistics that are similar to the ones in Table 5.1. The raw BETA is the coefficient from the regression. With a beta of 0.994, Apple has moved closely with the market over the past two years.

BLOOMBERG PROFESSIONAL® also calculates an adjusted beta. It is an estimate of a security's future beta. The adjusted beta is derived from historical data but modified by the assumption that a security's beta moves towards the

TABLE 5.1 Apple Inc: beta 2-year historical data estimate

Linear beta	Statistics	Beta +/-	Statistics
Raw BETA	0.994	BETA+(X>0)	0.838
Adjusted BETA	0.996	BETA-(X<0)	1.122
ALPHA (Intercept)	0.706	Avg Slope	0.98
R^2 (Correlation^2)	0.564	Convexity	-0.142
R (Correlation)	0.751	ALPHA (Intercept)	1.015
Std Dev of Error	2.892	R^2 (Correlation^2)	0.571
Std Error of ALPHA	0.287	R (Correlation)	0.756
Std Error of BETA	0.087	Std Dev of Error	2.842
t-Test	11.433	Std Error of ALPHA	0.373
Significance	0	Std Error of BETA+	0.15
Last T-Value	0.392	Std Error of BETA-	0.133
Last P-Value	0.652	Number of Points	103
Number of Points	103	Last Spread	4180.77
Last Spread	4180.77	Last Ratio	0.034
Last Ratio	0.034		

Source: BLOOMBERG PROFESSIONAL® (accessed 20 July 2021).

market average over time. It is found if you choose Linear in the control area. The calculation is:

$$\text{Adjusted Beta} = (0.67 * \text{Raw Beta}) + (0.33 * 1.0).$$

For Apple, this adjustment does not affect its beta too much as it already close to 1. This is the beta used in all the other functions in the BLOOMBERG PROFESSIONAL® platform.

The rest of the statistics report the goodness of fit of the regressions. The definition of these variables can be found in the help file by *clicking* on <F1> on the keyboard or the green help menu button.

Let's explore the options. In our main text, we report not only the beta estimation but also the Bull and Bear beta. This can be done here by clicking on the Beta +/− options. These estimates are also reported in Table 5.1 in the columns on the right. It shows that Apple Inc has a slightly lower correlation (0.838) with the market when the market is going up than down (1.122). Without hedging your investment for the market movement, holding Apple Inc will give an amplified downside risk exposure in a bear market. Note the above detail is for the period covering the Covid-19 crisis.

Tips

Multi-Security Regression Analysis
You can access this function in the BETA function and go to [96] Actions] then [Launch Multi-security Analysis].
The function also allows us to compare two different periods' beta estimations. We can do this by selecting a second range which BLOOMBERG PROFESSIONAL® has automatically populated for us (we can always customize these ranges).

Factor Backtesting (FTST)

In this section, we look into the function of factor backtesting. This is the function we used to create the results in the empirical evidence section.

FTST allows users to perform equity backtesting. BLOOMBERG PROFESSIONAL® is proud of their point-in-time, historical fundamental data that is free of survivorship, restatement, and lagging bias, and represents fundamentals as they were known in the market at each observation point. That includes over 2,000 fundamental data points, scoring models, and custom formulas.

One can think of this as an extension of the combination of the Equity Screening (EQS) function and the equity testing (BTST) function.

For example, we can test the hypothesis that low PE stocks tend to outperform high PE stocks by comparing the performance of portfolios of low and high PE stocks. However, FTST is more powerful than EQS as it allows the weighting of different factors.

The best way to learn this function is to go through the testing of one strategy. Let's look at the set-up of testing the beta strategy in the UK market.

Step 1 Creating a Model

Load this function by *typing* {FTST} and <Enter>. This will load up the main screen of the function.

Click [1) Create Model] to load up the screen for options.

First, select the pool of securities that we will use to test the factor. In this case, we choose constituents of the FTSE 350. To do this we click on [Universe] to edit our selection. We *type* {FTSE 350} in the amber search box and select {FTSE 350 INDEX}.

Second, we choose the [Analysis Period] by setting the frequency of rebalancing to annually and testing periods as {Relative, 15 years}. We use an annual rebalance and a testing period of 15 years.

Third, we set the analytic parameters including the number of buckets. The choices include quartile, quintile, and decile which will group our pool of stocks into 4, 5, and 10 groups, respectively. In this context, in the Analytic Parameters, we choose {Decile}. We also specify a benchmark {FTSE 350 Index} to compare the performance. The weighting we used is default {Equal} and the currency for our comparison is set to be {GBP}.

Finally, we have the specification of factors. In this example, we are going to study the CAPM beta as our sorting variable. In the yellow strip beneath the Factors heading, we *type* {beta} and select from the drop-down list {1-year} to specify the period for the beta to be estimated.

> **Tips**
>
> BLOOMBERG PROFESSIONAL® will not automatically refresh screens, even if the testing is done. To view the latest status, click on the refresh icon on the top-right corner.↻

To select, confirm the selection of this factor, please don't forget to *hit* <Enter> and observe that this factor appears in the factor list below. By default, it selects {H} in the ordering selection. There are two choices here: {H Higher Value is Better} and {L Lower Value is Better}. In this case of beta, according to CAPM, the higher beta should provide a higher expected return. By contrast, there is a line of literature advocating the benefit of betting against beta.[7] For this test, we chose {L}, in this case the smallest beta will be in Q1 and the highest beta will be in Q10.

Save the model by *clicking* on [Action] -> [Save] and name it {Beta_UK}.

Step 2 Backtesting

To start the backtesting, *click* on [1) Backtest] at the bottom-right corner. A message will appear indicating your testing is being executed and it will notify you when it is done through a message. *Click* [1) OK].

Step 3 View Backtesting Results

Once the model is completed, the results can be viewed by *clicking* on the magnifying icon next to the model in the main Factor Backtester screen.

The overview shows a chart (the top-left panel), summary statistics for the factor (the top-right panel) and detailed statistics by groups (the lower panel). Examining the detail of the decile return in Figure 5.8 we can see that return seems to behave in line with the CAPM predictions over the past 15 years – a lower beta earns a lower active return, while a higher beta earns a high return.

Investing in just Q10 earns an annual active return of 7%. So one way to have capitalized on this would have been to invest only in high beta securities in the UK during this period.

---

[7] A. Frazzini and L.H. Pedersen, 'Betting against beta'. *Journal of Financial Economics* 111(1) (2014): 1. They find that betting against beta (BAB) factor, which is long-leveraged low-beta assets and short high-beta assets, produces significant positive risk-adjusted returns.

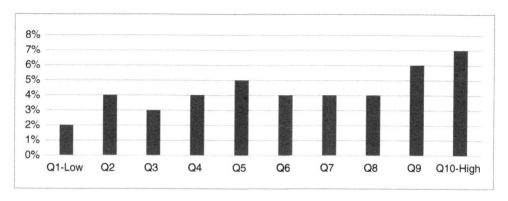

FIGURE 5.8   Annualized active returns of portfolios sorted by last year's betas 12/31/2005 to 12/31/2020.
Source: BLOOMBERG PROFESSIONAL®.

The Return tab of the function reports the plot of the return for the groups which are similar to the above and particularly the information coefficient.

The information coefficient (IC) is the correlation between the cross-section of factor values at each rebalancing and the realized forward returns. The value ranges from -1 to 1. The time length of forward returns depends on the specified rebalance frequency. Correlations are calculated for each time period of the backtest and then averaged.

This measure captures the predictability of the factor value (in this case, the stock's beta) in predicting the stock's next period return. A large positive number would indicate a good factor. Overall, the beta factor IC is close to zero. This suggests that beta is not a very good factor in explaining the cross-sectional return in the pool. Having said that, we notice that a factor with a low IC can still be useful in developing a strategy – as long as the relationship of the extreme deciles produces a strong contrasting return pattern, as is the case in the beta sorting in the UK market during this period.

The Turnover tab shows the turnover in each decile. Turnover is defined as the percentage of new stocks at each time of rebalancing as a percentage of the size of the portfolio in the last rebalance. A lower turnover is better for a strategy's implementation as it will not only save transaction costs but also reduce trading errors. We can see in Figure 5.9 that if one invested in the high beta stocks, on average about half of the stocks will change every year.

The Counts tab reports similar information as the Turnover tab but focuses on the number of stocks instead of the proportion of portfolio size.

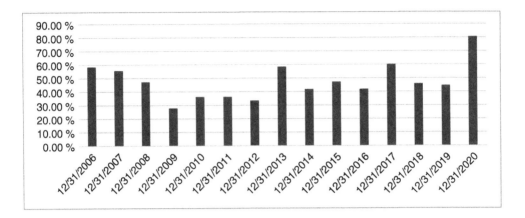

FIGURE 5.9   Turnover Q10.
Source: BLOOMBERG PROFESSIONAL®.

Finally, the Security Analysis tab allows us to look into the composition of the portfolios one point at a time. To examine the details of the portfolio characteristics, we can also export each of the portfolios so that we can use them in the PORT function as we did in the previous chapter. Just select [96) Output] -> [Export] to portfolio. From the export window, we can choose which decile of the portfolio we want to study and assign a portfolio name.

Multifactor Model

The benefit of using FTST instead of EQS is that it can combine multiple factors by calculating a combined factor score called the Z-score. For example, we can combine the famous Fama and French three factors together to partition stocks into 10 groups. To do this, at the end of Step 1 in our previous example, instead of selecting a factor, we *click* on [10) Composite] to add a new combined factor.

Following the previous example, we add each of the single factors first before we clicked Composite so that the system will take those factors by default when the composite window is loaded. We summarize the factor setting as follows in Table 5.2.

TABLE 5.2   Factor setting

Factors	Field descriptions	Weight (%)
Beta	1-year beta – Higher is better	33.3
HML	Price to book ratio 1 day ago – Lower is better	33.3
BMS	Market cap 1 day ago – Lower is better	33.3

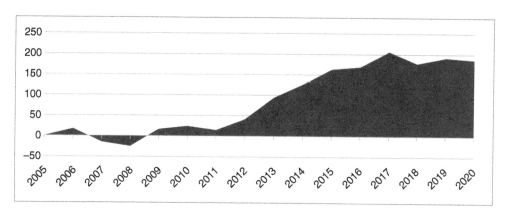

FIGURE 5.10 Fama and French 3 factor: FTSE 350 historical Q Spread return (%).
Source: BLOOMBERG PROFESSIONAL®.

Note that for the price to book and the size factor, the lower the better. We accepted the default weights (which equally weights the ranking of these three factors for each company) to form the new Z-score. We gave it the name of Fama-French 3 Factor and *clicked* [1) Save & Use].

We then ran the backtest (see Step 2 in the previous example). The program will then rank the stocks according to this Z-score and calculate the performance of the portfolios.

The results will be reported in a tab called Multi-factor. Figure 5.10 shows the Q Spread which is the return of a portfolio longing the stocks in the highest Z-score portfolio and shorting the stocks in the lowest Z-score portfolio.

The combined three-factor strategy provides a good overall cumulative return of 186% over the 15 years. One can export this portfolio and look into the detailed risk, return and characteristics in the PORT function.

EXERCISES

1. Construct a Fama-French factor model test for the Chinese and the US markets. Explore any additional factors to those we have discussed so far and consider changing some of the relative weightings. Reflect on the results and consider how the 'model' might be improved.
2. Estimate Netflix's beta and particularly examine the stability of the beta estimation over two different periods. What do you observe? Can this finding regarding the stability of beta estimation be generalized to other growth stocks, for example, Tesla? What is the implication for practical investment decisions?

CHAPTER 6

Behavioural Finance

Some Useful Insights

INTRODUCTION

Behavioural Finance (BF) started to take off in the very late 1970s and early 1980s but it was not until the 1990s and 2000s that it really got going. Even then, it faced a bit of an uphill battle against mainstream finance. We have been involved with BF since the start and we have witnessed its various twists and turns, and we could have written this chapter in many different ways, ranging from the philosophical to a straightforward list of empirical results. We will take the middle ground and do a bit of both. We will give a bit of background and then proceed to discuss the main 'behavioural biases' and the main 'anomalies' featuring in the academic literature. We will round off with some of our own results on anomalies from around the globe.

BACKGROUND AND SOME PHILOSOPHICAL INSIGHTS

In the late 1950s, Herbert Simon published work on bounded rationality. Basically, when making decisions, individuals have to confront a number of issues – the tractability of the decision problem, the information they have to make the decision, the limits of their brain to solve the problem, and the time they have to reach the decision. Take any decision (and even the simple ones rarely are) and the computation needed explodes. The common examples used are potting a ball in snooker or pool, and riding a bicycle. Let's take the former and bear in mind all of the above points. Potting a ball in a hole on the edge of a table involves a lot of computation. The strength of the arm, the straightness of the cue, the response of the ball to the cue tip, the speed of the cloth, the angle at which to hit the target ball if the shot is not straight, etc. There will be a formula to work all of this out but it is far beyond the human brain. So humans have worked out a solution – it is called practice. You are not sure why a shot works but with practice you will be able to replicate it without the need for complex mathematics. You will develop rules of thumb, heuristics, etc. If you are bored, consider the calculations needed to work out how to ride a bike. Both of these problems stretch the limits of AI and even walking is just being conquered by the scientists involved with robotics.

From the above it seems fairly obvious that Simon was onto something but he faced huge resistance from mainstream economics and finance, and this is not surprising, given the investments made in human capital in these mainstream subjects. We have covered these arguments in detail elsewhere but the gist is as follows. Following the Second World War, economists and finance academics had the aim of portraying themselves as scientists with the hope they would gain the same funding and respect as 'physical' scientists. To achieve this, they needed a general and replicable framework of analysis – a range of ifs and buts would not suffice. So a model based upon rational agents competing in 'free markets' was the way to go. The rational model was based on a number of restrictive assumptions about the individual and his/her behaviour and how they would operate within markets. It has the benefit of forming a coherent framework of analysis and discussion. On the back of this rational framework, departments, journals, and academic careers were built – the approach worked in the sense that these topics gained credibility on campuses and eventually fed the outside world (including the finance industry) with quantitatively trained employees. The professors were happy as they were feted and reaped significant rewards.

Given the above, it is not surprising that mainstream economics and finance have fought a long battle against the behaviouralists. We can still remember the arguments being waged in staff seminars in the late 1970s and early 1980s, and will cover some of these as we progress. However, before we cover some of the obvious defences, we need to tackle something far deeper. Before the Second World War, investment finance was taught via a series of case studies, recognizing the complexities of specific situations and the individuals involved. It was more of an art than a science. People weren't seen as irrational or rational per se, they were responding to situations – sometimes badly, sometimes well. Then came the mainstream with strict prescriptions on what was to be defined as rational with actions outside of the framework being seen as irrational. Just consider sunk costs. From the 'rational' perspective, they should be ignored as they cannot be changed. There are, however, good reasons why they may not be ignored – one example, being reputation (a human trait that makes a lot of contracting easier). Humans live their lives through time and have to connect with a range of individuals across time, and we have developed behaviours to make these 'transactions' easier. However, it is difficult to model such interactions and it suits the purpose of the mainstream to label them as irrational.

These notions of rational and irrational seem, on the face of it, harmless but they are far from being so from at least two perspectives. First, the rational framework underpinned the notion of the efficiency of free markets that has so dominated the globe for a number of decades. We have seen the benefits and costs (consider the crash of 2007) of such a viewpoint. Second, and this is even more insidious, if behaviour is seen as irrational, then we can promote activities to make individuals more rational. Richard Thaler came up with the idea of the 'Nudge'. Small activities by agencies (including government) can push individuals into being more rational, as defined by the mainstream. This paternalistic perspective is based on a received wisdom of what is rational and ignores the behaviours that have developed over many millennia. We are not arguing that all behaviours should be accepted but they should be given some thought and reflection before being branded irrational. Please note we are not arguing against markets, we believe in them very much. It is just we do not believe in the fiction at the core of mainstream economics and finance. Markets are messy, dynamic, make mistakes, competitive, innovative, etc. Essentially, we see a lot of value in the Austrian economists' view of the world – Google von Mises and Hayek. This is why we have written this book on investment *experts*. They understood parts of the messiness of markets and worked out how to make money from the actual operation of markets. They sometimes get it wrong but, in general, their insights give profits across the long term. If it was easy, we would all be millionaires.

Before we move on to looking at behavioural traits, we need to comment on one of the primary defensive arguments of the mainstream. They argue individual traits are not important because they cancel each other out via the 'law of large' numbers in markets. Essentially, the core is rational and the irrationalities around the core are unimportant. This argument basically makes the assumption that the core is rational through the sheer power of this way of seeing the world – rationality dominates 'irrationality'. And the argument is taken one step further; even if there is sufficient weight in the actions of the 'irrational' (this could be the herd), the market will correct itself and head towards the rational outcome. Please do not confuse this with reversion to the mean – there is no reason why the mean of a market should equate with the rational outcome. The mean is just the consensus of the majority. With that thought in mind, we now turn to the behavioural traits that have been explored in the literature.

KEY BEHAVIOURAL TRAITS:TERMED BIASES BY THE MAINSTREAM

In this section we consider a range of behavioural traits that could impact investment decision-making. As noted earlier, they are often seen as biases needing to be removed or reduced. Indeed, in some cases they may well be biases, but in other cases they may reflect the needs and wants of an individual. We will deal with them alphabetically as this seems as good an approach as any; trying to rank them in terms of importance is fraught with a range of issues. We will first define each trait in general terms and then consider how they may impact on investment decision-making. In the following section we try to bridge between these traits and the 'anomalies' that have been found via the empirical literature in finance. The bridging is rarely clean and a number of 'biases' may be behind an anomaly.

Affinity

Affinity refers to investment behaviour driven by the investment reflecting the values of the investor rather than cold, hard, financial calculus. Ethical investment may be caught under this heading. Investors may make such invest-ments because they reflect on the type of individual they wish to see themselves as (and for others to see them as) and/or they believe such companies have long-term potential. Investing in home country companies on grounds of patri-otism is also given as an example of affinity investing. Again, and this will be the case for all the behavioural traits discussed in this section, there may be good financial logic for making such decisions, or it may reflect other argu-ments in an individual's utility function. Investors may be willing to receive lower returns because the investment is providing benefits; for example, you feel good about supporting the local shop though it would be cheaper to go to the supermarket. Essentially, we need to be careful not to brand all activity that does not maximize the monetary return as being irrational and a bias. What we should be doing is making a full list of all the costs and benefits and then choosing the best of the set of net benefits, as choosing otherwise would be irrational.

Investors subject to affinity bias can make investments in companies making products or delivering services they like but don't examine carefully. Such investors may invest in their home countries at the expense of investing in foreign countries. Additionally, they may invest in 'sophisticated' investment products that convey status only to find they have invested in something they don't understand.

Anchoring and Adjustment

Anchoring is to do with the situation where an initial piece of information takes an undo weight on how a situation is assessed. For example, when purchasing a car, the initial price suggested forms the anchor and all other prices are seen as adjustments away from this initial, anchor price. So subsequent prices below the anchor price are seen as cheap, though they may be high compared to the market value. A lot of evidence suggests it is difficult to get rid of the anchor once it has been set, and this applies to both sellers and buyers. On eBay a seller may set the Buy it Now price far too high and well above market value, and then show reluctance to accept prices approximating market prices because they are well below their initial anchor price. Professional car traders use this bias (coupled with a notion of fairness) against buyers by asking the buyer to set the initial price on their trade-in – knowing that it will, in general, be set low.

In terms of investment behaviour, anchoring displays itself in a number of ways. For example, investors tend to make general market forecasts that are too close to current levels, given what might be suggested by historical fluctuation. They will tend to over-play recent evidence and anchor their forecasts on the percentage that a particular asset class might rise or fall based on the current level of returns. Similarly, investors (and securities analysts) tend to stick too closely to their original estimates when new information is learned about a company.

Finally, investors can become anchored on the economic states of certain countries or companies. For example, in the 1980s, Japan was an economic powerhouse, and many investors believed that it would remain so for decades. Unfortunately, Japan stagnated for many years after the late 1980s.

Availability

The availability trait refers to individuals judging the likelihood of an event by the ease with which they can retrieve data on similar events. The ease of availability of retrieval tends to dominate the probability of likelihood. For example, smokers cite an elderly relative smoking all his/her life as evidence that smoking can't be too bad for health.

Investors will choose investments based on information that is available to them (advertising, suggestions from advisors, friends, etc.) and will not engage in disciplined research or due diligence to verify if the investment selected is a good one.

There are three basic ways availability affects investment behaviour: (1) categorization; (2) a narrow range of experience; and (3) resonance. Taking these in turn, first, investments are based on categorical lists easily available in memory. Second, investments tend to follow a narrow range of life experiences, such as the industry worked in, the region lived in, etc. Third, investors will choose investments that resonate with their own personality or have characteristics that investors can relate to their own behaviour.

Cognitive Dissonance

Cognitive dissonance (CD) occurs when there is a tension between an individual's beliefs/preferences and the action he/she undertakes when new information becomes available on the consequences of past actions. Individuals have a need for consistency between their beliefs, etc. and the actions they take. This is the idea of being true to yourself. An example of CD is when an individual cares about the environment and buys a car that fits this preference. Only to find out the car he/she bought is far from environmentally friendly because the manufacturer has been fiddling the miles per gallon calculations (i.e. the VW/Audi diesel debacle). Individuals do not like such internal disharmony and will try to either explain away the situation (and salve their conscience) or they will take action – in the above example, this could involve selling the car.

CD has a number of potential consequences for investor behaviour. The most obvious is the holding of loss-making securities positions because of the desire to avoid the mental pain associated with admitting a bad decision has been made. An amplification of this type of behaviour is investors continuing to invest in a security after it has gone down (average down) to confirm an earlier decision. Finally, CD can cause investors to herd because they avoid information that counters an earlier decision.

Confirmation

The confirmation trait involves searching, accessing, recalling, and giving more weight to information confirming one's beliefs or actions. No one wants to be at fault or to have made errors, so it is a natural tendency to find information confirming beliefs and/or actions. For example, people like to find a bargain when shopping and after the purchase they will often search other shops and online retailers to confirm they have made the right purchase and it was indeed a bargain.

It is easy to see how a confirmation bias can cause investors to seek out only information that confirms their beliefs about an investment that they have made and not seek out information that may contradict their beliefs. This behaviour can leave investors in the dark regarding, for example, the imminent decline of a stock. Technical analysis can be prone to this type of bias by focusing on a limited number of screens and not being open to information from other sources.

Conservatism

Conservatism refers to the situation where individuals under-adjust their probabilities in the correct direction but by an insufficient amount, given new information. The traditional explanation of the conservatism bias referred to individuals anchoring on initial probabilities and struggling to move away from them. This does not, however, explain the reason for the struggle. What seems to be occurring is that people have difficulty in adjusting their subjective probabilities, given new objective data, the process of transformation is noisy and not well defined. This might be because the prior probabilities have been confirmed a number of times and are well cemented, while it is unclear how accurate the new information is and how much weight to place on it. The conservatism bias might, therefore, be quite a 'rational' response.

Conservatism bias can cause investors to cling (or react very slowly) to a view or a forecast, behaving too inflexibly when presented with new information. For example, if an earnings announcement depresses a stock, the conservative investor may be too slow to sell. Conservatism can relate to an underlying difficulty in processing new information and it is often an easier option to simply stick to a prior belief.

Endowment

The endowment effect is to do with things being valued more once they are owned. The effect has a number of aspects. People are more likely to retain an object after owning it than to go out and buy it. The effect may be because we over-value after ownership as compared to market value, the ownership giving us some insight into its value for us. There is little reason to believe the market value of an object measures the value to the individual. However, we may retain objects because we do not want to incur the transaction costs of selling. And here there is no reason to believe the transaction costs of selling are the same as those of buying. We would argue, in fact, they are higher for selling than buying. However, it could be the case that an individual has developed an emotional attachment to an object – think of Gollum in *Lord of the Rings*.

Endowment bias causes investors to hold securities as a result of decision paralysis, which places an irrational premium on the compensation price demanded in exchange for the disposal of an endowed asset.

Framing

A situation can be framed in a number of ways to emphasize the positives rather than the negatives. Framing is part of the art of marketing and politics. The best-known example from behavioural science is the Asian disease problem. A drug has been found that can cure 90% of the patients and kill the remainder; and this can be framed in two very different ways, elucidating very different responses. One way is to state the drug will kill 10% of the patients, the other is to state it will save 90%. Not surprisingly, the latter receives a far more positive response than the former. While there are a number of explanations of this trait, the most straightforward is concerned with bounded rationality. Due to time pressure and the desire to cut down on transaction costs, individuals take situations at face value and do not delve too deeply – this explains why marketing can be such a successful activity.

Framing can affect how the risk tolerance of investors is assessed. For example, when questions are worded in the 'gain' frame, a risk-averse response is more likely. When questions are worded in the 'loss' frame, risk-seeking behaviour is the likely response. Similarly, when an investment opportunity is framed in a very positive way, it is more likely to be taken up.

Hindsight

We have all heard of hindsight bias. The feeling we knew something all along, when in fact we did not. It is also referred to as 20/20 rear vision. It is seen as a bias because we too often did not see the event before it happened, we only feel we could have.

Not surprisingly, it has a number of possible levels. The simplest is misre-membering an earlier opinion/judgement – the notion that you said it would happen, when, in fact, you did not. The next level is the belief the event was inevitable when it was not – the notion that it had to happen. The third level involves the notion that you could have foreseen the event – the notion you knew it would happen.

Hindsight bias can lead investors to portray positive developments as if they were predictable and this can inspire excessive risk-taking because they believe they have superior predictive powers. Negative performance can lead to investors blocking out poor predictions to avoid the pain of loss. This type of behaviour can spill over into how investors evaluate money managers. Unfairly criticizing them when they perform poorly and over-praising them when they perform well.

Illusion of Control

Illusion of control is where individuals believe they can control events they actually have little influence over. This features in many aspects of daily life, one being the idea that most people feel safer driving rather being a passenger, even allowing for there being no difference in their driving skills.

Illusion of control can impact investors in a number of ways. First, and most obviously, it can lead to more trading than is necessary because of the belief of possessing more control over outcomes than is actually the case. Second, it can also lead to under-diversification because investors focus on companies where they feel they feel they have some amount of control over the companies' fate. Third, illusion of control contributes to over-confidence and this can lead to excessive trading.

Loss Aversion

There is a lot of evidence individuals feel the pain of a loss a lot more than the joy of a gain; this has been well captured by Kahneman and Tversky's Prospect Theory.[1] In contrast to mainstream theory that models situations in terms of the final wealth, Prospect Theory models situations as gains and losses as compared to the current position.

Not surprisingly, loss aversion has consequences for investor behaviour as investors hold onto loss-making investments too long, selling winners too early, and holding imbalanced portfolios as a result of the previous types of behaviour.

Mental Accounting

Without being aware of it in many cases, individuals use mental accounts to plan and control their financial activities. They code and categorize various expenditures into different mental accounts. Individuals wish to keep their various mental accounts in balance (different individuals will have different mental categories) and they will 'borrow' across accounts and across time to achieve balance in individual accounts. The mental accounting system will lead to behaviours such as delaying activities so as to maintain a balance and not closing an account in a loss position.

Mental accounting bias can have many effects on investor behaviour, with specific effects depending on the exact nature of an individual's mental accounting 'system'. If an individual separates income from capital and they only wish to spend from the income account, then they may chase dividends to the detriment of the capital value of the stocks. In terms of capital accounts, stock appreciation can lead to wealth effects and possibly increased risk-taking. However, stock price declines may lead to stocks being held (and this is risky) because individuals do not wish to close accounts at a loss.

Mental accounting is a large and varied topic and readers are encouraged to explore its many wonderous implications.

Over-Confidence

Over-confidence is a very well-established trait where individuals have a heightened sense of their skills, talent and judgement. Some 90% of

---

[1] D. Kahneman and A. Tversky, Prospect Theory: An analysis of decision under risk. *Econometrica* 47 (1979): 263–291.

Americans believe they are better than average drivers, which, of course, is statistically impossible. The consequences of such a trait are varied, and many accidents can be laid at the door of over-confidence, such as accidents that occur due to a miscalculation of the necessary skills (driving accidents) and accidents that continue to develop because of over-confidence in being able to deal with the consequences (Chernobyl).

In terms of investment behaviour, over-confident investors may ignore negative information and under-estimate downside risk and hold onto stocks they should not. Equally they may over-trade because they believe they have information/skills not possessed by others. As well as affecting trading, over-confidence may lead to under-diversified portfolios because of the belief in stock selection skills.

Recency

The recency bias leads to recent events being over-weighted. A good example is that people significantly increase the perceived risks of flying after an air crash; the recent events tending to distort the perception of the true under-lying probabilities.

Not surprisingly, the recency bias shows itself in many ways in terms of investor behaviour. Investors make projections based on small historical data samples, ignore fundamental values, and focus too much on recent upward price performance. Recency bias can cause investors to ignore historical facts concerning the bubbles, peaks, and valleys that naturally occur in any stock market.

Recency bias can also cause problems with asset allocation, with investors becoming infatuated with an in-fashion asset class.

Regret Aversion

When weighing up various actions, we may take into account how much regret we would feel. This is not an easy concept and it is best explained by examples. Imagine you have a boat and you no longer use it and the right thing to do is to sell it. But if you change your mind about sailing in the future, you might regret selling the boat. So part of your decision to sell the boat or not weighs up the potential regret you might feel in the future. Let's consider the case of classic cars. You have a Porsche you don't use and it has climbed in value to £35k. You should sell it because it has gained 100% in value and it is costing you money in storage. However, how would you feel if the appreciation continued and it was worth £70k in two years' time and you sold it now for £35k?

The regret of doing something is stronger that the regret of not doing something. Therefore, the default regret-free action is to maintain the status quo, holding a position for too long and taking too long to make decisions. For example, if investors have suffered losses in the recent past, regret aversion may lead to very conservative investment choices, avoiding markets that have recently gone down, holding loss-making positions and, thereby, avoiding the crystallization of the loss, investing in super-safe companies and, thereby, avoiding the consequences of a downside, and holding onto winning stocks too long just in case they keep on moving up.

Self-Attribution

When individuals claim the positive outcome of a random event as being down to their skills/knowledge, this is self-attribution. It is the down-playing of randomness and the over-playing of skills, etc.

After a period of good returns, investors may believe they are a result of skill and this may lead to increasingly risky decisions, trading too frequently, being selective in their 'news acquisition' (i.e. seeking information confirming their skills as a trader) and holding under-diversified portfolios.

Self-Control

This is a trait where short-term emotional activities stop us achieving our long-term goals. You may want to be thin but you do not have the self-control to stop eating cakes and biscuits. You wish to wake up sober every morning but you don't have the self-control to not drink that bottle of wine, etc. We are not robots and we have cravings and weaknesses that make up our everyday lives. Clearly, however, individuals vary in how far they can control their short-term desires.

The self-control bias can cause issues with investment behaviour with the basic principles of wealth creation being lost sight of; for example, the principles of compounding and diversification.

Status Quo

This trait is concerned with individuals preferring things to stay as they are. It can cause investors to hold securities they are familiar with or fond of, both of which can compromise financial performance.

KEY TRAITS IN THE MARKETS: TERMED ANOMALIES BY THE MAINSTREAM

There are hundreds of variants of return anomalies that have been documented in the market. An anomaly is normally defined as a violation of some form of market efficiency. When publicly available information can be used to formulate a trading strategy that can earn abnormal returns that cannot be justified by the systematic risk profile of the strategy, we refer to such a phenomenon as an anomaly. The most long-lasting anomalies are momentum, the size effect, value premium, and post-earnings announcement drift:

- **Momentum** is about price continuation, that is, stocks with higher returns in the past 6 to 12 months performing better in the next 6 to 12 months.[2] This has links to behavioural biases: under-reaction,[3] over-confidence about private information,[4] gradual information diffusion, and limited attention.[5]
- **The size effect** refers to the fact that smaller stocks earn a higher future return even after controlling for their systematic risk.[6] Size is normally measured by market capitalization. Links to behavioural biases: limited attention to small stocks (neglected stocks).
- **Value stocks** are stocks with a higher book-to-market ratio. The opposite is growth stocks which have a lower book-to-market ratio. Value stocks normally earn a higher return than growth stocks.[7] The book-to-market

---

[2] N. Jegadeesh and S. Titman, Returns to buying winners and selling losers: Implications for stock market efficiency. *Journal of Finance* 48 (1993): 65–91.

[3] N. Barberis, A. Shleifer, and R. Vishny, A model of investor sentiment. *Journal of Financial Economics* 49 (1998): 307–343.

[4] K. Daniel, D. Hirshleifer, and A. Subrahmanyam, Investor psychology and security market under- and over-reactions. *Journal of Finance* 53 (1998): 1839–1885.

[5] H. Hong and J.C. Stein, A unified theory of underreaction, momentum trading, and overreaction in asset markets. *Journal of Finance* 54 (1999): 2143–2184.

[6] E.F. Fama and K.R. French, Common risk factors in the returns on stocks and bonds. *Journal of Financial Economics* 33 (1993): 3–56.

[7] Ibid.

ratio is the book value of equity in the previous fiscal year over the market value of equity at the end of the previous year. Links to behavioural biases: paying too much for growth stocks (expectation error due to extrapolation of past growth).

- Since Ball and Brown[8] first discovered the **post-earnings announcement drift** (PEAD) anomaly (the anomaly refers to the fact that prices keep drifting in the same direction as the price reaction on the earnings announcement day), it has turned out to be one of the most puzzling and long-lived market anomalies. Links to behavioural biases: underreaction to new information and limits to arbitrage (transaction costs) slowing down the price adjustment.

Other anomalies are documented in the literature, see e.g. Cai et al.[9] Table 6.1 provides a summary.

Behavioural vs Alternative Explanations of Anomalies

The reason they are referred to as anomalies is because the predictability of comovements in stocks sorted by these firm characteristics cannot be explained in the traditional rational expectations framework. Barberis and Thaler[10] provide a good summary of the behavioural theory and experiments that can help us understand some of these anomalies.

Prospect theory by Kahneman and Tversky[11] provides a good foundation for us to examine investor behaviours with a different perspective from the rational expectations framework. It formalizes some of the behavioural traits we discussed above in a framework of analysis. Especially, loss aversion (investors feel more pain when experiencing a loss than a gain) and the disposition effect (investors are reluctant to sell assets trading at a loss relative to the price at which they were purchased[12]) can explain many investors' buying and selling decisions. Ask yourself if any of these findings also apply to you:

---

[8] R. Ball and P. Brown, An empirical evaluation of accounting income numbers. *Journal of Accounting Research* 6 (1968): 159–178.

[9] C.X. Cai, K. Kevin, P. Li, and Q. Zhang, Market development, information diffusion and the global anomaly puzzle. *Journal of Financial and Quantitative Analysis* (2021). Available at SSRN: https://ssrn.com/abstract=2839799.

[10] N. Barberis and R. Thaler, A survey of behavioral finance. In G. M. Constantinides, M. Harris, and R.M. Stulz (eds) *Handbook of the Economics of Finance*, vol. 1 (Oxford: Elsevier, 2003), pp. 1053–1128. https://doi.org/10.1016/S1574-0102(03)01027-6.

[11] Kahneman and Tversky, Prospect Theory.

[12] H. Shefrin and M. Statman, The disposition to sell winners too early and ride losers too long: Theory and evidence. *The Journal of Finance* 40 (1985): 777–790.

TABLE 6.1 List of return anomalies

Type	Anomaly	Short description
Accounting	Asset growth	Negative relation between the asset growth rate and subsequent one-year returns
Accounting	Investment-to-assets	Firms with a lower investment-to-asset ratio have higher returns
Accounting	Investment growth	Negative relation between investment growth and future returns
Accounting	Accruals	Negative association of accruals and stock returns
Accounting	Working capital accruals	Negative correlation of stock returns and operating accruals
Accounting	Net operating assets	Negative relation between net operating assets and stock returns
Accounting	Net stock issue	Net stock issue is negatively correlated with stock returns
Accounting	Composite equity issue	Firms with high composite equity issue have lower stock returns
Accounting	Book-to-market	High book-to-market ratio stocks earn higher returns
Accounting	Gross profits	Higher stock returns for profitable than unprofitable firms
Accounting	Distress risk (O-score)	Firms with high probability of bankruptcy have lower stock returns
Market-based	Short-term reversal	Firms with higher returns in past month have lower stock returns in following month
Market-based	Long-term reversal	Stock return reversal, i.e., winner stocks in past 5 years become loser stocks
Market-based	Maximum daily return	Negative relation between firm's extreme daily return in past month and stock returns in next month
Market-based	Trading volume	Negative relation between dollar trading volume and returns

1. Using discount brokerage data, Odean[13] finds that individual investors are more likely to sell stocks which have gone up in value relative to their purchase price, rather than stocks which have gone down. Do you like to sell on an up-tick?

2. People are loss averse (i.e. they feel much more pain from losses than for the same level of gains) and a more frequent evaluation of investment performance would discourage investors from investing in a risky asset as they will observe more frequent losses (at a monthly level) than if

[13] T. Odean, Are investors reluctant to realize their losses? *The Journal of Finance* 53 (1998): 1775 –1798. https://doi.org/10.1111/0022-1082.00072.

they evaluate across a longer horizon (at an annual level) for a given period of investment (e.g. 10 years). Essentially, do you check your portfolio return too often?

3. Thaler and Johnson[14] find that, after prior gains, subjects take on gambles they would normally avoid, and that after prior losses, they refuse gambles they normally would accept. Do you keep two separate mental accounts for your capital and profits/losses and treat them differently?

Some theories directly model the impact of investor behavioural bias leading to mispricing in the markets. These include the models by Barberis, Shleifer and Vishny[15] and Daniel, Hirshleifer, and Subrahmanyam[16] that assume prices are driven by a single representative agent prone to a small number of cognitive biases (conservatism, representativeness, or overconfidence). Conservatism and representativeness are seen as explaining the short-term momentum and long-term revision in the context of post-earnings announcement drift. There is also a family of 'extrapolating' models that can explain a wide range of anomalies (see Barberis, for a recent survey[17]).

In brief, investors' behavioural biases may cause prices to deviate from their fundamental value. However, mispricing cannot persist if there is smart money in the market spotting these opportunities and taking 'arbitrage' positions. Therefore, a second stream of the literature is focused on why arbitrage is limited. Why is there a 'free' lunch on the table?

It turns out that even when an asset is wildly mispriced, strategies designed to correct the mispricing can be both risky and costly, rendering them unattractive. As a result, the mispricing can remain unchallenged. For example, Greenwood, Shleifer, and You[18] show that even if one can call a bubble correctly ex-ante, the average return between the first identification of the price

---

[14] R.H. Thaler and E.J. Johnson, Gambling with the house money and trying to break even: The effects of prior outcomes on risky choice. *Management Science* 36 (1990): 643–660.

[15] Barberis, Shleifer, and Vishny, A model of investor sentiment.

[16] Daniel, Hirshleifer, and Subrahmanyam, Investor psychology and security market under- and over-reactions.

[17] N.C. Barberis, Psychology-based models of asset prices and trading volume. NBER Working Papers 24723, National Bureau of Economic Research, 2018. A list of anomalies includes (i) medium-term momentum, long-term reversal, and the value premium in the cross-section of average returns; (ii) excess volatility and time-series predictability in aggregate asset classes; and (iii) the formation and collapse of bubbles.

[18] R. Greenwood, A. Shleifer, and Y. You, Bubbles for Fama. *Journal of Financial Economics* 131(1) (2019): 20–43.

run-up and the peak price is 30%, confirming the adage that it is difficult to bet against the bubble.

Nevertheless, the list of anomalies we presented in this section has been shown to be a profitable strategy over a long period. Researchers have used these anomalies to create new pricing factors. The most recent asset pricing models are largely empirical findings driven, for example, Fama and French's[19] 5-factor model, Q-factor,[20] and the mispricing[21] models. From an investor's point of view, as long as these strategies earn after costs profit, it doesn't matter if the return from these strategies is categorized as a risk-premium or mispricing. This is why the factor investing approach (and extension of style investing) have become increasingly popular both as a strategic approach and for creating smart passive ETF products.

EVIDENCE

Identifying factors requires a large amount of historical data. The Factor to Watch (FTW) function in BLOOMBERG PROFESSIONAL® allows you to see which factors are systematically rewarded across segments of the equity markets, so you can identify the attributes of stocks on which you want to focus. This function provides the simple backtesting of a large group of known factors (about 180 different factors).

For example, Table 6.2 presents the return of the 15 selected strategies applied to FTSE 350 stocks as of 25 July 2021. We sort them by the 10-year cumulated return. It reports the net long-short return for the quintile portfolio sorted by the relevant variables.

For each metric, FTW ranks the securities in the universe from the highest to the lowest. It then compares the returns between the securities that fall in the top quintile (top 20% of the universe) versus those in the bottom quintile (bottom 20% of the universe). The portfolios are rebalanced every month and monthly returns are cumulated to obtain the yearly and multi-year returns.

For example, Table 6.2 shows that information derived from the analysts' forecast revision contains useful information to the market and following this

---

[19] E.F. Fama and K.R. French, A five-factor asset pricing model. *Journal of Financial Economics* 116 (2015): 1–22.

[20] K. Hou, C. Xue, and L. Zhang, Digesting anomalies: An investment approach. *The Review of Financial Studies* 28(3) (2015): 650–705. https://doi.org/10.1093/rfs/hhu068

[21] R.F. Stambaugh and Y. Yuan, Mispricing factors. *The Review of Financial Studies* 30(4) (2017): 1270–1315. https://doi.org/10.1093/rfs/hhw107

TABLE 6.2   NMX index net long-short (Q1–Q5) (%)

Style	Factor/Driver Name (15)	1D Ret	1W Ret	Prior Month	YTD Ret	1Y Ret	10Y Ret
Revisions	3M EPS Revision % (FY1)	0.25	0.53	4.84	12.17	10.19	284.94
Revisions	3M Target Price Change %	-0.62	0.65	-0.92	6.12	5.49	250.39
Momentum	PORT EU Momentum	-0.28-	1.77	-3.48	-9.72	-20.02	132.80
Profitability	PORT EU Profit	0.42	0.11	3.24	3.70	-19.41	58.66
Growth	1Y Fwd EPS Growth (FY) %	0.27	1.14	-1.90-	0.18	-16.24	45.35
Dividends	Dividend Yield (Indicated)	0.06	-1.64	1.66	4.36	-17.41	17.07
Surprises	EPS Surprise % (Last)	0.33	1.04	1.91	8.05	-3.90	8.23
Value	PORT EU Value	0.42	0.54	0.84	13.25	14.42	5.74
Sentiment	Sell Side Expected Return	0.64	0.71	1.11	3.56	29.57	-24.86
Technicals	14D RSI	0.61	-0.12	-0.01	-4.45	-10.48	-32.18
Size	Market Capitalization	0.40	0.00	1.13	-4.47	-19.95	-35.11
Growth	5Y Actual Sales Growth	-0.23	1.29	3.28	3.56	-1.66	-40.97
Leverage	PORT EU Leverage	0.06	-1.03	-1.25	-0.66	14.78	-42.29
Volatility	1M Volatility	0.28	1.67	-3.06	4.43	19.29	-46.79
Dispersion	Rev Est Dispersion (FY1)	-1.00	-1.12	-3.47	-4.52	9.01	-49.00

Source: BLOOMBERG PROFESSIONAL® (accessed 25 July 2021).

strategy of buying revised upward stocks and selling revised downward stocks earns strong positive returns. Both analysts' 'Revisions' strategies work well for this market.

Among the more traditional factors, momentum, profitability, and growth all do well for the 10 years but not for the last year. The oldest set of factors such as Size and Value do not perform so well.

International Evidence

Turning to the international comparisons, we report the 10-year cumulative returns for different markets. There are two important observations. First,

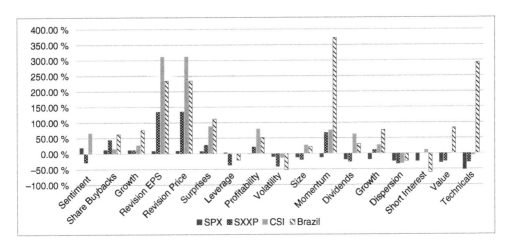

FIGURE 6.1   International evidence net long-short (Q1–Q5) (%).
Source: BLOOMBERG PROFESSIONAL®.

there is some consistency in the performance of the best strategies. Especially the analysts' revisions and momentum strategies have consistent top performance in these markets, as is the case for the UK. It suggests that when analysts update their view, the market will normally move in line with their updated view. This is encouraging as it indicates that analysts seem to have some real new insight that the market (average investors) do not know. Second, this evidence is also consistent with the view of market efficiency. For arguably the most developed market (the US market) and the most traded index (SPX), most of this publicly known information generates a very small return. By contrast, using similar information in emerging markets such as China (CSI) and Brazil, the same strategy can generate a much better return (Figure 6.1). Our study points out that market development affects the strength of different types of anomalies.[22] The key takeaway is that testing and understanding what is currently working in each market are important for creating strategies. The function such as FTW would give some indication for us to refine our strategy development with further tests.

---

[22] C.X. Cai, K. Kevin, P. Li, and Q. Zhang, Market development, information diffusion and the global anomaly puzzle. *Journal of Financial and Quantitative Analysis* (2021). Available at SSRN: https://ssrn.com/abstract=2839799.

SUMMARY

- We study behavioural biases in terms of their relevance to investment decisions for two reasons:
  1. to remind ourselves not to be influenced by our biases when making our investment decisions;
  2. to detect mispricing due to others' biases and take advantage of it.
- For the former, the effective approach is to understand the potential bias and build a checklist that may apply to your own investment habits. Try to document your trades systematically and analyse your trading patterns.
- For the latter, there are well-documented anomalies and pricing factors that are not necessarily driven by traditional risk factors.
- We show you can study and identify what works in a pool of securities you can trade and use the backtesting tool to develop your investment strategy.

PRACTICAL APPLICATION V: FACTORS TO WATCH

Whether it's risk or behavioural bias, a piece of information that can generate predictability of stock return comovements can be seen as a factor that affects the underlying return generating process. Therefore, we may simplify our investment research to the search for factors that can predict returns and then try to create a portfolio that can increase our exposure to such factors while reducing other risks. To do this, the best approach is to use factor-sorted portfolios and remove the effect of other factors by taking long-short factor portfolios in which other common risks borne by the two legs of portfolios are cancelled out. This is the approach promoted by the Nobel Laureate Eugene Fama when proposing his famous 3-factor model with Kenneth French. Since their paper, many factors and variations of specifications of factors have emerged within the literature. Some academics call it a factor zoo containing hundreds of different factors.[23] Therefore, selecting a factor that performs well becomes a real challenge, let alone explaining why it works.

In the BLOOMBERG PROFESSIONAL® system, there is a function, *FTW <GO>*, that does the up-to-date backtesting of factor performance. The testing

---

[23] G. Feng, S. Giglio, and D. Xu, Taming the factor zoo: A test of new factors. *Journal of Finance* LXXV(3) (2020).

on recent data is important for factor investing for one reason. Studies show that once an academic paper reveals a new factor that works in historical data, smart money (such as a hedge fund) will trade the strategy and, therefore, speed up the price correction process and reduce the profitability of the strategy. In this regard, well-known factors discovered earlier are not expected to perform as well as the newer factors in more recent data.

We can consider FTW as a collection of ready-made backtesting results which can be generated from either the EQBT or FTST functions that we studied in the earlier chapters. The key benefit of this function is to allow switching to different universes quickly and producing backtesting results for multiple strategies with a comparable setting at once. Let's take a look at some specifications in the following steps.

Step 1 Load the Function

Type {FTW} + <Enter>

Step 2 Selecting a Universe

This can be done by changing the selection from the source field drop-down menu. This is normally located in an amber box (input box) on the top left of the screen. In this function, it has a default setting of selecting the {United States}. The dropdown list contains all the major indexes from different regions including North America, Global, Europe (EMEA), Asia Pacific, and Latin America.

In this example, we select {NMX index FTSE 350 index} from the EMEA sublist on Page 2/4 of the dropdown menu.

By default, this function will produce results in the Quantile Spreads tab for *All sectors* and the *Monitor view* for the *Highlights style*. Each of these can then be customized. This view reports the name of a style such as Profitability, the factor variable name, and then the returns for this factor for various historical periods dating back from the time when this view is loaded. Unfortunately, the date of this analysis cannot be changed, only the current view is available.

Another limitation of this function is that only quintile analyses are available. Securities are equally-weighted within each quintile. This calculation does not consider transaction costs (which may be higher in emerging/frontier markets). Cumulative performance may also appear high in universes that have fewer securities, due to higher concentrations in each quintile. For historical backtesting with a more flexible setting, in previous chapters, we have shown we can do that in the EQS, EQBT, FTBT, or FTST functions. This function can be used as a quick preview of what is potentially important, hence the name Factor to Watch.

Step 3 Selecting a Style

The Highlights Category of styles presents those factors that the BLOOM-BERG PROFESSIONAL® system deems to be important in terms of their historical performance (best and worse). It provides a summary of all styles – selecting some representative factors in each style.

To understand these styles and their drivers better, we can select different subsets of styles.

To filter by factor style category, from the Style column dropdown menu we can see there are 30 subgroups of factors that we can choose from (Table 6.3). The example we gave in the main evidence section is from the {Highlights} group. If we select the {All} group, this will show all of the factors. There are more than 200 of them at the time of writing and they have varied market by market. BLOOMBERG PROFESSIONAL® is constantly adding new factors into the pool.

The All, Highlights, Curated, My Factors, and PORT are aggregated summaries of factors. From the {Earnings} onwards the specific categories of factors are inspired by academic findings.

In this example, let's select 'All'. We can see 167 factors can be calculated in the market.

TABLE 6.3 List of factor categories

ID	Subgroups	ID	Subgroups	ID	Subgroups
1	All	11	ESG	21	Size
2	Highlights	12	Growth	22	Surprises
3	Curated	13	Investment	23	Tax Rate
4	My Factors	14	Leverage	24	Technicals
5	PORT	15	Momentum	25	Trade Activity
6	Sentiment/Set-up	16	Profitability	26	Val vs History
7	Earnings	17	Revisions	27	Value
8	Accruals	18	Sentiment	28	Variability
9	Dispersion	19	Share Buybacks	29	Volatility
10	Dividends	20	Short Interest	30	Work Cap

Source: BLOOMBERG PROFESSIONAL® (accessed 25 July 2021).

Step 4 Comparing Factor Performance

To compare the performance of these factor strategies for different time periods, we can do that in the Movers View of the Summary page. In the Movers view, we can further refine our comparison period to different Horizons ranging from 1 day to 10 years, all of which are relative to the date of your access. For example, suppose on 25 July 2021, we are interested in which factor works for the FTSE 350 in the last year. We can choose the '1 Yr' from the Horizon dropdown menu. In Figure 6.2, we report the seven winners and losers.

We can see that the five-year beta calculated using monthly data is the winning factor. In other words, the higher the beta (systematic risk), the higher the return. This is consistent with what we have found in Chapter 5, where we studied the CAPM beta return in the UK market.

However, the comparison is a single dimension in that we only studied return and did not consider the risk profile. If you are an investor only invested in this portfolio but nothing else, the risk you should care about is the total risk (i.e., the total volatility). In other words, the ratio that you care about is the Sharpe ratio which is the mean return divided by its standard deviation, where the return is calculated by subtracting the risk-free return.To compare the

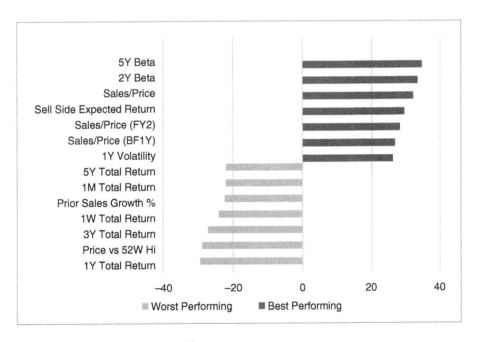

FIGURE 6.2   Factor winners and losers – 1 year.
Source: BLOOMBERG PROFESSIONAL®.

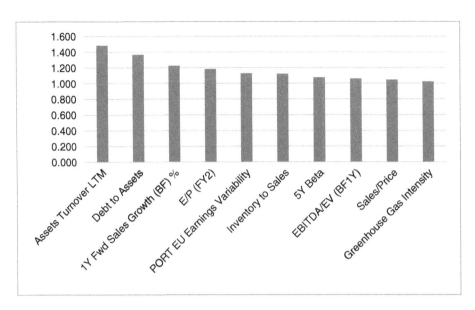

FIGURE 6.3   Top 10 strategies according to their Sharpe ratios – 1 year.
Source: BLOOMBERG PROFESSIONAL®.

strategy in terms of risk profiles, we can do that in the Strength-View. It reports, among other statistics, the Sharpe ratio of all of the strategies. In the following, we plot the top 10 strategies according to their Sharpe ratios. We can see that all of these strategies have a Sharpe ratio that is greater than 1 with the 5Y beta among them (Figure 6.3).

Step 5 Looking into the Strategy

If we sort the performance of the factors by their 10-year performance, it indicates that the '3M EPS Revision % (FY1)' factor performance is the best. If we want to know what stocks are in this portfolio at a given point in time, we can do that by *clicking* on the factor in the summary page. This will bring us to a page displaying the details for this factor for the universe we have chosen (FTSE 350). We report a selection of the top 10 stocks in Table 6.4.

We can see that the overall upward revision reflects an optimistic view of the potential post-pandemic economy across many different industry sectors. The 1-day return reminds us that all of these strategies need to be taken in a portfolio approach and require patience to realize the potential return. Returns for one security on a particular day will not necessarily be in line with the strategy's expected outcome. If such volatility in the strategy causes stress, then the best solution is not to check the return too often.

TABLE 6.4   Top 10 stocks in the '3M EPS Revision % (FY1)' strategy

Ticker	Sector	Industry	3M EPS revision % (FY1)	Quintile	1D Ret (%)
TLW LN Equity	Energy	Oil & Gas Producers	278.9	1	0.46
GRG LN Equity	Consumer Staples	Retail – Consumer Staples	102.7	1	1.94
VMUK LN Equity	Financials	Banking	69.6	1	1.20
OXB LN Equity	Health Care	Biotech & Pharma	65.7	1	-0.15
FGP LN Equity	Industrials	Transportation & Logistics	55.8	1	0.18
FXPO LN Equity	Materials	Metals & Mining	55.6	1	1.14
ATG LN Equity	Consumer Discretionary	E-Commerce Discretionary	49.9	1	3.30
CNE LN Equity	Energy	Oil & Gas Producers	47.4	1	0.15
NWG LN Equity	Financials	Banking	44.4	1	2.52
LLOY LN Equity	Financials	Banking	39.3	1	1.45

Source: BLOOMBERG PROFESSIONAL® (accessed 25 July 2021).

Overall, Factors to Watch provides a powerful tool to identify which factors are driving the movement of return in a market. It provides a good starting point to develop a quantitative approach to stock selection. We can take these factors further for portfolio strategy development by using the techniques we have learned in previous chapters. For example, using EQS and BTST to further examine the historical performance of the strategy and PORT to examine the risk and liquidity of the strategy.

EXERCISES

Using FTW to study one index of your choice, answer the following questions:

1. Which factor produces the highest 10-year return?
2. Which factor produces the highest Sharpe ratio for the 10-year horizon?

CHAPTER 7

Technical Analysis

INTRODUCTION

This is the penultimate chapter concerned with 'market approaches' to investing and its content is the one current traders/investors will be most familiar with. However, the previous chapters help us to understand the pluses and minuses of the techniques/approaches we discuss in this chapter.

If we return to Markowitz, in Chapter 5, the 'Portfolio Chapter', one of the key insights of Markowitz is that if the market has collective wisdom (and here we mean it is rational in terms of the risk and returns relationship), we can then use past data to predict future prices, etc. On this basis he used statistical techniques to estimate expected returns and variances to model an 'efficient frontier' of risk and return opportunities. If individuals know how they feel about such matters, they can then choose a portfolio of stocks to match their specific risk and return preferences. The predictability of expected return is driven by the fundamental risk and return trade-off. This all works well if the collective wisdom can be defined as 'normal' (rational) and not prone to extreme flights of fancy, and if the past forms a continuum into the future.

However, the behaviour of the financial markets (and their responses) in the financial crisis of 2008 and the Covid-19 crisis should tell us that everything is not always normal. Almost every economist is predicting (as of mid-April 2020) the West will be facing the biggest recession since the 1930s and possibly since the Great Frost of 1708/09 (the coldest winter for 500 years that led to many deaths – at least 600,000 in France by the end of 1710 – and a significant reduction in GDP). The FTSE 100 is 'happily' bouncing along in the mid-5000s betting on a V-shaped recovery once the lockdown is removed in May 2020.

There are a number of biases that explain why the markets are not adjusting to the economic reality that may well follow Covid-19. We could go through a number of these but we will just address the most obvious – and we discuss them in alphabetical order for ease: anchoring, availability, confirmation, and conservatism.

The world markets have been living through one of the longest bull runs in history and one explanation for the lack of adjustment to a new reality is that investors have firmly **anchored** their expectations in a bull market mentality. This anchoring tendency may be complemented by an **availability** bias – a number of the traders may never have seen a full-blown economic recession (the last big one was in the early 1970s) and there is no readily available data/memory on which to base an adjustment on. Also, in any 'bear' market, there are relief rallies and these give **confirmation** to the belief that the markets are still in a bull phase. Bear markets seem to be characterized by a number (up to 5) of down cycles before the penny finally drops and the reality of a bear market is accepted. Finally, there is the **conservatism** bias and this complements/links to the previous biases. Here investors are conservative in adjusting to new information and this may again explain why the markets are struggling to adjust to the new economic regime that has emerged on the back of Covid-19.

So here we have a bit of a conundrum. If past data are to be useful to investors, they have to contain patterns that can be discerned and acted upon. Effectively, prices should not perfectly impound prices or there would be no gain to be achieved. Equally, if past prices are not adjusting in some form to the new reality, then they will be of little use. What we need is for past prices to reveal some information on the future but be neither perfect nor zero in their information content. We believe this to be normally the case but when faced with 'truly unique' situations (i.e. Covid-19), past prices may be of little use and more fundamental economic analysis will be a better bet on the presumption markets cannot ignore/escape economic reality forever. This is well illustrated by one of the veteran traders on Wall Street – Jim Rogers.

I expect in the next couple of years we're going to have the worst bear market in my lifetime.

The impact of the coronavirus on economies will not be over quickly because there's been a lot of damage. A gigantic amount of debt has been added.

The Chinese economy is opening again, people are going back to work. Factories, restaurants are opening again. I am looking at life, and life is not such that we are all going to take the bus and take boats again.
(FXStreet.com *16 April 2020*)

Given the above caveat, we now move on to briefly introduce technical analysis. Technical analysis is a method/set of tools using patterns (shapes) of past data on stock prices to help make predictions on where prices will go next. The idea is the same as before, past prices reveal the collective wisdom of the market and we learn from the past how specific patterns/shapes precede up or down future price movements. We cover the basic elements of technical analysis in a later section.

BACKGROUND

There are many, many technical analysts we could have chosen to illustrate the approach. Given the long history of technical analysis, we have changed tack for this chapter and decided to discuss the technical analysts who have contributed to the approach over the past century.

TECHNICAL ANALYSTS

Jesse Livermore (1877–1940)

Before we move on to some of the best-known names in Technical Analysis (TA), it would be remiss not to mention Jesse Livermore – often seen as one of the founding fathers of TA. One of the reasons he is not always included in the lists of TAs might be his extremely colourful life. Unlike some of the other experts mentioned in this book, Livermore started out on a poor farm and he soon learnt in his early teens he could make a lot more money by taking 'bets' (leveraged positions) on stocks via the 'bucketshops' that were common in the US in the late 1800s. Note, the stock markets were largely unregulated in the US until the early 1930s (following the Wall Street Crash of 1929) and information on companies was patchy and piecemeal. In this type of environment, rumour and emotion are powerful forces driving stock prices up and down. Livermore quickly realized he was as much betting on the 'collective wisdom (madness)' of the market as the fundamentals of companies. His favourite book was *Extraordinary Popular Delusions and the Madness of Crowds* by Charles Mackay (1841).

Given the nature of the trading environment Livermore learnt to watch price trends and take long and short positions. He is best known for his large 'short' bets and these formed the base of his many fortunes. He took large short bets before the San Francisco earthquake in 1906 and the Wall Street Crash in 1929. The former seems to have been a case of luck (unless his timing was perfect) but the latter is likely to have been based on his insight into the madness of crowds. However, you need a certain 'devil may care' personality to take such bets and live with the possible negative consequences. As already noted in previous chapters, we have dabbled with short positions but the pain of them going wrong is just too great, given our personalities. Also in the current environment (April 2020), the market is showing signs of extreme irrationality – rising 3% on some rumour of a vaccine, then falling the same amount on a negative rumour. This is the type of market where it is easy to 'lose your shirt'. However, it is clear Livermore had the personality (but this might be questioned by the nature of his demise – see shortly) to take such bets and enjoy the positive fruits. There can be no doubt he was a risk-taker and a 'live life to the full' character. He bought fancy houses and apartments, very expensive yachts and even his own rail carriage (remember what was happening in the US in the late 1800s and early 1900s). He was bankrupted three times, married three times and seemed to have a taste for dancing girls. Even with a robust, risk-taking personality – living life in such a fast lane takes its toll and he eventually committed suicide in 1940, the suicide note stating he could no longer take the hard work and disappointment. He died with significant debts.

There are many lessons to learn from the life of Jesse Livermore and a more detailed read will pay dividends. The lessons we take is to understand how markets are driven by many factors, not least rumour and emotion, and also to understand your own personality and how you balance the pleasure of gain against the pain of loss.

Charles Dow (1851–1902)

While we started out with Jesse Livermore, Charles Dow is seen by many as the founding father of Technical Analysis. This to our mind is a bit of a stretch as his individual insights would have been lost in the mists of time without some key individuals following in his footsteps (see shortly). Nonetheless, his life and contribution to finance do bear further discussion.

Dow was born in 1851 on a farm in Connecticut and received no formal education in finance or seemingly more generally. Remember this was a time of the 'Wild West' and the same buccaneering spirit and lack of law featured in the business/financial activities of the US. However, by his mid-twenties, he had established himself as a reporter, working his way across a number of local newspapers. By the age of 26 (in 1877) he was writing business stories for the *Providence Journal*. He was known for his accurate writing and unbiased reporting, and he appears to have been a natural researcher. While Dow eventually became well known for the Dow Jones Index and Dow Theory (we will cover this in some detail in a later section), he was essentially a newspaper man – and this is well illustrated by his founding of the *Wall Street Journal* in 1889 at the age of 38. This newspaper is still known worldwide for its accurate reporting of the news. But we are getting ahead of ourselves.

In the late 1870s, Dow had the good fortune to accompany a number of 'business people' on a trip to the silver mines of Colorado. From the insights he gained, he realized that reporting on financial news was valuable but he had the wrong base, i.e. Connecticut. He moved to New York in 1880 and began working for a financial news bureau. By 1882, he had formed his own financial news agency with Edward Jones – Dow, Jones and company. From this beginning, they developed more and more detailed news reporting that culminated in the *Wall Street Journal*. Its mantra was the honest and accurate reporting of the financial news for all. He set up wire connections with a number of the financial centres of the US and key overseas centres (e.g. London).

However, while Dow's focus was financial news, he is best remembered for the Dow-Jones Industrial Average that he established with his partner in 1896 and for Dow Theory. The DJ index initially tracked the closing prices of 12 industrial companies and published on a daily basis the average closing price of these companies. This was accompanied in 1887 by an index for railroad stocks. From his interest in tracking prices, and to a lesser degree volumes, he started to lay the foundations of Dow Theory. He believed that by looking at the rise and fall of markets, it was possible to predict the direction of the market. By recording the highs and lows of his industrial and rail indices on a daily, weekly, and monthly basis, he could analyse how these reflected/predicted more general market movements. For example, he believed that if both indices reached new highs at a similar time, then a shift in outlook had occurred and a 'new bull phase' was in operation.

Hamilton, Rhea, Gould, and Magee

Dow's original insights were not developed into a coherent theory and those who followed were critical to its development in their different ways. As this is not intended to be a history book, we have grouped them together. W.P. Hamilton (1867–1929) built on Dow's work and he became the fourth editor of the *Wall Street Journal* and was at the helm of the paper for the two decades before his death. He used the notions of tides, waves, and ripples to analyse stock market movements. The tides (long-term trend of 4 or more years) were the long-term movement/sentiment of the market – either bullish or bearish. The waves are what happened on a weekly and monthly basis. The ripples were the daily movements and seen as largely irrelevant. He used these movements with some basic rules to call major changes in the market, for example, he made a final appeal about the froth of the market three days before the Wall Street Crash.

Robert Rhea died in 1939 (we have been unable to find his date of birth) and had not been a well man for most of the 1920s and 1930s. Nonetheless, he is seen as the man who added the most rigour to Dow Theory. He collated and refined the ideas of Dow and Hamilton in his 1932 book, *The Dow Theory*.[1] He used his insights to call the market bottom in 1932 and the top in 1937. His investment letter 'Dow Theory Comments' attracted many subscriptions and he lived a comfortable life off the back of these before his untimely demise. While Rhea used 'Dow insights' to call the market, it is Edson Gould (1898–1983) who has by far the longest track record of TA success and this led to the moniker 'Dean of Technicians'. He began work in the 1920s and he kept going until his death; he was part of a number of well-known US financial firms such as Moody's and Smith Barney. Like Rhea, he made a number of very accurate market predictions but he also made most of his money writing about the market. In the early 1960s, he established a publication, 'Findings and Forecasts' which attracted a wide subscription and was eventually sold to Anametrics in the late 1960s. He developed Speed Lines to assess trends, which are still widely used today (we discuss these in the section on Key Findings). The last name in this section is John Magee (1901–1987) – the man who wrote the bible on Technical Analysis, *Technical Analysis of Stock Trends* in 1948.[2] Magee charted everything on stocks, prices, volumes, averages, etc. and then attempted to identify shapes such as triangles, flags, bodies, shoulders, and so on . . . Not

---

[1] R. Rhea, *The Dow Theory: An Explanation of Its Development and an Attempt to Define Its Usefulness as an Aid in Speculation* (Colorado Springs, CO: Rhea, Greiner, 1932).

[2] R. Edwards and J. Magee, *Technical Analysis of Stock Trends* (Boston, MA: John Magee Inc., 1948).

surprisingly, he is known as the father of Chartism. As for others in the section, he seems to have used his knowledge to benefit clients more than himself. A very different picture emerges when we consider Quant Investors in Chapter 8.

KEY LESSONS

We now move on to the key lessons to be gained from Technical Analysis.

Dow Theory

We could have written this section in many different ways, given the huge breadth and depth of the subject – these are not surprising, given its long history. The approach we have eventually adopted is to focus on Dow Theory, as everything derives from it. We will leave other aspects of TA until Practical Application VI; we will, however, only cover the key essentials as there are many excellent books and websites devoted to the intricacies of technical analysis.

Dow Theory, as already noted, assumes market movements comprising three elements: the main movement (tides), the medium swing (waves), and the short swing (ripples). The main movement may last for many years (consider the recent bull market) and is seen as rarely being shorter than one year. It can be either a bull or a bear trend. Within the main movement exist intermediary movements (medium swings) that will be seen for a few weeks or months before they are reversed. So, in a main upward movement, there will be medium upward swings adding to the movement and downward swings detracting from it. Finally, there are short swings (lasting only a few days/weeks) that are essentially noise.

Figure 7.1 shows how these movements/swings interrelate. Figure 7.1 illustrates the primary and intermediary trends in a hypothetical price according to Dow's Theory. An upward main movement is considered as continuing so long as each medium downward swing ends up higher than the last. The main movement is seen as being over when the last downward medium swing is lower than the previous and the next upward medium swing does not achieve the level of the last one. While we will shortly discuss other 'signals' emanating from Dow Theory, we should discuss some of the underlying assumptions. First and foremost, there is the assumption that market prices impound the available information, and in this it is similar to the efficient market theory of academic finance. However, the nature of the trends add another layer of subtlety. Basically, the trends are driven by different types of traders. The first part of the trend (phase 1 – the accumulation phase) is

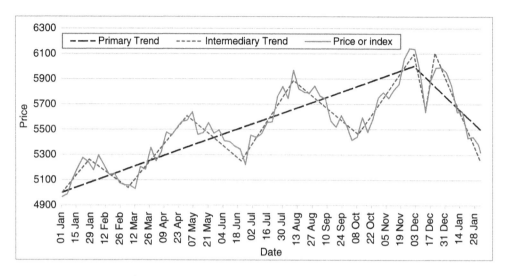

FIGURE 7.1   Primary (main) and intermediary trends in price.

driven by investors in the know – they are actively digging out news. Eventually, their actions start to drive prices higher and the other traders (momentum/noise traders) catch on to what is happening and drive prices much higher (absorption phase) and this might continue until speculation becomes evident. At this point the 'smart investors' begin to distribute their holdings to the market (distribution phase). Such a pricing process has been modelled in the behavioural asset pricing literature by Hong and Stein.[3]

Dow also saw evidence of a primary movement when a range of indices all point in the same direction and when the volume levels are supportive. Finally, while Figure 7.1 shows a clear turning point in the primary movement, there is some debate over how much evidence is needed to call a change of movement – it is, not surprisingly, a matter of judgement and there will be many false dawns before day eventually breaks. We now turn to some of the signals that might be used to call a turning point.

Head and Shoulders

Dow Theory argues that specific shapes precede a turning point and this is one of the best known. A Head and Shoulders shape at a peak predicts a significant price drop (see Figure 7.2). They rarely occur and while they have been shown to have some credibility with individual stocks, this is not the case for the overall market.

---

[3] H. Hong and J.C. Stein, A unified theory of underreaction, momentum trading, and overreaction in asset markets. *Journal of Finance* 54 (1999): 2143–2184.

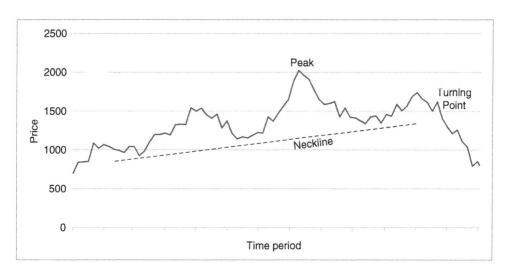

FIGURE 7.2   Head and Shoulders pattern.

The earlier discussion about the types of investors that drive trends can be seen in the shape of the Head and Shoulders. When the share price has been on a rising trend with significant volumes for quite some time, the smart investors will realize it has been going on long enough and they start to distribute their shares. The price starts to fall back to the neckline. The price fall will entice more investors into the share and the price will rise to the top of the head (Peak). More selling by the smart investors pushes the price down to the neckline on the right-hand side of the head. There is a small rally, on typically low volumes, but this peters out and if it pierces the neckline by a significant amount (2–3% drop), then a turning point has occurred and the 'herd' that rushed in, will now start to stampede out. This process can be seen as a tug of war between the optimists and pessimists near the end of a trend. As the optimists fail to push the price to continue with the existing trend signal, the pessimists win in the end.

So far, we have looked at diagrams of price movements to try to understand trends and turning points. However, there is more to the TA's arsenal than diagrams, graphs, and shapes – there are also a number of metrics and ratios that can be used to complement the more visual aspects of the art. Again, there are many of these and we just focus here on the best known. When looking at a current price, you will often mentally be comparing it to some average (month, quarter, year, etc,) and if the price has too big a **deviation** from the average, you will start to ponder. What is going on here is an implicit belief in averages and the reversion of prices to the average. By looking at the average and past movements around the average (some measure of deviation, variance, etc.), you will be able to gauge if the present deviation is beyond the normal. For example, if it is a long way above the average and beyond the normal deviation, then this may signal that the price is about to turn. There is a large family of TA strategies that feature the moving average as a part of the signal construction.

Another indicator of a turning point is **volatility**. Again, a stock will have a normal level of volatility and if this suddenly shoots up, it indicates there is a divergence of opinion as to where the stock price should be moving – and this indicates a potential turning point. Figure 7.3 shows the quarterly relationship between the S&P500 and the volatility index (Vix). It shows spikes in VIX generally coincide with the market turning.

A variation of volatility is the measure of **relative strength**. For a given period (say, 10 days), it sums up the gains on the positive days (say it gained 10 points on each of the 6 gain days = 60) and divides it by the total market movement for the same period (say we had 5 points lost on each on the loss days = 20). Therefore, in this example we would have a relative strength of 60/ (60+20) = 75%. TAs believe any relative strength measure outside the range 30–70 is indicative of a potential turning point, in this example, prices would be predicted to turn down.

The final metric we consider here is the **advance/decline ratio** (ADR) that is used to predict market turning points. For any given period (let's take a day), the total number of advancing stocks is divided by the number of

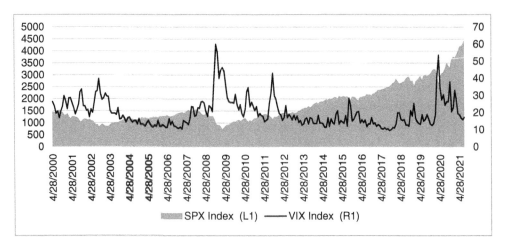

FIGURE 7.3   Volatility and turning points.
Source: BLOOMBERG PROFESSIONAL®.

declining stocks. If a sequence of this ratio starts to turn downwards, then a bull sentiment may be turning down, etc.

This section has covered some of the basic ideas coming out of Dow Theory and some of the 'logic'. What should be apparent is that while trends can be seen as continuing, the really hard call (this is similar to being a contrarian) is to predict a true turning point. Of course, if this was easy, we would all be millionaires (we keep saying this) and we could forget about hard graft. However, given the many different investors and other agents that make up the market, it is perhaps not surprising, it is difficult to spot the 'true' main trends and turning points, given all the other currents and eddies that make up the 'flow of the market'. In short, the market does not efficiently price every asset but it is competitive. When you discover a useful pattern to predict future price movement, it will work for a while but soon you will notice that others have also spotted this and the profit of the strategy will drop and the search for 'new angles' continues. Technical Analysis is used to identify return predictability and it doesn't matter whether the predictability is driven by risk or biases. To separate an opportunity from the noise is likely to take a lot of data and analysis and we, accordingly, turn to the key lessons of the Quant Investors in Chapter 8.

APPLYING THE LESSONS

Technical Analysis (TA) is a huge subject and we will just give a taste here of some of the basic principles/tools that can be used. While some traders will use only TA to guide their investment decisions, a lot of traders use the tools in conjunction with fundamental analysis. The latter being used to identify stocks with potential and TA being used as a confirmation/timing device. And this moves us on to a key issue. There are many ways to address how to invest and it is important you come up with an approach that suits your personality (especially risk appetite), the time you have available, and what basically interests you. For example, if you are interested in broader macro effects on the economy, you will want to consider investing at the market and/or industry level. The length of focus is likely to be relatively short term and may focus on 'indices' breaking out significantly from, say, a 30-day moving average. Of interest here is the Buffett Indicator that divides the market cap of a country by its GDP. It is basically trying to work out if the market is over-/fair/under-valued by normalizing via GDP. Buffett has argued this is one of the best indicators he uses and it has predicted a number of 'turning points'. A ratio below 70% is seen as being under-valued, 70–90% as fair value, and above 100%, alarms begin to ring. Before the Dotcom crash the US Indicator was approximately 160%, before the financial crisis it was 120% and in March 2020 it was 150%. Even after the recent corrections, it stands at 127% on 22 April 2020, and so you can draw your own conclusions.

Whereas if your interest is at the company level, you are likely to undertake fundamental analysis and adopt a longer-term investment horizon, with the TA just being used to confirm you are buying/selling at the right time. No matter which approach you adopt, you will need to ensure you have the appropriate data sources and the trading platform(s). Finally, be aware you will make mistakes (in the calculation, in the assessment of data, in the execution, etc.) and it is best to start small – the big gains will still be there in the future.

We now move on to a number of the TA tools. We only cover a few to give a flavour of what is possible. Each of the tools casts a slightly different light on stock price data and, if used together, they should help to form a more comprehensive picture. But, remember, no one tool is perfect and even when combined, they can be misleading. The trick here is to be constantly aware of false signals and, if in doubt, don't invest – you may miss that great uptick but you also may avoid that disastrous plummet!

Since there are many TA rules, picking one of them is seemingly a task as difficult as selecting stocks. The basis of the TA analysis is that history will repeat itself. Backtesting these strategies using historical data gives some indications of which strategy works historically. We will first introduce the main categories of TA strategies and a sample of the specific strategies in each category. The main purpose is to understand the basic definitions and intuition. We can leave the detailed calculations to the software. We will then examine some empirical evidence through the example of backtesting the strategies on the FTSE 100 index and its constituents in the next section. We will highlight the key statistics and practical considerations that need to be attended to when selecting and applying these strategies.

We will cover the following categories of TA:

- Moving Average
- Moving Average Bands

- Momentum/Oscillators
  - Ups and downs
  - Different periods
  - Highs and lows
- Trend Analysis

For each TA category, we will give a brief definition of the idea, its calculation and the practical application of the idea in a trading strategy. We then present a snapshot of its application in the FTSE 100 index during a one-year period. The main focus of these snapshots is to visualize the indicator and the strategy in action. We will formally present the comparisons of these strategies in the next section. Readers who are more interested in the testing results can skip the definitions below and use them as reference when reading the evidence of backtesting.

Moving Average

Moving Average (MA)

The moving average (MA) is the foundation stone of technical analysis as originated from Dow Theory. Its significance will be seen as we progress through some of the most popular TA strategies. With or without MA in their names, most of the strategies use the concept of MA in their construction. It is critical to understand this concept and its intuition.

A moving average measures the average of the price level over a period of time (e.g. 5 days). This average is likely to move (unless the series is constant) as new data come in (e.g. when new daily data come in, the oldest observation in the previous 5-day observations will drop out and the new daily data will be used as part of the 5-day average). There are many variations of using MA in forming a new signal as we can see from the list above. *A simple MA* strategy is where the price stays above a moving average, there is a buy signal, and there is the opposite signal if it remains below. Different lengths of moving average can be compared and here we have cross-over strategies. For example, if the one-day price cuts across in an upward movement a 20-day moving average, there is again a buy signal.

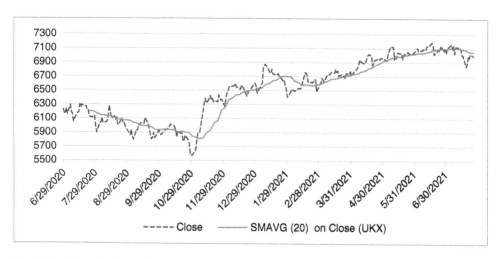

FIGURE 7.4   Simple moving average.
Source: BLOOMBERG PROFESSIONAL®.

TABLE 7.1   Simple moving average performance summary

Statistics	Long	Short	Total
Trades	23	23	46
Wins	4	4	8
Losses	19	19	38
% P&L	-6.09	-17.4	-23.5

Source: BLOOMBERG PROFESSIONAL®.

To illustrate the following, Figure 7.4 and Table 7.1 show the simple moving average strategy applied to the FTSE 100 index over a one-year period. It shows that there are 23 buy and sell signals respectively but only four out of the 23 times is the strategy is correct, therefore, making a loss overall.

Exponential Moving Average (EMA)

The exponential moving average is calculated by applying a percentage of today's closing price to yesterday's moving average value. It places a greater weight and significance on the most recent data points. It reacts more significantly to recent price changes than a simple moving average (SMA), which applies an equal weight to all observations in the period. There are other MA calculations that have been developed which are just variations of how the average is calculated such as the *Triangular MA* and the *Weighted MA*.

Figure 7.5 and Table 7.2 illustrate an EMA strategy as applied to the FTSE 350 for one-year period. We can see it generates less signals and performs

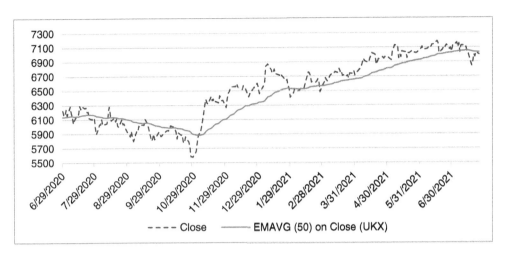

FIGURE 7.5   Exponential moving average.
Source: BLOOMBERG PROFESSIONAL®.

TABLE 7.2   Exponential moving average performance summary

Statistics	Long	Short	Total
Trades	7	7	14
Wins	2	4	6
Losses	5	3	8
% P&L	12.39	-1.68	10.71

Source: BLOOMBERG PROFESSIONAL®.

better than the SMA, in that it has a higher winning ratio and generates a positive 10.71% for this one-year period which, however, is still lower than buying and holding the index over this period (14.67%).

In summary, the above MA strategies can be seen as momentum strategies. When the short-window MA or daily price 'breaks through' the long-window MA, it suggests there is a strong short momentum to continue in that direction. The next set of strategies use moving averages to construct 'Bands'; by contrast, these are reversal strategies.

Moving Average Bands

Moving Average Envelopes

MA Envelopes (MAE) use a historical moving average (e.g 15-day) and percentage-based support (e.g. 3% lower than the average) and resistance levels (e.g. 3% higher than the average) for a selected security. These support

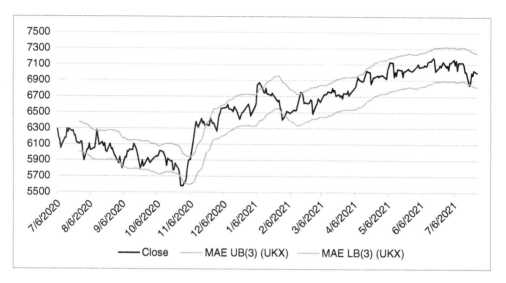

FIGURE 7.6   Moving Average Envelope.
Source: BLOOMBERG PROFESSIONAL®.

TABLE 7.3   Moving Average Envelope performance summary

Statistics	Long	Short	Total
Trades	4	3	7
Wins	4	1	5
Losses	0	2	2
% P&L	19.92	1.19	21.11

Source: BLOOMBERG PROFESSIONAL®.

and resistance levels form a moving average 'envelope', which you can use to gauge a security's trading activity. The idea behind the use of MAE is that prices are mean-reverting after extreme price movements. The moving average is one way to capture the mean. Moving Average Envelope (MAE) strategies go Long when the close price crosses to below the Lower Band of the MAE and Short when the close price crosses to above the Upper Band.

Applying a 15-day MAE on the FTSE 100, we can see that it generates seven signals (Figure 7.6). Among them five are correct, the strategy generates a 21.11% return during this one year, beating the Buy & Hold strategy (Table 7.3).

Bollinger Bands/Trading Envelopes (TE)

Bollinger Bands are another way of defining a band based on a simple moving average. They are similar to the MA Envelope but instead of choosing the

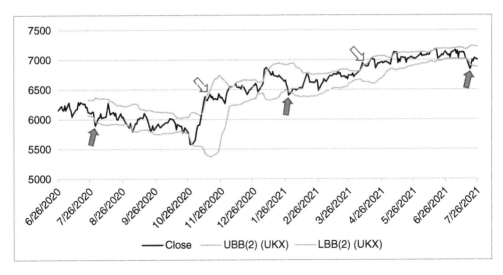

FIGURE 7.7 Bollinger Bands.
Source: BLOOMBERG PROFESSIONAL®.

TABLE 7.4 Bollinger Bands performance summary

Statistics	Long	Short	Total
Trades	3	2	5
Wins	3	0	3
Losses	0	2	2
% P&L	12.15	-4.02	8.14

Source: BLOOMBERG PROFESSIONAL®.

percentage arbitrarily and fixed (e.g. 3% as in the above example), John Bollinger used a number of standard deviations from a simple moving average to define the variable bands. In BLOOMBERG PROFESSIONAL® they are also reported under the name of Trading Envelopes. These bandwidths become narrower during less volatile periods and wider during more volatile periods. Normally two standard deviations are used from 20 days of the historical average. Bollinger Band Strategies go Long when the close price crosses to below the Lower Band and Short when the close price crosses to above the Upper Band.

Applied to the FTSE 100 for a one-year period, it shows that Bollinger Bands have a more volatile band as compared to the MAE above. It generates even fewer signals and the success rate in this period is 60% with a positive return that is lower than the buy and hold strategy (Figure 7.7 and Table 7.4).

Ichimoku (GOC)

The General Overview Chart (GOC) displays the Ichimoku Kinko Hyo equilibrium analysis that was developed by Goichi Hosoda, and is commonly referred to as an Ichimoku chart. It is a moving average-based trend identification system. These charts combine three technical indicators to define a price trend. Close and mid-prices are manipulated to generate a pattern of signals that are plotted 26 days in the past, 26 days in the future, along with the current price data. Practitioners of the Ichimoku technique use these charts to identify short-term momentum, long-term trends, and price objectives. It is quite an elaborate system which took him 30 years to perfect.

The Ichimoku strategy goes Long when the Conversion line of the Ichimoku indicator crosses from above the Base line and Short when the Conversion line crosses from below the Base line.

Applying the above to the FTSE 100, we can see the Conversion and Base lines are very volatile (Figure 7.8 and Table 7.5). Out of the 13 signals, only four are correct and the strategy has a negative return for this particular period.

In summary, these strategies try to identify bands that the price will normally operate within. They are reversal strategies, as when the price moves out of the band it is predicted that the future price will move back into the band.

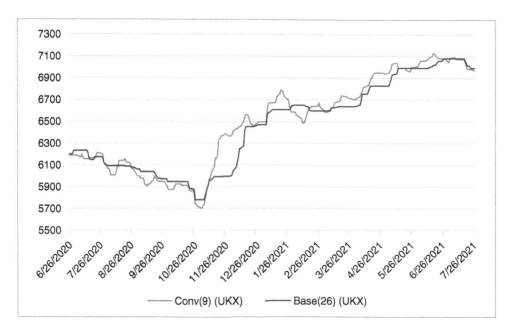

FIGURE 7.8   Ichimoku (GOC).
Source: BLOOMBERG PROFESSIONAL®.

TABLE 7.5 Ichimoku (GOC) performance summary

Statistics	Long	Short	Total
Trades	6	7	13
Wins	3	1	4
Losses	3	6	9
% P&L	4.16	-10.94	-6.78

Source: BLOOMBERG PROFESSIONAL®.

Momentum/Oscillators

The Relative Strength Index (RSI)

RSI, developed by J. Welles Wilder, measures the velocity of a security's price movement to identify overbought and oversold conditions. Wilder introduced a series of new TAs in his 1978 book *New Concepts in Technical Trading Systems*.[4] The term overbought (oversold) is used in TA to describe a price as being too high (low) as compared to its fundamental level due to positive (negative) investor sentiment. Therefore, we expect a subsequent correction in the price. RSI is used to recognize potential turning points to help make entry/exit decisions.

RSI values are calculated from closing prices in a historical period (e.g. 14 days). It measures the relative strength of the moving average of UP closes and of DOWN closes. The statistics are standardized to be in a range between 0 and 100 (see Practical Application VI for the details). A high RSI normally indicates a stronger strength for a buy and vice versa. However, a sell signal is triggered when the RSI value is greater than 70 as it indicates an overbought condition. Similarly, an RSI indicator falling below a value of 30 indicates an oversold condition and a buy signal is usually triggered when the indicator crosses 30 from below as the indicator is rising back to the central band.

Applying a RSI 14 days to the FTSE 100 generates very few signals in a single year. At the time of writing (July 2021), there is one sell signal generated which so far turns out to be incorrect. There is one near buy signal which happens on 17 October 2020 when the RSI value is at 30.7 (Figure 7.9 and Table 7.6).

---

[4] J.W. Wilder, *New Concepts in Technical Trading Systems* (Greensboro, NC: Trend Research, 1978).

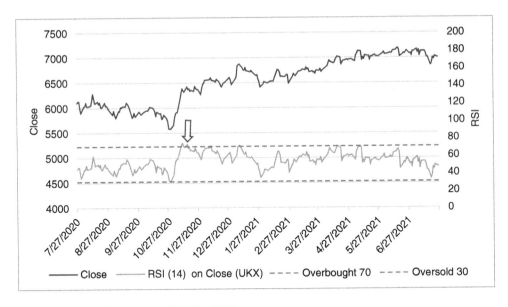

FIGURE 7.9   Relative Strength Index (RSI).
Source: BLOOMBERG PROFESSIONAL®.

TABLE 7.6   Relative Strength Index (RSI) performance summary

Statistics	Long	Short	Total
Trades	0	1	1
Wins	0	0	0
Losses	0	1	1
% P&L	0	-11.08	-11.08

Source: BLOOMBERG PROFESSIONAL®.

Moving Average Convergence/Divergence (MACD)

Gerald Appel developed MACD as an indicator of the change in a security's underlying price trend. The theory suggests that when a price is trending, it is expected, from time to time, that speculative forces 'test' the trend. MACD shows the characteristics of both a trending indicator and an oscillator. While the primary function is to identify turning points in a trend, the level at which the signals occur determines the strength of the reading. It can be considered a special version of MAO.

The MACD line uses the difference of two exponential MAs (e.g. 12- and 26-day) and then the moving average (e.g. 9-day) of the MACD line as a Signal line. The MACD strategy goes Long when the MACD line crosses above the Signal line from below and Short when the MACD line crosses down below the Signal line from above. Similar to the MAO, it measures the strength of the exponential MA's signal relative to the recent period.

MACD tends to generate more signals as the following example shows (Figure 7.10 and Table 7.7). The Signal line and the MACD line cut each other and generate signals. In this particular period, however, it does not generate a profitable strategy.

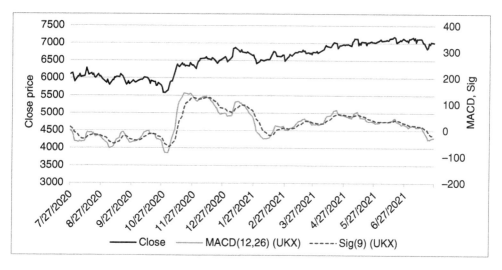

FIGURE 7.10 Moving Average Convergence/Divergence (MACD).
Source: BLOOMBERG PROFESSIONAL®.

TABLE 7.7 Moving Average Convergence/Divergence (MACD) performance summary

Statistics	Long	Short	Total
Trades	14	14	28
Wins	3	3	6
Losses	11	11	22
% P&L	-8.06	-20.24	-28.3

Source: BLOOMBERG PROFESSIONAL®.

The Williams %R

The Williams %R oscillator identifies whether a security is trading relatively high or low in relation to the highs and lows of a lookback period (e.g. 14 days). The oscillator is defined as WLPR = -100*(N Period Highest High - Close) / (N Period Highest High - N Period Lowest Low). Similar to the Rex oscillator, it tries to capture the relative position of the close price. For example, if the close price is near to its high in the last 14 days, this measure will be closer to zero. By contrast, if the close price is near to its low, WLPR will be closer to -100. The Williams %R Strategy is a momentum strategy and it tries to identify a continued strong trend. This is achieved by identifying the extreme positive sentiment (i.e. go long when WLPR is above -20 moving towards 0) and extremely negative sentiment (i.e. go short when WLPR is below -80 moving towards -100).

The William %R is very successful in the one year when it is applied to the FSTE 100. Some 17 out of 21 signals are correct and the strategy earns a before cost profit of 23.08% (Figure 7.11 and Table 7.8).

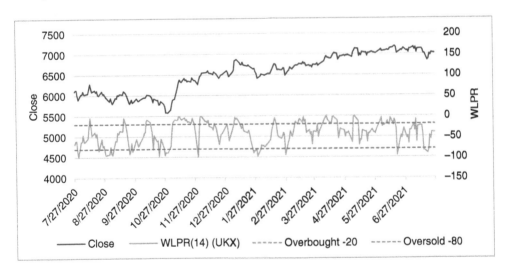

FIGURE 7.11   The Williams %R.
Source: BLOOMBERG PROFESSIONAL®.

TABLE 7.8   The Williams %R performance summary

Statistics	Long	Short	Total
Trades	9	8	17
Wins	8	6	14
Losses	1	2	3
% P&L	20.76	2.32	23.08

Source: BLOOMBERG PROFESSIONAL®.

The Commodity Channel Index (CMCI)

The Commodity Channel Index (CMCI), developed by Donald Lambert, measures the difference between the current price and the historical average price.

CMCI = (HLC3 – N Period Simple MA of HLC3)

/(0.015 * N Period Mean Deviation of HLC3)

where: HLC3 = (High + Low + Close) / 3. Intuitively, when the CMCI is above zero, it indicates the price is above the historic average. When CCI is below zero, the price is below the historic average. High readings of 100 or above, for example, indicate the price is well above the historic average and the trend has been strong on the upside. However, the trading signal comes when this trend is reversed. A sell signal is triggered when the indicator crosses 100 from above, suggesting an overbought situation. Similarly, a buy signal is triggered when the indicator crosses -100 from below, signalling a correction to the oversold position is likely.

Similar to other oscillators in the category, CMCI produces a good outcome for the FTSE 100 in one year beating the index (Figure 7.12 and Table 7.9).

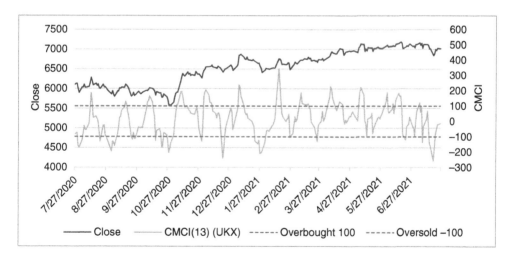

FIGURE 7.12 Commodity Channel Index (CMCI).
Source: BLOOMBERG PROFESSIONAL®.

TABLE 7.9   Commodity Channel Index (CMCI) performance summary

Statistics	Long	Short	Total
Trades	11	10	21
Wins	9	6	15
Losses	2	4	6
% P&L	21.88	3.69	25.57

Source: BLOOMBERG PROFESSIONAL®.

K Bands

Keltner Bands, illustrated by Charles Keltner in 1960, are bands drawn above and below a centreline to illustrate bullish and bearish breakouts. The basic idea is that price movement will be confined within a 'typical' range, given its historical average and range. The centre line is a simple moving average of the 'Typical Price' ((H+L+C)/3). The bands are then drawn above and below the centreline based on a simple moving average of the trading ranges (H-L). The defaults for both the centre and band Moving Average periods are 10 days. The values for the Upper and Lower Bands are often set to 100, i.e. 100% of the MA of the trading ranges over the previous 10 days. This setting defines a band that the price should normally move along that is within two times of the historical trading range around the moving average value. When the price moves outside this band, there is 'force' to bring it back into this band. Therefore, the K Band strategy goes Long when the close price crosses below the lower Keltner Band and Short when the close crosses above the upper Keltner Band.

K Bands is the best winning strategy for the FTSE 100 during this one year. It has a winning ratio of 75% and a return of 44.47%, beating the buy and hold by nearly 40% in this one year (Figure 7.13 and Table 7.10).

Trend Analysis

Most of the technical analysis indicators we have discussed so far use the historical data to display the relationship between the current price and the Signal line. The interpretation of the signals is an implicit forecast of the future movement. Trend analysis takes the obvious step of including a forecast in the signal construction.

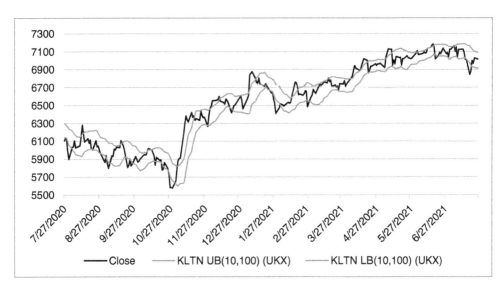

FIGURE 7.13   K Bands.
Source: BLOOMBERG PROFESSIONAL®.

TABLE 7.10   K Bands performance summary

Statistics	Long	Short	Total
Trades	10	10	20
Wins	9	8	17
Losses	1	2	3
% P&L	30.17	14.3	44.47

Source: BLOOMBERG PROFESSIONAL®.

Parabolic SAR

The parabolic Stop-And-Reversal (SAR) indicator was also developed by J. Welles Wilder Jr. The SAR points are a function of price movement and time. The parabolic SAR indicator appears on a chart as a series of dots that follow price, using an acceleration factor (AF) that increases with the velocity of price movement. The intuition is to use the distance between the current close and the recent extreme (max or min) to 'predict' the next period price, given the assumption of how fast the price will accelerate to that extreme. A dot is placed below the price when it is trending upward, and above the price when it is trending downward. A buy signal is generated when the next period's SAR is higher than the current period (i.e. when the dot switches its position from above the price to below the price in the chart) indicating the price is changing from trending downward to trending upward.

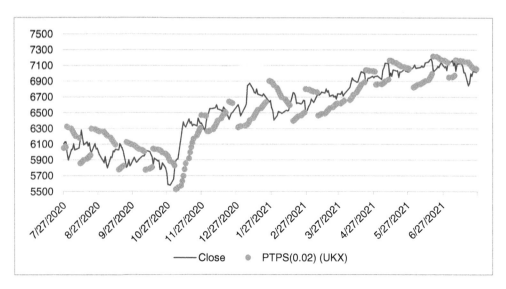

FIGURE 7.14   Parabolic SAR.
Source: BLOOMBERG PROFESSIONAL®.

TABLE 7.11   Parabolic performance summary

Statistics	Long	Short	Total
Trades	11	12	23
Wins	3	1	4
Losses	8	11	19
% P&L	-5	-19.11	-24.11

Source: BLOOMBERG PROFESSIONAL®.

This strategy generates quite frequent signals. However, during the one year we tested for the FTSE 100 it performs poorly (Figure 7.14 and Table 7.11).

SUMMARY

The above should have given you a feel for a few of the tools used by TAs but remember there are many available. None are perfect and TAs use a range of tools to confirm their suspicions/expectations of future price movements. However, the really smart investor does not take any of these indicators at face value and jump to easy conclusions – instead, they reflect on what might happen if the signals are false and misleading, what are the consequences for wealth? From this perspective, the signals from TA should be 'one of many' bits of analysis, and the wise person only moves when they stack up in the round. Let us finish with an example. It is 2 May 2020 and the UK is still in lockdown with the prospect of another four weeks of 'house arrest' and most economists are predicting economic Armageddon. Against this backdrop, the FTSE 100 has spent most of the week climbing from a level of 5500 (still too high, given economic conditions) to 6000. The market has disconnected from economic fundamentals and anybody investing on the basis of technical signals is betting on the market and not business fundamentals. To put this into perspective, the S&P 500 has had its best month (it rose 12.7% in April) since 1987 and its best April since 1938 (and this was an interesting year, given what followed in 1939). And here we return to Buffett's Indicator – by any measure of future GDP and the losses that will be incurred, the market is significantly overvalued.

EMPIRICAL EVIDENCE

Dow Theory has been around for a very long time and this is a plus and a minus in terms of empirical evidence. The plus is that we have potentially a lot of data. The minus is that the theory may have worked for specific periods and markets but not in all cases, and here the conclusions will need to be nuanced. The need for nuance is amplified because, as we have seen, the signals to predict a turning point are far from 100% objective and depend on how TAs see the various trends and metrics coming together. As we have said many times, if this was easy we would all be very rich. There is also the danger of a look-back bias when undertaking the empirical analysis, i.e. the signals are obvious with hindsight but would they have been so clear at the time? And this is the problem with Laura Sether's[5] following conclusion, 'the historical record appears to support its remarkable effectiveness'. We will come across this issue again shortly.

Testing of Dow Theory

It is not surprising, given the longevity and widespread interest, that others have tried to assess the performance of Dow Theory. In 1947, Richard Durant[6] analysed the performance of Dow Theory from 1897 to 1946 and found it beat a traditional buy and hold strategy by a factor of more than 10. However, a famous paper by Alfred Cowles in 1933 cast doubt on the predictive power and money-making potential of Dow Theory.[7] Essentially, Cowles found that

---

[5] L. Sether, *Dow Theory Unplugged: Charles Dow's Original Editorials and Their Relevance Today* (Cedar Falls, IA: W & A Publishing, 2009).

[6] R. Durant, *What Is the Dow Theory?* (Detroit, 1947).

[7] A. Cowles III, "Can stock market forecasters forecast?" *Econometrica* 1(3) (1933): 309–324. https://doi.org/10.2307/1907042.

returns from a buy and hold strategy outperformed a Dow Theory timing strategy. As always with empirical work, care needs to be taken before reaching a firm conclusion. Brown, Goetzmann, and Kumar revisited the Cowles data and came to the opposite conclusion.[8] As usual, the devil is in the detail and the reasonableness of the assumptions being made. In the original work of Cowles, raw returns were compared and here the buy and hold strategy wins. However, in the work of Brown et al., they note that through the application of Dow signals, a participant would often be out of the market (i.e. zero risk) and if risk-adjusted returns are considered, then Dow Theory has the edge – effectively, it had higher Sharpe ratios. Whether one should focus on raw or risk-adjusted returns is a matter of personal preference.

Another way of analysing the potential of Dow Theory is to see how many times its potential predictions may have been correct. Martin Pring[9] found between 1897 and 1990 that it was correct more than 90% of the time with buy signals and 80% of the time with sell signals. However, we come back to the same problem of 'look-back bias' – how many investors would have used the signals at the time, that is, how strong/credible were the signals, given all the other news? Perhaps, the biggest criticism of Dow Theory is that the signals come too late, given all the other information/uncertainties and this is especially the case if Dow's advice of waiting for confirmation is taken before acting to avoid errors!

BLOOMBERG PROFESSIONAL® Backtesting

Let's work through the backtesting evidence for the FTSE 100 index. Figure 7.15 presents the backtesting results for a set of TA strategies we introduced in the previous section (see Practical Application VI for details of strategy backtesting).

Figure 7.15 reports the backtesting on the FTSE 100 Index across one year between July 2020 and July 2021. We can see the best performance is the K Bands with a 44.47% annual gain and the worst is the Rex Oscillator with a loss of 35.5%. It is important to note the above statistics only use one year of data on one index. To understand the relative performance of these strategies in a more general setting, we need to enlarge the sample. We present two examples of such experiments.

---

[8] S.J. Brown, W.N. Goetzmann, and A. Kumar, The Dow Theory: William Peter Hamilton's track record re-considered (February 1998). NYU Working Paper No. FIN-98-013, Available at SRN: https://ssrn.com/abstract=1296408

[9] M. Pring, Introduction to Technical Analysis (New York: McGraw-Hill, 1997).

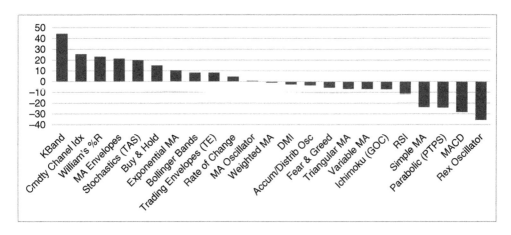

FIGURE 7.15 Return from backtesting TA strategies on FTSE 100 Index between July 2020 and July 2021 (% total return).
Source: BLOOMBERG PROFESSIONAL®.

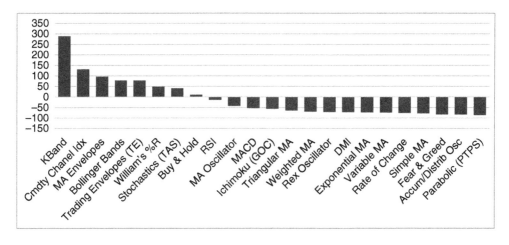

FIGURE 7.16 Return from backtesting TA strategies on the FTSE 100 Index between July 2000 and July 2021 (% total return).
Source: BLOOMBERG PROFESSIONAL®.

Our first approach is to extend our testing period to a longer horizon: 20 years. We report the backtesting on the FTSE 100 index in the period from July 2000 to July 2021 (Figure 7.16).

We can see that there seems to be some consistency in the 20 years-evidence and the 1-year evidence. K Bands and some other oscillators seem to be able to beat the buy and hold in this market. It is important to note that during these 20 years we have had three big crises (Dotcom, subprime, and the Covid-19 pandemic) and Brexit. Each time there is a big drop in the index followed by a strong bull run. Using some technical indicator that is able to capture the market sentiment to time the turning point seemed to be an appealing idea. The question is, which one to follow?

We now turn to international evidence in these TA tests. Table 7.12 shows the summary for the CSI 300 (China), Nikkei 225 (Japan), and Dow Jones Industry (USA). It reports the total percentage return of the strategy for the 20-year period between July 2000 and July 2021. We can see that different

TABLE 7.12　International evidence

CSI 300		Nikkei 225		S&P 500	
Strategy	**% total R**	**Strategy**	**% total R**	**Strategy**	**% total R**
Triangular MA	1764	Exponential MA	112	*Buy & Hold*	**205**
DMI	1761	*Buy & Hold*	73	KBand	104
Weighted MA	1686	Weighted MA	24	Exponential MA	43
Simple MA	753	MA Envelopes	21	Stochastics (TAS)	36
Ichimoku (GOC)	650	MACD	19	Bollinger Bands	21
Exponential MA	478	DMI	18	Trading Envelopes (TE)	21
Parabolic (PTPS)	394	Triangular MA	16	Ichimoku (GOC)	4
Fear & Greed	286	Parabolic (PTPS)	-9	Triangular MA	0
Buy & Hold	278	Ichimoku (GOC)	-13	DMI	-9
MACD	196	Bollinger Bands	-13	MA Envelopes	-15
Variable MA	195	Trading Envelopes (TE)	-13	MACD	-24
MA Oscillator	-84	KBand	-24	RSI	-26
Rex Oscillator	-94	Cmdty Channel Idx	-44	Fear & Greed	-26
MA Envelopes	-97	William's %R	-47	Weighted MA	-28
Accum/Distrib Osc	-98	Fear & Greed	-48	Cmdty Channel Idx	-33
Rate of Change	-98	Simple MA	-56	Simple MA	-34
KBand	-98	MA Oscillator	-56	William's %R	-44
Cmdty Channel Idx	-99	Rex Oscillator	-58	Variable MA	-56
William's %R	-99	Variable MA	-69	Parabolic (PTPS)	-75
Stochastics (TAS)	-100	Stochastics (TAS)	-73	MA Oscillator	-84
RSI	-100	Accum/Distrib Osc	-75	Accum/Distrib Osc	-91
Bollinger Bands	-101	RSI	-77	Rate of Change	-95
Trading Envelopes (TE)	-101	Rate of Change	-78	Rex Oscillator	-96

Source: BLOOMBERG PROFESSIONAL®.

versions of the moving average do well. Especially in the Chinese market, some of these technical rules can be exploited to have significant gain. In general, it reflects our general observation about market efficiency. For the US market, arguably the most efficient stock market, we can see that the 'market' is hard to beat. None of these strategies is able to beat the buy and hold return. Similarly for the Japanese market, we see only one winning strategy over the buy and hold. The key lesson here is that technical indicators may be more likely to work in the less efficient and emerging markets.

SUMMARY

We have learnt the following lessons from the above discussion and the simple empirical tests:

- There is no consistent performance across the list of common technical indicators discussed; in short, there is no easy money.
- A Buy & Hold passive strategy is hard to beat, especially across horizons greater than 3 years.
- The ultimate advice from Dow, ironically, is to invest in a stock index – an idea pioneered by Dow in his creation of the Dow Jones Transportation Index.
- A 'good' technical indicator is more likely to be 'found' in short-horizon tests. This can be due to data mining.
- However, the fact that Buy & Hold is more often than not beaten by some of these TAs suggests there is an opportunity to use TA to improve short-term performance.
- The question is, which one to choose? Further selection and rotation techniques will be required to develop a strategy that can consistently perform.
- Our cross-sectional tests on multiple markets suggest that MACD and RSI seem to do well across all of the markets tested.
- Overall, when using technical indicators, there is no one strategy that performs for a long period. This is why quantitative fund managers need huge machine learning power to go through the data to identify which strategy is more likely to work and then adapt it dynamically (see Chapter 8).

PRACTICAL APPLICATION VI: A WALKTHROUGH OF TECHNICAL ANALYSIS

The best place to start exploring technical analysis on BLOOMBERG PROFESSIONAL® is the Technical Study Browser (TECH function). The TECH <GO> serves as a gateway to all technical studies.

In BLOOMBERG PROFESSIONAL®, a technical strategy is referred to as a piece of study. We can see there are more than 100 standard studies provided by BLOOMBERG PROFESSIONAL® and there are many more by third parties, which are often subscription-based products. For the standard categories, we have the following notable strategy types:

- Momentum/Oscillators
- Moving Average and Bands
- Patterns
- Statistical
- Support Resistance
- Trend Analysis

Definition

For each of the studies, when selected, a brief definition of the study is given and further options, such as the function to run the study, are given. To find out more about this study, you can *click* on [6) More>>].

To apply the study to a security, we first load the security. In the discussion of the lessons we apply the studies to the FTSE 100 index. In this example, we demonstrate the application of the RSI function to a selected company: Vodafone. To do this, we load the security Vodafone and then we enter {RSI} + <Enter> to load the RSI function.

Backtesting

To see how this strategy performs with a strictly rule-driven investment approach, we can use backtesting. To do this, we load the backtesting function. We *type* BTST <Enter> while the security, in this case, Vodafone, is loaded. BTST allows users to run a pre-configured multi-strategy analysis for the currently loaded security or group of securities, so you can assess the effectiveness of a variety of trading strategies over the date range of the analysis.

Strategy Definition

Before we look at the multi-strategy comparisons, let's continue with the examination of RSI. Clicking the pencil icon next to RSI will take us to the Strategy Definition page. It has predefined the RSI (14) as the factor. The trading strategy can be sub-categorized as follows:

	Action		Condition		
1	Cover & Go long	When	RSI	Crosses above	30
2	Cover & Go short	When	RSI	Crosses below	70

Simulation Control

Clicking the Simulation Control tab will display the testing parameters. These include whether we allow both long and short trades or just focus on one leg of the trade. If it is too costly to do short trades, one can test only taking the long side and see what the profit looks like. There is also an important parameter, such as the window of the test with the maximum of 25 years. There is also a setting for currency. For transaction costs, one can account for the commission both in terms of per trade or proportion to the value. Finally, the simulation also allows for price slippage as a form of opportunity cost. For example, if the market is moving fast, there will be a gap between the signal generated and the trade executed. Adding an additional cost to each trade will estimate a more realistic and conservative outcome of the strategy.

The default strategy is long and short with an initial investment of $100 million. The strategy will enter the position the next day once the signal is generated using today's closing price. The entry trade price for the strategy is set to the next day market's opening price. But this is not necessarily always available; for example, not all investors can participate in the market opening auction. A more conservative approach can be taken by assuming a trade can be transacted at the next day's market close instead of open.

Strategy Analysis

Once we are happy with the simulation control setup we click on [Analyze] to see the simulation result (Figure 7.17 and Table 7.13).

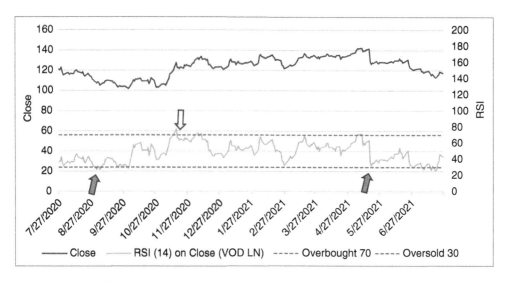

Figure 7.17   Vodafone RSI.
Source: BLOOMBERG PROFESSIONAL®.

TABLE 7.13   Vodafone RSI performance summary

Statistics	Long	Short	Total
Trades	2	1	3
Wins	1	1	2
Losses	1	0	1
% P&L	9.4	1.45	10.85

Additional Stats	Stats
Avg Duration	76
Sharpe Ratio	0.65
Sortino Ratio	1.17
Total Return	10.85
% Max Return	17.38
% Min Return	-6.58
% Winning Ratio	66.67
% Losing Ratio	33.33
% Max DD	19.56
Max DD Length	119
Recover From Max DD	N/A
Recover Period	N/A
% Max Increase	25.64
Increase Length	32

Source: BLOOMBERG PROFESSIONAL®.

TABLE 7.14 Comparison of TA strategies: Vodafone

Strategy	Long	Short	Total	%Total
Stochastics (TAS)	7	7	14	51.44071952
MA Oscillator	12	13	25	41.10621058
William's %R	8	7	15	36.07532236
Accum/Distrib Osc	71	70	141	30.70400512
Cmdty Channel Idx	9	8	17	27.86355622
Bollinger Bands	5	4	9	17.389491
Trading Envelopes (TE)	5	4	9	17.389491
KBand	8	7	15	13.12327292
RSI	2	1	3	10.84943878
Exponential MA	7	7	14	5.98752514
MA Envelopes	5	4	9	5.26026456
Buy & Hold	1	0	1	-3.22580328
Rate of Change	65	64	129	-9.10335942
DMI	10	10	20	-9.44779796
Triangular MA	8	8	16	-12.95399772
Variable MA	14	14	28	-17.91842396
Parabolic (PTPS)	13	12	25	-20.58456888
Weighted MA	9	9	18	-20.72140236
Rex Oscillator	51	50	101	-28.00343482
Simple MA	12	12	24	-31.78397982
MACD	12	12	24	-32.34136548
Fear & Greed	11	11	22	-34.06062346
Ichimoku (GOC)	6	6	12	-34.33527064

Source: BLOOMBERG PROFESSIONAL®.

From the report we can see that it generates three signals with two of them being correct and the overall strategy earns 10.85% with a Sharpe ratio of 0.65. However, to evaluate the performance of the strategy, one needs to compare the performance with the buy and hold benchmark and also other strategies. By default, the BTST produces a multi-strategy comparison.

Comparison of TA Strategies

Let's return to the comparison screen and see what is working for Vodafone across this year (Table 7.14). Table 7.14 sorts the strategies by their total profit for the year. It shows that the best strategy Stochastics (TAS) generated a paper gain of 51.44%. This strategy trades 14 times. We can also see the RSI, although not as good as other strategies, at least beats the buy and hold in this period.

Application

Suppose you would like to adopt or follow a strategy. The first thing you can do is to set an alert for this strategy by clicking on the bell shape △ next to the strategy in the multi-strategy display.

It will prompt you to save the strategy to your account. Then you can edit the alert parameters.

The Alert frequency is set as once per day. For higher frequency alerts there is an option to set as frequently as 30 seconds. You can set this strategy for the next 365 calendar days. For the delivery method, most of the options are related to delivering the alert within the BLOOMBERG PROFESSIONAL® platform. To obtain an alert when you are not logging into BLOOMBERG PROFESSIONAL®, you should choose Message. The alert will deliver to your BLOOMBERG PROFESSIONAL® message (see the tips for forwarding alerts to your non-BLOOMBERG PROFESSIONAL® email address).

Tips

Forwarding Alerts to Your Email Address
   Type MRUL {go}; select ALRT MSG Type; select Forward the MSG to and input your email address. You can have multiple emails entered, separated by a semicolon.

In summary, the use of the BLOOMBERG PROFESSIONAL® system for TA studies has two advantages. First, it has comprehensive and high-quality historical data for backtesting. Second, it has a good collection of the standard algorithms, with a flexible structure to integrate them into a more advanced system.

EXERCISES

Conduct BTST for a security of your choice and answer the following questions.

1. What is the best strategy if we conduct the analysis at the end of 2000?
2. If from year 2000 onward, we do the test annually and pick the winning strategy of last year to the next year, can this strategy beat the market?
3. Is your finding consistent if you try the same test on another security?

CHAPTER 8

Quants and Alternative Investments

INTRODUCTION

This final chapter discusses the Quants approach to investing and it is a natural follow on to the Technical Analysis in Chapter 7. Quant investing (often known simply as Quants) is not a million miles away from Technical Analysis, it is just more sophisticated in its pattern recognition. It uses the huge power of modern computers, statistical techniques, and massive amounts of data to spot the smallest of patterns and how these might proceed, given price movements. Technical analysis was first developed in the late 1800s/early 1900s, well before the advent of computers, and used the human eye to spot patterns and shapes, Quants is just the modern-day equivalent. However, this does not mean Technical Analysis is redundant. A lot of retail investors do not have the elements needed to make Quants work for them, also they will rarely have the investment size needed to make the most of the fraction of percentage gains that often characterize Quant analysis.

However, what makes Quants a stand-alone investment approach is the emergence of the data-driven economy, given the rapid development in information technology. If data are the new 'oil' that companies and nations compete to obtain, the financial investment decision will naturally evolve by gathering more data and it does not matter if you rely on a fundamental or technical approach to formulating your investment decisions. The quantitative investment approach could well be the dominant force in the investment services industry in the next 20 years. A byproduct of the Covid-19 lockdown is the acceleration of the trend to go digital and automation.[1]

The rise of artificial intelligence (AI), in combination with Big Data, makes concepts previously unquantifiable possible to capture and forecast. One example is Warren Buffett's investment in Occidental Petroleum in 2019. Two days before the announcement of the $10 bn investment helping Occidental's acquisition of Anadarko Petroleum, senior management from Occidental Petroleum flew to Omaha to have a secret meeting with Warren Buffett. This secret, however, was decoded by an alternative data company call Quandl who tracks flight details of private jets. Clients of Quandl, most of them are hedge funds, would receive an alert about this unexpected visit, triggering speculation of a potential investment opportunity.

Similarly, using satellite images, alternative data companies can help track the traffic flow of a company's warehouse car park providing useful information to 'nowcast' sales. Speech processing and textual analysis of a director's speech during a conference call can abstract the mood and confidence of the speakers about what they said. In the past, these were science fiction, and mainstream economists would see them as third-order importance or not relevant at all. With the evolution of the data infrastructure and financial markets, more data-driven strategies are being tested and implemented. In this chapter, we offer a brief walkthrough of Quant investing history and we will encounter some of the richest and most influential individuals, due to their ability to use data and machines for automating investment decisions. We will learn about some of their secrets of success and the danger of catastrophic failures.

BACKGROUND

Jim Simons

While we have covered quite a few technical analysis experts in the Chapter 7, in terms of Quant investors, we will focus mainly on Jim Simons, the best known of this type of investor – however, we touch on other Quant investors

---

[1] Credit Suisse is investing more in technology as part of the overhaul of its investment bank, with chief executive Thomas Gottstein saying that Covid-19 has 'accelerated' trends, including digitization. Meanwhile, UBS chief executive Sergio Ermotti said during the bank's second quarter earnings call that the pandemic had sped up clients' 'shift to digital'. https://www.fnlondon.com/articles/ex-goldman-veteran-marty-chavez-virus-will-speed-up-tech-takeover-of-wall-street-20200804

as we progress through the chapter. Quant investing, as we discussed in the introduction, is the use of powerful computers, Big Data, statistical techniques, and large amounts of money to make the most of 'small percentage' gains. Given all of this, it is not surprising that Quant investors tend to be a secretive bunch. An extensive search revealed nothing of real substance beyond what is available for Jim Simons, hence the focus.

Jim Simons was born in the US in 1938 as the single child of a Jewish shoe manufacturer. He showed early promise in mathematics and he is as well known as an outstanding mathematician as an investment expert. Unlike many experts in this book, he showed no real interest in investment until relatively late on in his life – compare this to Buffett. His mathematical/statistical techniques have no need to understand company finances, corporate life, etc., unlike the Buffett approach. In many ways, he could be applying his techniques to any large data (e.g. dust particles from space) but he happened on data that could offer very significant (in fact, almost unimaginable) monetary rewards.

Simons has a BSc in mathematics from MIT and he completed his PhD at Berkeley in 1962. After completing his doctorate, he went to work for the National Security Agency and focused on breaking codes. From 1964 to 1968, he worked for the research division of the Institute for Defense Analyses (and taught mathematics at MIT and Harvard). In 1968, he then became a full-time academic and was chairman of the mathematics department at Stony Brook University until 1978. He has received outstanding awards for his mathematical work and he is still active – giving academic presentations, etc. He is famous for his work on pattern recognition and contributed to the early work on string theory.

He established Renaissance Technologies (RT) (his hedge fund) in 1982 and brought a lot of his academic insights into play. Basically, RT (and the associated Medallion Fund that is only open to family and friends – see later) use Quant methods (often automated) to look for non-random movements in big, financial data. His early successes seem to be based on a lot of intuition (where to look for the non-random movements) and luck, and seem to derive from the fairly solid premise that most series of financial data have a tendency to mean revert. He also started to understand the importance of momentum and how markets can get carried away (cf. Jesse Livermore in Chapter 7).

Many see Simons as the greatest investor of all time, given the performance of his funds – his Medallion Fund made an average annualized net (after fees) return of 39% across the period from 1988 to 2018 and nobody comes close to this level of consistent performance. The performance has been helped by the very long bull run (see later) and his ability to attract Quant investor stars (mathematicians, physicists, signal specialists, and statisticians). By 2019, he had $55 billion under management in his funds. One of the attractions of working with Jim Simons is the ability to be part of the Medallion Fund with its impressive returns – this only being available to 'family and friends'. To put this performance into context – $1 invested in 1988 in Medallion would be worth $20,000 in 2018 (net of fees), while investing in the S&P 500 would have led to $20 and even investing with Buffett would 'only' have given $100.

In terms of the Renaissance Technology fund, that is open to the investment community, there has been some controversy over how its performance has lagged behind that of the Medallion Fund. The controversy may have been added to by the 'high' charging structure of RT. While the normal practice in the hedge fund industry is to have an annual charge of 2% and a 20% performance fee, RT went for a 5% (annual fee) and 44% (performance fee) structure – aggressive from most perspectives. But given the performance any investor achieved post fees, then the charges may well be more than reasonable. Another area of controversy has been RT's use of complex 'basket' options to shield the day-to-day trading gains from income tax (estimates suggest the tax shields may have saved RT more than $6.8bn over a decade). However, even the best models cannot cope with 'black swan' events. RT lost 7% in February 2020 and it is down 12% on the year to date (early April 2020). But these short-term losses have to be set against the staggering long-term gains that have been produced by an unemotional attachment to the results of models. We doubt Simons would be willing to swap the rigour of his approach for the intuition of Jesse Livermore.

While Simons may have been criticized for some of his tax practices, there can be no doubt over the scale of his philanthropy. He and his wife (Marilyn) have been in the top 50 of US Givers since the list was launched in 2013. In 2015, they donated $298 million for education and research in maths and science – this placed them in the top 10 Givers for that year. Such giving does not include funds given to Foundations – and Simons has a significant Foundation for similar activities.

KEY LESSONS

A 25-Sigma Event

We have noted that Quant investors are a 'secretive bunch' and this is because they work on small margins of 'performance' and big bets. To let others know the source of the small margins would be to give away wealth and potentially create losses for themselves if too many others 'piled' into the market, backing the 'same bets'. Because of this we have again changed tack in this chapter and we are going to 'walk through' the lessons gained by Goldman Sachs in their use of Quant models at the height of the financial crisis in 2007. As we will see, it is a salutary lesson on understanding the risks as well as the benefits of Quant models. We have already seen some of the benefits when we discussed Jim Simons.

At the height of the financial crisis, David Viniar, the Goldman Sachs CFO, stated he was seeing value reductions in their Quant position that you should never see in a number of lifetimes, never mind it being repeated on a number of consecutive days. He referred to it as a 25-sigma event which is about equivalent to winning a lottery in the UK more than 20 times in a row.[2] Its Global Equity Opportunities fund suffered such heavy losses that it took the unprecedented step of putting $2 bn of its own capital in the fund in August 2007. Other Quant funds suffered similar large-scale losses. PDT (Process Driven Trading), led by Peter Muller, lost $600 million of Morgan Stanley's money over just two days. For the two funds of Renaissance Technologies, Medallion lost more than $1 billion that week, a stunning 20%; RIEF (Renaissance Institutional Equities Fund) was down nearly $3 billion, or about 10%. In the industry, this is known as the 'quant quake'.

What should have been learnt from this episode is that Quant models do have risks attached to them, and if they go wrong on a leveraged position (and they usually are, given the small percentages involved), they can end up being very costly, very quickly.

So what went wrong with the Goldman Sachs' position? A lot of the Quant funds at the time were using sophisticated variations of value stocks and momentum – in a sense, what else is there? These strategies worked well until somebody decided to pull their money from the Quant fund. To meet the cash

---

[2]K. Dowd, J. Cotter, C. Humphrey, and M. Woods, How unlucky is 25-Sigma? (2011). https://arxiv.org/ftp/arxiv/papers/1103/1103.5672.pdf

demands they had to reverse their long and short positions and this just made matters worse for other Quant funds using similar strategies, e.g. selling long positions forces prices down and the cascade begins. What the Quant boys had not allowed for was the risk that other Quant players had similar strategies and there was a potential for a stampede once some 'bad news' emerged, e.g. a quarter of Renaissance's holdings are shared by rivals Quant funds which clearly increases the systemic risk of the Quant world as a whole.

In addition to the tail risk of a number of players responding in the same way to an event, there is the additional risk of any marginal gains being short-lived. The Quant guys are searching Big Data sets for every margin of success, and they often use the same data, the same techniques, and read the same academic research (i.e. one piece of literature of interest might be the one on anomalies) – so it would be surprising, in the extreme, if any given strategy (even allowing for secrecy) would have much longevity. What lessons should be taken from this case? First, do not expect Quant strategies to have a long shelf life. Second, there needs to be a constant search for new margins. Third, leveraged positions can turn costly very quickly and the effectiveness of risk control would make or break a fund or even the wider financial ecosystem.

APPLYING THE LESSONS: QUANT INVESTING

As noted on a few occasions in this chapter, Quant investors are by nature secretive and because of this, it is difficult to fully describe what is going on in any particular fund. What differentiates Quant funds from other non-Quant funds are the information sources. Quants build their advantage on algorithms and data, while traditional hedge funds work on their private information through network insiders and industry experts. To this end, all of the lessons in this book are data-driven interpretations of the insights of expert investors. And they can all be implemented via rules and data-driven strategies. We will see they belong to families of style/factor investing promoted by funds such as AQR Capital.

Early Quant Funds and Their Strategies

The goal of quantitative finance is to identify predictability which is the same as what the traditional economic model tries to achieve. What is different between these two is the starting point. Traditional economic models start with theories and principles that are supposed to guide human behaviour and inter-action to predict how these agents' behaviours will lead to a set of predictable outcomes in equilibrium. Quants start with the data and use whatever tech-niques are available to help them identify patterns that are likely to persist in the future (i.e. the patterns have statistical significance and are not merely random observations).

This is why the best Quants do not have backgrounds in business or eco-nomics. It would take a lot of courage for an economist to trust a model without knowing what are the underlying drivers of the system. By contrast, a researcher from natural sciences would feel at ease in trusting what the data and mathematical model tell them.

Having said that, one of the world's most famous hedge funds, **Long-Term Capital Management** LP (LTCM), was led by economists and not just any economists. Myron S. Scholes and Robert C. Merton led LTCM and have the distinction of both being Nobel Prize laureates in Economics. The rise and fall of this fund offer many valuable lessons to fellow Quant investors.

LTCM's main strategy belongs to a broader category of **statistical arbi-trage**. Statistical arbitrage often involves two steps. First, identify a pool of securities that have high comovements (guided by economic reasons, e.g. two leaders in the same industry or by evidence of high historical correlations). Second, monitor the pair to identify divergence in the pair's price movements and take positions in betting on the convergence of the prices to their long-term relationship. Hence, such a strategy is also known as convergence trades. This approach is a natural extension to some of those TA strategies we dis-cussed in Chapter 7 but involves data from more than one security. LTCM enjoyed great success when applying this in the fixed income markets gener-ating more than 50% return annually and attracting billions of inflow in the period between 1994 and 1997, managing close to $7 billion in the summer of 1997.

Most of the Quant strategies, such as statistical arbitrage, spot only small profitability opportunities that require frequent trading. Therefore, to make it worthwhile, **large leverage** is needed to improve the overall return. This sig-nificantly increases the liquidity risk of the funds. The LTCM fund eventually needed a government bailout in 1998 due to their inability to continue funding their leveraged positions during the Russian financial crisis.

One aspect of Quant strategies is the frequency of their trades. Since the markets are competitive, arbitrage opportunities are small and short-lived. High-frequency trading (HFT) is an integral part of many Quant strategies.

For example, **ultra-high frequency trading (UHFT)** is made possible due to the modernization of stock exchanges partly due to the pressure from Quant hedge funds. Among them, E.D. Shaw was referred to as 'King Quant' by *Fortune* magazine in 1996 because of his firm's pioneering role in high-speed quantitative trading.

David Shaw holds a PhD from Stanford University in 1980 and became an Assistant Professor of computing sciences at Columbia University. He joined Morgan Stanley in 1986 in their automated proprietary trading group and set up his own hedge fund (D. E. Shaw & Co) in 1988 which specialized in preparatory algorithmic trading. Although his fund was also affected by the Russian crisis in the late 1990s, it survived and recovered. Another Quant expert in the late 1980s, Ken Griffin, installed a satellite dish on his dormitory roof at Harvard to get up-to-the-second quotes and was using high-powered computers to make statistical-arbitrage trades from a fund of $13 billion.

These experts use similar statistical arbitrages in spotting arbitrage opportunities in a very short timeframe; eventually, competing in milliseconds in the twenty-first century. One example of UHFT is the use of order book information. Signals are constructed based on the order imbalance to anticipate next trades and the funds step in to provide liquidity on both the buy and sell sides of the market – acting like dealers and earning the appropriate 'spread'. Therefore, modern UHFT eventually becomes an arms race with firms competing for fast computing power and differential speed of connection to the exchange server – in this situation, milliseconds matter. Co-location (locating computers owned by HFT firms and proprietary traders in the same premises where an exchange's computer servers are housed) has become a lucrative business of exchanges.

However, there is also a dark side to HFT. HFT trading firms are very secretive about their activities; while their growth in the market has been fast and significant. For example, Citadel Securities, formed in 2002, is the HFT market-making arm of Citadel LLC, the financial institution founded by Ken Griffin in 1990. Citadel was managing over $30 bn in assets across multiple investment strategies by 2018. Another of the biggest players is Getco LLC, a proprietary algorithmic trading and electronic market-making firm based in Chicago. It was founded in 1999 by two former floor traders – Stephen Schuler and Daniel Tierney. A proprietary private company means they only trade owners' money and, therefore, they do not need to disclose their finance or explain how they make money to anyone. However, by 2009, firms like Citadel and Getco quickly had become significant players in the US stock market and accounted for

10–20% of the daily trading volume of many US stocks, including highly traded names such as General Electric Co., Oracle Corp. and Google Inc.[3] HFT firms are the new 'market makers' in the US network of stock exchanges: such as the CME, Eurex, NYSE Arca, NYSE Arca Options, BATS, Nasdaq, Nasdaq Options, Chi-X, BrokerTec, and eSpeed.

At the same time, many traditional brokerage firms started experiencing increasing transaction costs. Quotes on their trading terminal became untradable. When they placed their orders on their terminals, as soon as they hit the enter button, the quotes disappeared and their trades were executed at worse prices. The links between the rise of HFT and the 'illusion of quotes appearing on trading terminals' were discovered by traders in the Royal Bank of Canada. The story of the battle between the traditional brokers and HFT is vividly depicted by Michael Lewis in his international bestseller, *Flash Boys*.[4]

Ironically, the origin of this was triggered by one piece of regulation by the Security and Exchange Commission (SEC). To make sure brokers executed at the best price on behalf of their clients in the network of exchanges in the US, the SEC passed the Regulation National Market System in 2005 and implemented it in 2007. It requires brokers to find the best quote in the whole system for their clients, otherwise, they risk losing their licences. To comply with this regulation, all brokerage firms need to have an aggregate view of all the available quotes and route the orders to the exchange in order of their price priority. Naturally, all these tasks are best done by an algorithm executed by a network of machines. It serves the purpose until an HFT spots what a difference a millisecond can make in this segmented market.

Why does speed matter? When a broker hits enter for a large order, their algorithm will route the order to the exchanges which have the best quotes. Large orders will be split according to the market depth (the number of shares at that best quote) sending part of the order to the exchanges with the best quotes and the rest of the order to the exchange with the next best quotes. The basic trick an HFT can do is to post quotes for stock in many exchanges with the best price but a small depth (e.g. selling Apple at $150, 1000 shares). When a broker posts a large buy order (e.g. buying 1 million shares of Apple), one of the split orders will reach one of the exchanges faster than the other (due to the different connection speed and distance to stock exchanges). The HFT will

[3] S. Patterson, 'Meet Getco, high-frequency trade king'. WSJ.com, 27 August 2009. Online.wsj.com. (accessed 26 June 2011).

[4] M.M. Lewis, *Flash Boys: Cracking the Money Code* (London: Penguin Books, 2015).

transact with this trade to gain the information of this buying interest from this broker. Then they will: (1) withdraw all their other best quotes in other exchanges; (2) buy from the existing best quotes from those markets (e.g. at $149); and (3) post a worse selling price on the system (e.g. at $151). In doing so, they are anticipating the rest of the split orders to arrive in the other exchanges. The only way they can do this is because of two things: (1) brokers' orders reach different exchanges at different times (there is the latency between hitting the enter key and reaching the stock exchange); and (2) HFTs have faster speed access to all markets than the broker, hence co-location is valuable. Since brokers' connections with the exchanges have variable speed, one of their split orders will arrive first before the rest. The HFT uses the best execution rule by posting the best price to obtain potential trading interest and front-run the rest of the orders in those markets where it takes 'longer' for the brokers' orders to reach. And the difference only needs to be in less than one millisecond. The consequence, among other things, is that the quotes on most of the brokers' trading terminals are not obtainable and their transaction costs are higher on average.

Style/Factor Investing Fund

Arbitrage strategies have scale-up limitations and this is part of the reason why successful Quant funds limit access to their funds and even return monies to investors in order to maintain an optimal size. For example, before being hit by the Russian crisis, LTCM returned $2.7 bn to investors in Q4 of 1997, citing concerns about the shortage of opportunities. The limitation is due to the **market impact** of their trades. Since the expected gain is small and requires frequent trading, small transaction costs can take away all the gain, especially when they are needed to trade a large position. A more scalable Quant fund emerges from what we have learned through this book: style investing that later became known as factor investing.

AQR Capital Management was one of the early adopters of style investing. It was founded by Clifford Asness, a University of Chicago PhD. The basic strategies such as Value and Momentum are often referenced in their strategies and in many other Quant funds, such as Alpha Architect. The important advance in their approach is a multi-strategies approach that produces a more diversified quantitative approach. Importantly, through the search for factors, they can identify and engineer a portfolio that has a low correlation with other asset classes. AQR is constantly looking for new ideas from the academic world. It awards a $100,000 annual prize to up to three papers (sharing the overall prize money) to encourage and acknowledge academics whose research promises to be of significant use to institutional investors.

A look at some of their recent winning papers confirms the direction of their search in factor investing. For example, the 2019 winning paper, by Kelly Shue from Yale, proposes that the difference in low and high price stocks is due to the non-proportional thinking of investors; more specifically, it shows the price level will affect investors' bias. Stock price movements are often reported and discussed in the dollar rather than percentage units, which may cause investors to think that news should correspond to a dollar change in price rather than a percentage change in price. Non-proportional thinking in financial markets can lead to return under-reaction for high-priced stocks and over-reaction for low-priced stocks. The research finding can be used to refine existing strategies by taking price level into consideration. It also partially resolves the puzzle of why companies manage their price levels by stock splits. For example, Apple Inc. carried out two significant splits of 7 to 1 and 4 to 1 in 2014 and 2020, respectively, to keep its share price lower than $100.

Macro-Based Quants

Ray Dalio started building his systematic approach to investing in commodity futures in the 1970s. His quantitative approach to global markets earned the trust of sovereign and large pension funds around the world. His hedge fund, Bridgewater, was the world's largest eight straight years in a row with a total fund of $124.7 billion at the end of 2017. The models developed by Dalio in the early days were economic theory-driven, coupled with standard econometric techniques to understand the systematic causal effects among the major markets. His success originated in his conviction in collecting, analysing, and building a systematic model to understand the flow of information and money across the markets. In particular, he built a multi-asset system, including interest rates, stock, currencies, and precious metal systems that would enable him to see a broader picture than the other normally narrow-focused fund managers. Dalio is not shy of sharing his insights. Through his systematic data collection and analysis, he famously and correctly predicted a few market downturns, including the 2007–2008 crisis.

In his book, *Principles*,[5] Dalio talks a lot about his principles and how he has developed them. There is an interesting insight regarding how he 'interacts' with his system. The biggest problem facing all Quant managers is how far they should trust their models and when and, if ever, they should over-rule the machine. During the stock market crash of 1987, investors were failed by sophisticated models and LTCM saw historic losses when they stuck to their arbitrage algorithm in 1988. These instances taught Jim Simons of Renaissance to over-rule his Quant model during 'the quant quake' in August 2007. Dalio's approach with his system is to 'learn' with it. He systematically documents his reasons for decision making and compares his decisions with those made by the machine and explores the reasons for any differences. Sometimes through the investigation, he finds out that it was because he overlooked certain data and the system taught him something new. On other occasions, he realizes something is missing in the model and he adds new criteria. This 'cultivating' approach to 'machine learning' is a good approach until 'deep and true' artificial intelligence emerges.

The Rise of Artificial Intelligence and Alternative Data

Renaissance Technologies, founded by Jim Simons, is arguably, as discussed in the introduction, the most successful Quant fund ever. The firm employs statistical arbitrage and pattern recognition in their strategies. The founding of their equity Quant unit was led by members of a former IBM speech recognition team (Peter Brown and Robert Mercer) who joined Renaissance in 1994. What is the similarity between speech recognition and predicting stock prices? According to this team, both of these processes can be viewed as being guided by a hidden Markov model: the output of a sequence in which each step along the way is random, yet dependent on the previous step. They developed a system that enables them to run a fully automated trading system (with very little human interference), trading between 150,000 and 300,000 trades a day. The importance of their contribution to the success of the Medallion Fund, the flagship fund of Renaissance, is evidenced by the fact that both of them became co-CEOs when Jim Simons stepped down in 2009.

With the digitalization of so many aspects of our lives (think of the Internet of Things), there is now a huge amount of data that was not available before. This gives machines some advantage over humans in terms of

---

[5] R. Dalio, *Principles: Life and Work* (New York: Simon & Schuster, 2017).

digesting and reacting to new information. Although the human brain is the most advanced intelligence we know of, the machine has the advantage of carrying out procedures more consistently and with less obvious biases. As instantaneous information and constant volatility are the new realities of global markets, the advantage of machines is much more apparent when fast and frequent decisions are required. And this is precisely the core of the competition in the Quants world. The abundance of Big Data has led to new waves of innovation in Artificial Technology, driven in part by technology giants such as Google.

Two Sigma, a hedge fund founded by a team with members from D. E. Shaw in 2001, is another leading proponent of AI. In addition to their in-house algorithm development, they also tap into the power of the internet through 'crowdsourcing'. They openly run many competitions for the use of AI in investment, such as the Halite AI Programming Challenge. There are other similar coding-trading platforms such as Quantopian, which is backed by Point72.

Investors who are looking for an edge could also try to obtain data from alternative sources, such as social media sentiments, weather forecasts, major shipping ports' traffic, job advertisements, etc. In exploring these new possibilities, hedge funds have increasingly begun to hire *data analysts*.[6] For example, to gauge the economic recovery from Covid-19 in an area, real-time energy consumption proved useful. Some of the alternative data methods use old data but a new technique to process them. For example, news-reading algorithms can be used to spot a change of sentiment and inform investment decisions.

Providing alternative data has also become a vital and valuable service to the hedge fund industry. Even before coronavirus struck in 2020, total annual spending on such alternative information by fund managers alone was predicted to reach more than $1.7 bn (alternativedata.org).

EMPIRICAL EVIDENCE

Performance of Hedge Funds

At the end of 2017, according to Institutional Investors, five of the six biggest funds (based on the 2018 ranking) relied largely or fully on computers to make

---

[6]https://www.ft.com/content/586b4ea6-48f4-11ea-aee2-9ddbdc86190d (accessed 27 July 2021).

their investment decisions. They are Bridgewater Associates ($124.7 bn), AQR ($90 bn), Renaissance Technologies ($57 bn), Two Sigma ($52 bn) and D.E. Shaw ($39 bn).

However, while these firms have been successful in attracting fund flow, their performance is not overly impressive (Figure 8.1 and Table 8.1).

Figure 8.1 reports a comparison of returns from various hedge fund indexes and the S&P500 index. We can see the two composite indexes: HFRIFWI and HFRXGL both underperformed SPX significantly over the past 15 years. Many of these hedge funds use quantitative strategies. A plot of the quantitative hedge fund index will produce a similar pattern. This evidence suggests that

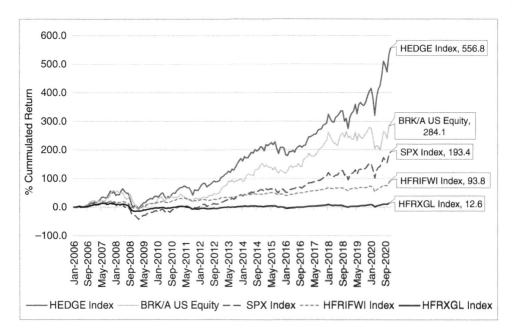

FIGURE 8.1 Hedge fund return comparisons, 2006–2020.
Source: BLOOMBERG PROFESSIONAL®.

TABLE 8.1 List of hedge funds and equity indexes

Security	Brief description
HEDGE Index	Wells Fargo Hedge FD TR Index
BRK/A US Equity	BERKSHIRE HATHAWAY INC-CL A
SPX Index	S&P 500 Index
HFRIFWI Index	Hedge Fund Research HFRI Fund Weighted Composite Index
HFRXGL Index	Hedge Fund Research HFRX Global Hedge Fund Index

TABLE 8.2 Market beta of HEDGE fund index

Linear beta	Stats
Raw BETA	1.031
Adjusted BETA	1.02
ALPHA (Intercept)	0.451
R^2 (Correlation^2)	0.887
R (Correlation)	0.942

Source: BLOOMBERG PROFESSIONAL®.

beating the market is difficult even for the 'sophisticated' investors. It was backed by this evidence that Warren Buffett was confident in winning his bet against hedge fund managers. By contrast, his fund was able to outperform the market during the same period by more than 90%.

Among the indexes, the HEDGE index is an unusual one. It can be considered as a hybrid of hedge fund and market wisdom. This index measures the performance of the 100 largest positions in equities and equity-related securities that are listed on the NYSE or NASDAQ, reportable on Form 13F and are held by hedge funds or managed accounts advised by alternative managers. A large aggregate concentration of a holding indicates the collective wisdom of the hedge fund managers. Focusing only on holdings in publicly listed companies that are larger in size captures the market's wisdom as it is closer to the passive indexing of selecting the largest companies in a market. To be included in this index, the market capitalization needs to be greater than $500 million.[7] This index evidently outperforms the market although it has a close correlation with the market. We report the estimation of the beta using SPX as the market index (Table 8.2). It shows that this index has a very similar risk profile to the market but earns a 0.45% monthly alpha during these 15 years. This outperformance suggests some skills in the hedge fund managers collectively in selecting securities in their portfolio.

Not surprisingly, this fund contains well-known stocks such as Facebook, Apple, Alphabet, Amazon, and Microsoft. What makes the difference is probably the selection from those less well-known or glamorous stocks. One can look further into such a list online. For example, Hedgefollow.com

---

[7] See Wells Fargo Research methodology document:
https://www.wellsfargoresearch.com/Indices/Download?indicesId=12e1ee33-a906-4453-b611-b32dbbd5b70b&fileType=Index%20Methodology (accessed 27 July 2021).

maintains a list of stocks with the highest number of hedge fund owners according to Form 13F filings.[8]

Academic Literature on AI and Alternative Data in Finance

There is some emerging academic literature examining the use of AI and alternative data for investment decisions.

Gu, Kelly, and Xiu use a variety of machine learning techniques (including boosted regression trees, neural networks and random forests) to predict monthly stock returns. They use a set of 90 'factors' and eight macro variables as their main predictors.[9] Their key conclusion is that machine learning methods, and neural networks in particular, significantly outperform both a simple three-factor model like the Fama-French (1993)[10] model and a linear regression model that uses all available factors. For example, a value-weighted long-short decile spread strategy that takes positions based on stock-level neural network forecasts earns an annualized out-of-sample Sharpe ratio of 1.35, more than doubling the performance of a leading regression-based strategy from the literature.

Similarly, Guida and Coqueret apply extreme gradient boosted trees to build enhanced diversified equity portfolios.[11] Their goal is to predict the 12-month (sector-relative) performance of individual stocks using a large number of features. They report significant gains in risk-adjusted performance on a simple multifactor portfolio. The factor exposure of the resulting strategy, nevertheless, remains consistent with a traditional multifactor portfolio. The authors conclude that tree-based models can be useful to avoid 'crowding' in quantitative strategies.

Another branch of the literature examines news sentiment. Before the popularity of the internet, Klibanoff et al. examined the front page of the *New York Times* and report that country-specific news affects country fund prices.[12] A series of larger-scale textual analysis studies were conducted by Paul Tetlock and published in the *Journal of Finance* from 2007 to 2010. In his

---

[8] https://hedgefollow.com/stocks

[9] S. Gu, B. Kelly, and D. Xiu, Empirical asset pricing via machine learning, *The Review of Financial Studies* 33(5) (2020): 2223–2273.

[10] E.F. Fama and K.R. French, Common risk factors in the returns on stocks and bonds. *Journal of Financial Economics* 33(1) (1993): 3–56.

[11] T. Guida and G. Coqueret, Ensemble learning applied to quant equity: Gradient boosting in a multifactor framework. In T. Guida (ed.) *Big Data and Machine Learning in Quantitative Investment* (Hoboken, NJ: John Wiley & Sons, 2019).

[12] P. Klibanoff, O. Lamont, and T.A. Wizman, Investor reaction to salient news in closed-end country funds. *The Journal of Finance* 53 (1998): 673–699.

study, 'Giving content to investor sentiment: The role of media in the stock market', he uses 'bag-of-words' algorithms to construct quantitative news sentiment scores from a *Wall Street Journal* column.[13] The study results showed that high media pessimism forecasts falling stock market prices.

Uhl, Pedersen, and Malitius use a commercial news sentiment database provided by NewsAnalytics from Thomson Reuters.[14] The database contained more than 100,000 Reuters news items per week from 2003. They show that by using aggregated company news and macro news sentiment, a tactical asset allocation strategy switching between equity and bonds can produce a Sharpe ratio of 1.5, compared with the benchmark's 0.7.

News sentiment is also found to be an important media affecting other anomalies or factor returns, such as momentum and accounting-based anomalies. Hillert et al. show that companies subject to greater media coverage exhibit a higher degree of momentum.[15] This effect is contingent on the article tone and reverses in the long run. Similarly, Engelberg, Mclean, and Pontiff study a sample of 97 stock return anomalies and find that anomaly returns are 50% higher on corporate news days and are six times higher on earnings announcement days.[16] These types of study suggest the use of news sentiment can be a potential source for enhancing the alpha of existing strategies.

Bai and Cai demonstrate an application of adaptive machine learning on predicting the volatility index (VIX) with nearly 300 economic variables. They demonstrate some promising out-of-sample forecasts that can be translated into a profitable quantitative strategy.[17]

SUMMARY

- The debate over fundamental vs technical approaches comes to a simple conclusion – they do not need to be mutually exclusive.

---

[13] P.C. Tetlock, Giving content to investor sentiment: The role of media in the stock market. *The Journal of Finance* 62 (2007): 1139–1168.

[14] M. Uhl, M. Pedersen, and O. Malitius, What's in the news? Using news sentiment momentum for tactical asset allocation. *Journal of Portfolio Management* 41(2) (2015): 100–112.

[15] A. Hillert, H. Jacobs, and S. Müller, Media makes momentum. *Review of Financial Studies, Society for Financial Studies* 27(12) (2014): 3467–3501.

[16] J. Engelberg, R.D. Mclean, and J. Pontiff, Anomalies and news. *The Journal of Finance* 73 (2018): 1971–2001. doi:10.1111/jofi.12718

[17] Y. Bai and C.X. Cai, Predicting VIX with adaptive machine learning (14 June 2021). Available at SSRN: https://ssrn.com/abstract=3866415

- While fundamental value will prevail in the long run, investor psychology will significantly affect asset prices in the short run. In some cases, the mispricing can persist for a long time.
- As John Maynard Keynes puts it: 'The market can remain irrational longer than you can remain solvent.'
- To capitalize from other investors' mistakes, sophisticated investors, such as Jim Simons, dedicate their time to searching for rule-based investment strategies to discipline their trades.
- With easy access to computing power and data through the internet, quantitative investment strategies will not be accessible just to hedge funds.
- This chapter provides a link between the expert ideas and the quantitative implementation through online platforms.
- All of the examples we provided in other chapters can be adopted to develop a systematic quantitative investment strategy.
- The key lessons about transaction costs, leverage, and liquidity need to be borne in mind when translating paper testing to live system implementation.
- Risk management is the key to the success of a Quant strategy.

PRACTICAL APPLICATION VII: QUANTS TOOLS

In this Practical Application section we introduce tools in BLOOMBERG PROFESSIONAL® which are relevant to developing and implementing quantitative strategies. It is important to point out that the screening (EQS) and backtesting tools (EQBT, BTST) are also an essential part of Quant strategy development for factor and technical investing strategies. In the following sections we focus on spotting arbitrage opportunities and accessing alternative data.

Simple Pair Trading Strategy

We demonstrate in BLOOMBERG PROFESSIONAL® how to identify high correlation securities and analyse their historical movement to spot divergence and pair trading opportunities.

Step 1 Correlation Finder (CFND)

The classic example is Coke and Pepsi. In BLOOMBERG PROFESSIONAL® we load the Coke security and the CFND (correlation finder) function. The CFND function allows you to study the correlations among the different peer groups and indexes. When we did this analysis on 14 July 2020, it had a 94% correlation with Pepsi during the 20 days period. Overall, during the pandemic period, stocks correlations have been very high for a given industry. This is a good starting point to examine the pair trading strategy as the two stocks are argubly most aligned at this point.

Step 2 Spread Analysis

To examine this highly correlated pair's price movement, we can load the historical return analysis (HS). HS <GO> is a charting tool that allows users to examine return for a long-short strategy.

To perform the analysis, we first load {KO US} and then load the {HS} function – this will load the Spread Analysis window. We specify {KO US Equity} in the Buy and {PEP US Equity} in the Sell entry boxes. Since the per-share prices are not comparable between the two securities, we normalize the two securities' prices to start with 100 and track the percentage change over time (Figure 8.2).

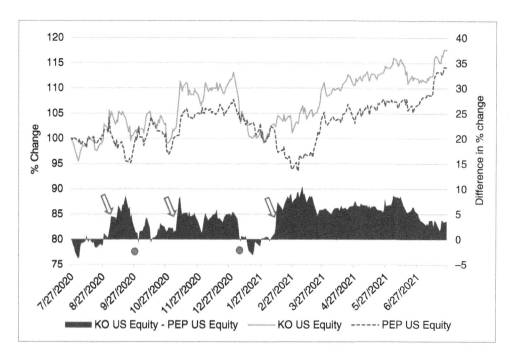

FIGURE 8.2   Spread analysis: Coke vs Pepsi.
Source: BLOOMBERG PROFESSIONAL®.

We can see that in this period Coca-Cola performs slightly better overall. Nevertheless, the two continued to comove together and cross each other. To take advantage of such divergence and convergence we need to use a quantitative rule to decide when to enter and exit the trade.

Step 3 A Pair Trading Example

To illustrate, we can consider entering this paired trade whenever the deviation is greater than 5% and exit when this difference is close to zero. When converging, it will generate about a 5% return. We can see it makes three trades in this period, all of which involve shorting Ko and longing Pep (Figure 8.2). It generates a cumulative return of 13.94% before costs with the last one still waiting for its convergence (Figure 8.3). It is important to know that this is a relatively low-risk strategy and market-neutral. It will be a good strategy to include in a portfolio to reduce overall market risk.

M&A Arbitrage

MARB < GO> allows you to monitor real-time merger and acquisition (M&A) arbitrage spread data, so you can identify deals that have potential arbitrage opportunities. You can sort the data by market measurements, region, and other deal characteristics, as well as displaying related charts and transaction details. You can then customize your view by creating custom templates.

The snapshot in Table 8.3 shows the key data for the ongoing potential M&A deals, including the identity of the target and acquirer, the deal size, and

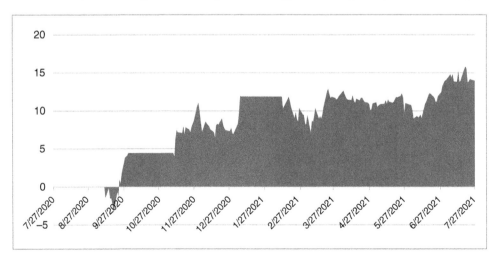

FIGURE 8.3   Cumulative pair traded return %: Coke vs Pepsi.
Source: BLOOMBERG PROFESSIONAL®.

TABLE 8.3 M&A arbitrage

Target	Acquirer	Deal Size (M)	Announced Date	Announced Premium in %	Payment Type	Offer Per Share	Target Price	Current Premium in %	Annualized Premium in %	Expected Completion Date
ELY CN	1859507D US	228.57	06/21/21	63.52	C/S	1.46	1.3	12.31	69.11	09/30/21 EXF CN
Private	132.02	06/07/21	Cash	Cash	6	5.53	8.46	47.53	09/30/21	CHNG US / UNH US
12806.69	01/06/21	40.96	Cash	25.75	21.95	17.34	40.31	12/31/21	CMO US	BESP US / 1064.99
07/26/21	19.2	7.3	6.38	6.38	14.51	33.73	12/31/21	AJRD US	LMT US	3597.15 / 12/20/20
26.22	Cash	51	47.05	8.4	19.52	12/31/21	COHR US	IIVI US	7033.89	03/25/21 / 16.12
C&S	281.13	253.03	11.11	16.41	03/31/22	FBC US	NYCB US	2626.15	04/26/21	Stk
44.19	42.36	4.31	10.02	12/31/21	ATH US	APO US	7215.38	03/08/21	25.87	67.34
64.07	5.11	9.92	01/31/22	CLDB US	FMNB US	97.63	06/23/21	21.7	C/S	26.62
3.76	8.74	12/31/21 FOE US		Private	2460.32	05/11/21	28.18	Cash	22	20.83
8.3	03/31/22									5.62 / 11.67 / Stk / 27.62

Source: BLOOMBERG PROFESSIONAL®.

the announcement day. Of special note is the announced premium, which measures the difference between the offer price and the market price of the target company at the time of the deal-making public. The higher the premium, the larger the room for the price increase for the target company as the deal nears its completion. It also displays the current (post-announcement) target company's price which, when compared with the offer price, can be used to calculate the current premium. An arbitrage strategy can be deployed by longing the target with the highest current premium. The risk of this strategy comes from the uncertainty of the successful completion of the transactions. It is often the case that larger premiums suggest greater such risk. Further research into the pairs and the key shareholder and regulatory concerns would lead to a better assessment of the arbitrage opportunity.

Alternative Data

Supply Chain Analysis (SPLC)

SPLC provides a comprehensive supply chain breakdown for a selected company, so you can analyse the revenue exposure of the central company, its suppliers, and its customers, as well as track the performance of a company against its peers. SPLC also provides access to related functions that allow you to further analyse the performance of the selected company or peer companies.

For example, supply chains can provide a lot of useful data about downstream activities. One way of estimating how many iPhones Apple is producing can be inferred from the suppliers' sales of the iPhone's raw material to the iPhone factories.

A typical supply chain database will contain important information, such as the proportion of revenue that is attributed to the specific supplier or customer, so that the significance of the relationship can be evaluated.

There is academic evidence showing that the share price movements of suppliers and customers are interlinked. For example, Pandit, Wasley, and Zach show that suppliers' stock prices react to their customers' earnings announcements.[18]

---

[18] S. Pandit, C.E. Wasley, and T. Zach, Information externalities along the supply chain: The economic determinants of suppliers' stock price reaction to their customers' earnings announcements. *Contemporary Accounting Research* 28 (2011): 1304–1343.

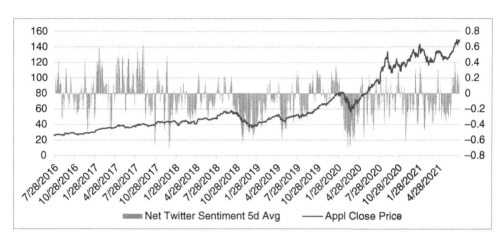

FIGURE 8.4 Intraday tweet volume and sentiments: Apple Inc.
Source: BLOOMBERG PROFESSIONAL®.

Intraday Tweet Volume and Sentiments

GT <GO>, the social activity chart, allows you to plot intraday tweet volume, positive/negative sentiment, and a list of the latest related tweets alongside pricing action for selected securities in a line chart. The following topics explain how to use a chart to analyse securities in GP <GO>.

Figure 8.4 plots the 5-day moving average net Twitter sentiment for Apple Inc. and its closing price. We can see that simple sentiments like this often serve as a contrarian signal. For example, if we go short whenever the average net sentiment is positive, this will generate 63% over these five years before costs. Such a strategy may not be attractive for investing in stocks like Apple as it has experienced significant growth during this period, as a Buy & Hold strategy will yield a return of 450%. However, this is a hindsight conclusion! A short-sentiment strategy may work if applied systematically.

Environmental, Social, and Governance Analysis, ESG <GO>

ESG < GO> provides an overview of a company's environmental, social, and governance (ESG) performance, both over time and versus its peers, so you can assess risks and opportunities that may impact a potential investment.

For each company, the summary screen of the function shows the key measures for the three categories of environmental, social, and governance. Environmental measures include greenhouse gases, energy consumption, water consumption, and waste generation in proportion to their revenues.

The social aspect of the matrix includes gender equality, employment turn-over, and safety measures. Finally, the governance measures cover the quality of corporate governance, including board independence and board attendance. The system provides statistics to track relative performance by comparing a company's history to its peers.

The relevance of such data on valuation has been studied in the academic literature. For example, Khan, Serafeim, and Yoon show that it is important to read these metrics in combination with the company's core business.[19] They show that firms that score high on all issues of ESG outperform others by 1.5% per year but the result is not statistically significant. By contrast, firms that score high on material issues and low on immaterial issues outperform others by 4.83% per year. Materiality is measured by the relevance of the matrices to the core business according to the Sustainability Accounting Standards Board Materiality Map.[20] For example, measurement related to water usage is more important to the mining and extraction business, while affordability is more important to a health care business.

In summary, there are many tools and data which can be useful to derive and implement a quantitative or data-driven strategy.

EXERCISES

1. Use the correlation finder to identify the peers of Toyota. See if you can derive a profitable strategy using the spread analysis.
2. Use the sentiment analysis function to download data for a less well-known company from S&P 500 constituent. Examine the profitability of the short-sentiment strategy.

---

[19] M. Khan, G. Serafeim, and A. Yoon, Corporate sustainability: First evidence on materiality. *The Accounting Review* 91(6) (2016): 1697–1724., Available at SSRN: https://ssrn.com/abstract=2575912 or http://dx.doi.org/10.2139/ssrn.2575912
[20] https://materiality.sasb.org/

Appendix I. Introduction to BLOOMBERG PROFESSIONAL®

The BLOOMBERG PROFESSIONAL® terminal is built on **functions** and **securities**, organized by asset class and the common workflows of financial professionals. Understanding functions, securities, and how to find and interact with them is the key to getting the most from the depth and breadth of BLOOMBERG PROFESSIONAL®'s offerings.

Functions are applications designed to provide targeted information and analysis on either the broad financial markets or on a specific security. Functions are grouped together by workflow and are discoverable through a hierarchy of menus. Each function has a mnemonic (short name) used to identify and access the function quickly.

For example, if we want to get a fast view on the world equity market, we use the WEI function which will bring the relevant world equity index onto the screen with further related subfunctions for us to look further into each equity index. The design of putting the most relevant information and sub-function together is what BLOOMBERG PROFESSIONAL® means by common workflows (the workflows that are commonly used by financial professionals when they analyse a particular set of information).

Securities are the financial instruments you can analyse. You can load a security to the system, then run a series of functions to find information about the security or perform deeper analysis. The millions of securities in BLOOMBERG PROFESSIONAL®'s databases are organized by market sector and ticker. For example, to see data related to IBM, the format is IBM US Equity.

BLOOMBERG PROFESSIONAL® provides two main ways to find and interact with functions and securities:

Command Line is at the top of every BLOOMBERG PROFESSIONAL® screen. The entire system is discoverable from the command line. As the name suggests, the command line is where you enter commands to drive the system, but it is also a search bar to find what you need which is similar to a Google search. For example, if you type {IBM} in the line, it will bring up the functions and securities that contain IBM ordered by relevance. Quite often if it is a company's name you type in, the main equity security of the company will appear in the top two under the securities section.

To access a function directly, just *type* its mnemonic in the command line, then *hit* <GO> (the enter key in a normal keyboard). For example, to run the World Equity Indices (WEI) function, just *type* {WEI}, then *hit* <GO>.

Menus provide a way to browse the full breadth and depth of BLOOMBERG PROFESSIONAL®'s offerings to find what you need. All BLOOMBERG PROFESSIONAL® functions are organized into menus, which start with overall market analysis and allow you to drill down to security-specific analysis. Exploring the menus is a very good learning experience to understand what is the common workflow for a given topic. For example, once a security is loaded, *click* on the [Related Functions] menu and this will bring up a selection of the most relevant functions to this type of security. For example, load a government bond (e.g. CT10 Govt) and see what related functions are available. It will include Fixed Income Relative Value (FIRV) instead of Relative value (RV) when an equity security is loaded.

Help Pages are online user guides designed to help you find answers specific to one function. They include an explanation of the business solution the function provides along with how-to instructions, definitions, calculations, and links to related documents and videos. This is the best place to learn more about what a function can do and explore different features. To load a help page, when a function is loaded, *click* [F1] or *click* the green Help menu button on top of the screen. The help page can be printed as a PDF file for note-making and as a reference manual.

EXPLORING BLOOMBERG PROFESSIONAL®

The best way to learn BLOOMBERG PROFESSIONAL® is to explore the topic of your interests in the system. Here are a few ways to start exploring.

Explore Topic-Related Functions from the Resource Centre: BPS <GO>

This will be the best first landing page you should go to for resource to get you started with the system. It includes basic topics such as 'Getting started' to more specialized topics such as 'Portfolio & risk analytics' and 'Risk management'. Drilling down into these topics will lead you to resources that introduce you to different functions for the relevant task. These include cheat sheets (a list of common used functions under the topic), white papers, and sometime videos and work examples.

Explore Common Workflow by USER <GO>

Workflow is a set of functions that help you achieve your research aim. For example, they include Market Surveillance, Sector Analysis, Issuer Analysis, Security Selections, Relative Value, New Issues, Index Analytics, News, and Research and Collaboration Tools. Once you are familiar with some basic functions, you may use them to identify resources that you may not be aware of for your research objective. Under each of these headings you will find many suggested functions for the relevant tasks. For example, under Sector Analysis, you will find functions such as Bloomberg Intelligence (BI) presenting data, news, and analysts' analyses of different industries.

Learn More from Bloomberg University BU <GO>

This landing page gives information about seminars and training events for your continued learning of the system.

Appendix II. Methods of Valuation

INTRODUCTION

One issue with using a value approach to building a share portfolio is that you need a means of assessing the value of a company. And, of course, there is no single method that gives you the right answer. Before we get into the various valuation metrics, and these are really a shorthand to valuation, we should consider the economic and commercial forces that lead to value creation. The list below will not be exhaustive but it will give you a feel for what might be considered when reflecting on the financial valuation metrics.

We start with the external forces that will impact on the profitability and the long-term wealth creation potential of a company, we will then go on to look at internal factors.

EXTERNAL

In considering external factors, the best place to start is Porter's Five Forces model (Figure A.1). This model takes the lessons from decades of research in industrial economics and business studies and presents them in an easy-to-understand framework.

As can be seen from Figure A.1, competitive rivalry is at the core of the model. While most companies will be aware of their immediate competitors, Porter's model deepens this understanding and broadens the discussion to other factors in the business. A lot of these factors drive the value creation of companies and an awareness of them is critical. When reflecting on these factors, it is worth keeping in mind some of the current global brands – Amazon, Google, Facebook, Tesla, Ford, etc.

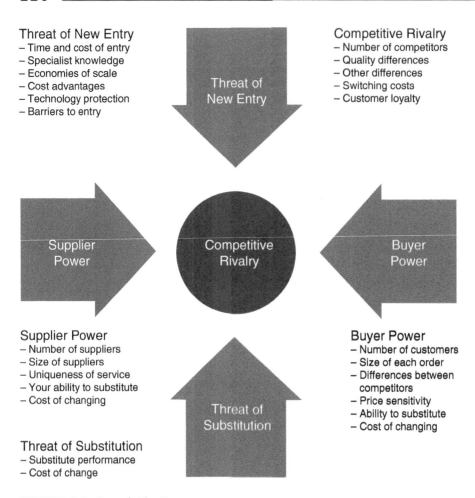

Threat of New Entry
- Time and cost of entry
- Specialist knowledge
- Economies of scale
- Cost advantages
- Technology protection
- Barriers to entry

Competitive Rivalry
- Number of competitors
- Quality differences
- Other differences
- Switching costs
- Customer loyalty

Supplier Power
- Number of suppliers
- Size of suppliers
- Uniqueness of service
- Your ability to substitute
- Cost of changing

Threat of Substitution
- Substitute performance
- Cost of change

Buyer Power
- Number of customers
- Size of each order
- Differences between competitors
- Price sensitivity
- Ability to substitute
- Cost of changing

FIGURE A.1   Porter's Five Forces.

1 Competitive Rivalry

In the short term, a lack of competitive rivalry is good as a company will be not be subject to price and cost pressures but in the long term it may be negative, in that a lack of competition may not promote the necessary innovation – effectively a company can become complacent until it is too late.

Competition is an interesting force in that one normally equates the strength of competition with the number of competitors, but this is far from the case in real life. It is the quality of the competition and not the quantity. Strong competition can come from a single competitor if it is of the right type, while if an industry is made up of a single strong player and a set of weak competitors, there is likely to be a lack of competition. Just consider the case of

Amazon – the retail industry has lots of competitors but does Amazon really have a credible competitor? Jeff Bezos has been clever in building a competitive position which now looks almost unassailable – this might be behind the Amazon share price that has had a 100-fold increase since 1997; a company that has built revenues to $50bn in 2018 but still makes minimal reported profits.

So what leads a company to have a strong competitive position? As a start, it may be price competitive because it has efficient operations and supply chains. If you consider supermarkets in the UK, the new entrants (Lidl and Aldi) gained significant market share on being price competitive on a limited range of products within fairly low cost locations. They also had the benefit of there being fairly low switching costs in this industry. If you consider banking, we have the opposite condition of high switching costs that protects relative inefficiencies.

A company can also compete on quality. At the top end of the automotive industry, the competition is as much about quality competition (within a price bracket) as price competition. The real question is what drives quality and here we have quality of the basic materials/inputs and how they are combined, plus the indefinable characteristic of style. Just consider an Aston Martin. Such brands build a quality that is hard to replicate and a brand loyalty that discourages customers switching to rivals. This type of customer base provides a company with many benefits – including the opportunity to innovate without the loss of the customer base, barring an obvious styling disaster. Apple has built a very loyal customer base, with fairly high switching costs, on the back of a perceived quality and a stream of innovations. It has tested the loyalty of this customer base with a few poor product launches but its ongoing competitive model has served it well with its stock price increasing approximately 400-fold across the past 30 years.

The power of the likes of Amazon and Apple are also derived from the four other forces in Porter's framework – buyer power, supplier power, threat of substitution, and threat of new entry. When these are combined in an 'optimal' manner, it gives a great deal of latitude in the market place.

2 and 3 Supplier and Buyer Power

Supplier power affects how easy it is for the supplier to increase prices and/or the buyer to force price reductions. Let's consider Aldi. It is well known to deal robustly with suppliers – arguing that if they do not agree to a price point and strict terms of delivery, other suppliers will happily jump on board. The power over suppliers is also driven by the Aldi growth model – not to play ball will risk losing out on a growing revenue stream. So for many suppliers, Aldi will be a prime customer to have but we are reminded of a comment by a senior partner in a national law practice: 'some clients just are not worth having'. We are also reminded of a case back in the 1980s, when Jaguar was starting to outsource more and more of its component manufacture under strict quality control conditions and open book shared accounting. One of us (Keasey) interviewed a supplier of pistons who was over the moon to have just become a recognized supplier to Jaguar. Six months later he was ruing the day he had signed the contract. The size of the order and the delivery conditions had led to Jaguar becoming his major customer (by quite some margin) and at the same time squeezing out his other customers. Jaguar made the most of this situation by placing ever stricter requirements on the supplier to the point where he noted: 'I have just become a low cost sub-unit of Jaguar with all of the risks and none of the benefits.' A definite case of having power over a supplier. Such power allows a company to be price competitive via cost efficiency. Its one weakness is control over the quality of the supply unless there is strict quality control measurement. This is the same problem that assails the subcontracting model.

In the above case, Jaguar had a lot of power over the piston supplier, while the latter had little power over its major customer. In its heyday at the top of the British car industry, Jaguar seemed to have quite a lot of power over its suppliers – though it seemed to want to use this power to increase volumes rather than prices. This began to change in the 1970s when German manufacturers were able to provide similarly priced machines with greater reliability. The rest is history with the indigenous car industry falling away through quality issues and the march of overseas manufactures: Japan for lower-priced cars and Germany for upper-end vehicles.

4 and 5 Threat of Substitution and New Entrants

A threat of substitution adds competitive pressure because too much of a price increase will lead to a loss of customers. Substitution can come from within the industry or from outside. Consider transport. A car manufacturer can face threats of substitution from other car makers but also the car industry can face such threats from other means of transport. At the moment traditional car makers are facing substitution threats from the likes of Tesla but a major factor holding back the switch to electric cars is the lack of a charging infrastructure.

A lack of substitution can also come from the cost of switching – a good example being banks and the associated hassle of changing direct debits, standing orders, etc.

The threat of new entrants can also help to constrain existing companies to maintain prices and quality. If they don't, new entrants will be attracted in by the promise of extraordinary profits. Barriers to entry will allow existing players to restrict entry. Staying with the banking example, customers (until recently) demanded a branch network and banks need a given amount of capital (by regulation) to operate. Both of these are barriers to entry and restrict entry. A further barrier is scale in many industries. Amazon has built a significant entry barrier through the scale of its distribution network. Steelworks have similar scale barriers to entry. Many other industries have scale barriers (consider pharmaceuticals) but these can eventually be reduced through innovation – smaller and more efficient power generation units are already challenging some of the larger power providers in the UK, this especially being the case in the renewable energy field.

In summary, value can be sustained through reducing competitive forces. Understanding the nature of such forces facing a company can help you gauge its longer-term potential.

INTERNAL

The internal operations, management, and governance of a company play critical roles in the creation and sustaining of value. The trouble is that these are not easy to gauge, given that a lot of companies are far from transparent. One simple adage to always bear in mind is 'if it looks too good to be true, it normally is'. Recent examples that spring to mind are Patisserie Valerie (PV), Neil Woodford (NW), etc. PV maintained a high and consistent margin for many years. Those with experience in business know this is highly unlikely as events always come along to cause problems. Similarly, NW's maintenance of high returns look with hindsight to be superhuman – only being achieved (or giving the impression of being achieved) through investment in highly illiquid and unquoted stocks. The problem with both of these examples is that it was not easy to gather the information needed to make the correct conclusion before it was too late. The only signal that something was awry was the 'too good to be true' adage.

Nonetheless, it is possible to gain some insight (before looking at the financials) as to the efficiency of internal forces.

Look at the Board and Governance – the names of directors (both executive and non-executive) are freely available and it is relatively easy to track the associated performance histories of directors. While the past is not a perfect indicator of the future, it is a guide. Under this heading consider the banking experience of those running HBOS before its collapse. You may also want to consider how much say the chairman has vis-à-vis the CEO – he/she is there, after all, to constrain the excesses of the CEO. Consider how much voice Keith Halliwell had versus Mike Ashley in the running of Sports Direct. In a similar vein, it is always worth considering if the non-execs are mere ornaments foisted on the company through governance regulations rather than experienced business personnel.

Coming down the organization, it is possible to understand the structure and whether it makes sense, given the nature of the business environment and the company, or is it a hangover from previous growth and/or mergers? In terms of the latter, it is also worth noting whether the acquiring company has the means to derive value out of the merger or is it going to be a distraction and a destroyer of value? Mergers are often undertaken as a consequence of management hubris (for example, consider what happened to the Royal Bank of Scotland under the merger-driven growth of Fred Goodwin) and this needs to be borne in mind, as does expansion into overseas territories.

Finally, the web has a lot of news and opinions on companies. These cannot always be relied on but they can be a source of insight. For example, the Glassdoor database records the opinions of employees on their companies. While some comments will have to be discounted because of 'disgruntlement', this can be an excellent source of up-to-date perspectives. We are reminded of the 'skip a layer' philosophy of management. If you really want to know what is going on with a layer of management, never talk to the reporting layer (they have too much to lose) but go one layer further down.

In summary, before looking at financial metrics, there is now a lot of information about companies available via a variety of web sources. The problem you may have is that there is too much information and making the decision of what to consider may be fraught and time-consuming. However, if you intend to be a long-term investor, such analysis could well pay dividends but it could be too costly if you are a short-term stock holder – such investors need more mechanical and immediate valuation metrics – to which we now turn.

VALUATION METRICS

Not surprisingly, given the complexities of a business, there are many factors to consider in valuing a company. Before we start, the eventual value of a business is what someone is willing to pay for it and what someone is willing to sell it for. In listed companies, the value of the shares reflect what the owners think the company is worth and, remember, investors come in many shapes and size – from the large pension fund with a long-term outlook and armies of analysts to the private investor working from the back bedroom. These different investors have different objectives and information sets, and will view many of the factors discussed above (for example, brand value) differently. So the share price of a company will reflect the objectives of the investor base as well as their perceptions of the value within the company.

Valuation metrics fall into two basic groups: one set being based on the asset value of the business and the other on the profitability/cash flow potential. ALL of the techniques look fairly simple on paper but they need to be applied with a degree of skill and scepticism. Remember, a lot of the data being used to calculate the following metrics is prepared by the company and 'verified' by its auditors – and we should all be aware of the number of auditing scandals over recent years (Patisserie Valerie springs to mind again). In addition, the financial data are often delayed and may not paint an accurate picture of the current health of the company – this especially being the case for younger and growing companies.

So, before, we discuss the various metrics, keep asking yourself – does the picture that is emerging make sense?, does it fit it with the news I have been reading?, does it reflect what is happening to the industry and competitors?, have major events occurred that are not reflected in the financial numbers, etc.?

Balance Sheet Valuation

Balance sheet valuation is a very defensive valuation metric and is based on the idea on what value would be gained if the assets were sold and all debts cleared – a net asset valuation. It pays no attention to the profit-earning ability of the company.

As always, the devil is in the detail but before we discuss such matters, it is worth considering the suitability of this metric. If you are a virtual software provider, the asset base is likely to be minimal and any net asset valuation is likely to massively undervalue such a company. Whereas a chemical business needs significant assets and such a valuation will cast some light on the overall value of a business. What these examples point towards is that the actual activities of a business should shape its balance sheet and to assess a balance sheet you should be aware of what a typical balance sheet in a particular industry should look like. For example, a bank (dependent on debtors and creditors) will have a very different balance sheet profile compared to a chemical business, or compared to a doctor's surgery.

Once you feel you know what a balance sheet should look like, you can start to delve into the detail. **Fixed assets** will be valued at historic cost less depreciation unless there has been a revaluation (this normally applies to land and buildings). The written down book value may seriously over-/under-estimate the value of these assets – of course, the value really depends on their use.

Examples

Let me give you some examples. Many years ago I (Keasey) was invited to value Silver Cross (the pram manufacturer). At the time it had a significant plot of land for its manufacturing premises and a lot of written down machinery. The book value of the machinery was almost zero but it had been well maintained and could continue producing prams for the foreseeable future – the production value of the assets was far greater than the book value. In fact, if the assets were valued on a replacement value with new machinery, they would have cost a small fortune but at the time their sale value was fairly minimal, given the number of factories closing. So the actual value of the machinery all depended on the intended use. The plot of land was significant and it had not been revalued and at the time there was a surplus of such plots for sale, given the demise of manufacturing. If the land had been acquired and held, then a significant uplift would have materialized, given the subsequent building booms.

This reminds me of another valuation situation I was involved in. We were purchasing a business with a very nice head office. The head office had not been revalued and nobody on the seller side seemed to understand the value of the HQ and its site. We ended up buying the business for a price that was equal to the asset of the HQ that we sold soon after acquiring the business.

Similar valuation issues apply to the **stock and debtor** parts of current assets; while cash has a face value – the actual amount paid may veer from this value depending on the precise situations of the buyer and seller. If a company is bought via a share swap and the buyer is cash poor and is struggling to raise funds, a premium may be paid. Alternatively, if the buyer is cash-rich, it may only be willing to buy the cash at a discount – of course, the seller may be able to strip the cash out but this may not be tax-efficient.

Getting back to stock and debtors, their value depends on their quality and market potential. The stock figure includes finished goods, work in progress, and raw materials – and the value you see in the balance sheet will reflect the mix of these three, the accounting valuation conventions used to measure their value, and the views of the auditors. Just remember these stock valuations can be way off the mark. Consider a computer hardware company. The finished goods could have been on the shelf a while and have suddenly been made obsolete, the components in work-in-progress may have a design fault and are worthless and/or they are also obsolete. It could even be the case that there may be costs of disposal – so rather than being an asset, they are a liability. Finally, the debtor book may be aged and partly uncollectable or there may be a large amount owed by a corporate that is on the verge of bankruptcy – consider how much suppliers to Carillion lost out when it went to the wall.

Working capital is made up current assets less current liabilities – short-term monies borrowed and trade credit. The 'quality' of these current liabilities can be critical to the short-term survival of a business. While current assets may seem to be sufficient to cover short-term liabilities in total amounts, the highly liquid assets (cash) may be insufficient to cover short-term liabilities; and here the quality of the relationship with the creditors is important. I am reminded of a case where a company X had factored its debtors to a finance company chaired by the Australian corporate raider, Bruce Judge. The X company was growing quite rapidly and it was unable to pull in cash from its debtors at the same speed as it needed to pay its creditors. Factoring the debtors seemed a good solution but company X did not do its due diligence on the finance company. For a couple of months all went well, and company X was matching its cash demands. However, Bruce Judge had seen an opportunity – he had hold of all of company X's invoices and he suddenly shut off his cash flow underpinned by the invoices. Company X had neither cash nor invoices and Bruce demanded a controlling equity stake before he turned the cash tap back on. Effectively the company was being held to ransom. Thank goodness the company had some significant institutional shareholders who helped bridge the cash gap until the invoices could be cancelled and reissued. There is a lesson to us all here – never lose control of your cash flow.

This nicely leads us to the final part of the balance sheet, the **funding side**. If we first consider the balance sheet from a shareholder perspective, we should subtract the total debts from the previous balance of fixed assets plus net working capital (current assets minus current liabilities) to understand the equity (shareholder) value of the business. However, the quality of the overall funding side of the business is important because it can indicate funding safety. If a company has borrowed a lot, then it may struggle to fund the interest and repayments on the debt – in other words, it is overgeared. Some have argued that companies can be undergeared because a lack of debt (which has tax benefits) means that the company cannot pursue profitable project opportunities. However, not all debt providers are equal and we need to consider the make-up and quality of the debt as well as the overall quantity. A single debt provider may leave a company open to abuse, while there are costs to managing a diverse debt portfolio. On the one hand, consider Robert Maxwell's use of a highly diverse debt structure to stay one step ahead of the fund providers – no single provider fully understood the gearing of the Maxwell empire. On the other hand, consider the case of the large number of small firms that tied themselves to RBS and went bust through loans being called in at short notice 'for no good reason'.

In a similar vein the structure of the equity base can also be important. A few influential institutional investors can bring order to a company through their monitoring activities. They can also help with fund raising when needed and they will occasionally bring project opportunities.

Overall, the balance sheet valuation metric looks simple but given the need to understand the detail and the quality of its various components, it is far from a quick exercise.

Price Earnings Ratio or Profit Multiplier

With this metric some measure of profitability is multiplied by some multiplier. The basic idea is that if a company is making £1,000 profit per annum and the accepted multiplier for that specific industry is 5, then the company is valued at £5k. If this amount is paid then, *ceteris paribus*, it will take 5 years for the purchase price to be recouped. Not surprisingly, there are a number of notions of profit that can be used (and we will see these differ, depending on the nature of the purchaser) and the multiplier can vary from a low number to the mid-30s (we have seen higher with some of the tech companies). In fact, some of the multipliers in the dotcom boom were infinite as companies floated on the stock market with no history and no immediate prospect of profit. To be fair, the prices being paid for such stocks was on the back of the notion that the companies would eventually be game changers and massive profits would flood in. This seems to be the case for Telsa that has a higher market valuation than Ford but only makes a fraction of its profits. However, if we ignore the stratospheric multiples for tech stocks, for small firms it is usual to pay between 3 and 5, and this can increase up to 12 for larger, listed companies with growth potential – these may even go into the mid-teens. This differential multiple is one reason why larger companies buy up smaller companies. Assuming away any integration issues, the larger company can in theory create value out of thin air by the simple act of purchase. Of course, there are integration issues and the small matter of properly valuing the company in the first place.

The profit measure you want to focus on is the likely profit that could be achieved when the business is bought and, as you can see, this will differ substantially if the business is to be kept as a stand-alone unit or integrated and sharing overheads. Let's consider a simple example to start with. Imagine you are buying a small firm and the owner has being trying to flatter his profits by taking a minimal salary of £10k per year. You are aware that a more realistic salary would be £50k and, therefore, the profit figure should be adjusted down by £40k. Other costs will also need to be examined to ensure they reflect what would be reasonable from a going concern perspective.

EBIT and EBITDA: it is difficult to avoid these notions in modern-day business and you need to be aware of them. If you take the net profit and add back interest and tax (if they have been taken away as part of the profit calculation), then you will end up with earnings (profit) before interest and tax (EBIT). This is often used by companies when valuing acquisitions because the interest and tax considerations will change once they become part of a larger group. However from a shareholder/investor perspective, the measure makes little sense because the interest and tax will have to be paid before any wealth is transferred to them. EBITDA takes the adjustment process one step further by adding back depreciation and amortization. This is a measure of profit before any adjustment for financing costs or the devaluation of assets (depreciation and amortization are accounting adjustments and are open to 'interpretation'). EBITDA gives a feel for what profits a business can cleanly generate and it is a close cousin to the notion of operating profits. From a shareholder perspective, the same comments apply here as they do for EBIT.

Comparables

One of the easiest valuation techniques is to look at comparable companies and see how they stack up relative to the business of interest. Of course, two assumptions need to be valid for this method to have credibility. First, the comparable businesses are indeed comparable and this is difficult to achieve as companies will often have different mixes of business components. Second, the valuation of the comparables is assumed to be fair. Overall, allowing for such assumptions, this is a relatively quick means of gaining an outline valuation.

Discounted Cash Flow

Academics and theoreticians hold this technique in the highest regard for its properties but, as we will see, it is not that easy to apply to company valuation. We will cover this technique in a bit of detail but interested readers should do a Google search as there is no shortage of expanded discussions of the approach.

Profit differs from cash because it makes allowance for the change in value of assets (depreciation and revaluations) and because of the timing differences between making sales and orders and eventually receiving cash. In the very long term, cash must equal profits and the two differ in the short term because of accounting adjustments. The DCF technique focuses on cash because this is the ultimate goal of any project or business (cash is king, etc.) and it avoids the noise of accounting adjustments. In simple terms, if we could add up all future cash flows, this would equate to the value of the business. However, a pound today is worth more than a pound next year because of the opportunity to earn interest and, therefore, we have to discount future pounds back to a present value to make them all equivalent.

So it all seems very straightforward but is far from being so from an investor valuation perspective. There are a number of issues. First, how do we work out the future cash flows? Do we proxy via operational profits, EBITDA, dividend streams, etc.? All of these will be noisy approximations of the cash generation. Second, how far do we look into the future to consider the cash generation? The investors in the tech companies and the likes of Tesla must be looking well into the future, given the current levels of cash burn. Third, in theory we should add to the cash stream residuals values when the business is sold or fails – not easy to calculate. Fourth, we have to discount future cash flows by a discount factor that is supposed to be the cost of capital for the business – and as most companies have a mixture of equity and debt, this will need to be a weighted mix of the cost of equity and the cost of debt. While academics spend many a chapter and paper arguing about how to properly calculate the cost of capital, most investors will struggle to derive an estimate and, not surprisingly, therefore, the best that can really be done is to take a factor that approximates current borrowing rates (say, 3–5%) and add a bit to reflect the risk of the company; the higher the risk, the greater the add on. Similarly, if risk is a concern, you may wish to restrict the length of the cash flow series being considered.

Before we finish, it is worth noting that Warren Buffett is a fan of the DCF approach and, therefore, it can't be all bad. We suspect, however, that he will be using a relatively simple 'cash generative' framework. In other words, he will be looking at gross margins, the sales volume, and trying to take account of any cash burn in terms of investments and overheads. This is all broad brush but if you understand the basics of the business you are thinking of investing in, you should be able to get a feel for its cash generative qualities. Might explain why Warren Buffett only invests in businesses he understands and he has stayed clear of the cash-hungry tech companies.

About the Companion Website

This book includes a companion website, which can be found at www
.investwithstyle.org. This website includes the following:

- Screening results of the strategies described in the book and updates.
- Additional discussion of style/factor investing which has been inspired by the experts and latest academic research.

Index